STORY PHYSICS

STORY PHYSICS

HARNESSING THE UNDERLYING FORCES OF STORYTELLING

LARRY BROOKS

WRITER'S DIGEST
BOOKS

WritersDigest.*com*
Cincinnati, Ohio

17 16 15 14 13   5 4 3 2 1

Distributed in Canada by Fraser Direct
100 Armstrong Avenue
Georgetown, Ontario, Canada L7G 5S4
Tel: (905) 877-4411

Distributed in the U.K. and Europe by F+W Media International
Brunel House, Newton Abbot, Devon, TQ12 4PU, England
Tel: (+44) 1626-323200, Fax: (+44) 1626-323319
E-mail: postmaster@davidandcharles.co.uk

Distributed in Australia by Capricorn Link
P.O. Box 704, Windsor, NSW 2756 Australia
Tel: (02) 4577-3555

Library of Congress Cataloging-in-Publication Data

Edited by Rachel Randall
Designed by Terri Woesner, adapted by Claudean Wheeler
Production coordinated by Debbie Thomas

DEDICATION

For Laura, the co-author and Senior Executive Editor of my life.

ACKNOWLEDGMENTS

I would like to thank the many people who have helped make this book possible, especially Andrea Hurst, my agent, and Rachel Randall, my eagle-eyed editor at Writer's Digest Books. Also, my many talented writer friends, who have kept me focused and positive in the midst of the eternal debate about how to write stories: Martha Miller, Sue Bronson, Mary Andonian, and over 6000 Storyfix.com readers who never let me forget that this stuff works. And, of course, my family, especially my wife, Laura, my son, Nelson, and the clan Mattern, for your love and unconditional support when the story isn't working.

ABOUT THE AUTHOR

Larry Brooks is the best-selling author of six novels, all psychological thrillers. His latest novel, *Deadly Faux,* is being published by Turner Publishing in October 2013, concurrent with the re-release of his five previous titles, including the *USA Today* bestseller *Darkness Bound,* and *Bait and Switch*, a "Best Books of 2004" selection by *Publishers Weekly.* He is the author of *Story Engineering: Mastering the Six Core Competencies of Successful Storytelling* (2011, Writers Digest Books), winner of the 2011 Next Generation Indie Awards in the Nonfiction Book category, and the creator of Storyfix.com, named one of the "101 Best Websites for Writers" by *Writer's Digest* magazine. He lives with his wife, Laura, in Scottsdale, Arizona, and is currently working on his next novel and some nonfiction projects.

TABLE OF **CONTENTS**

PART THREE:
The Power of Process

PART FOUR:
Story Physics in the Real Writing World

INTRODUCTION

In my many years as a writer, writing teacher, and blogger, I've never run into anybody who claims to know *everything* there is to know about storytelling. And I'm the first to say, often joining a chorus, that I don't either.

I offer this admission not so much from a position of humility—something of which I am rarely accused—but as a morsel of wisdom gleaned alongside more than a few missteps, the vast sum of which keep my occasionally misinterpreted ego (it's passion, actually; I've been too humbled by this business to allow my ego to get out of whack) in significant check. The more you know, the more you realize how complex and deep the craft of writing can be at a commercial level, and that many of the choices we must make in our stories are imprecise and a matter of degree. Stories are like people: Despite the fact that we are made of the same stuff and display the same moving parts, no two of us are completely alike, nor are any two *writers* exactly alike in their approaches. In both cases, the interior landscape creates something unique and compelling. Therefore, in counseling process, each writer's preferences and idiosyncrasies need to be regarded, evaluated, and appreciated separately.

That said, regardless of the differences, certain universal and fundamental storytelling principles and physics *do* apply. Almost without exception.

Physics are everywhere. They influence everything, literally *and* literately. Like a flowing river or the inherent power dwelling within an atom, they can be used to our advantage. Or, as is too often the case, they can be minimized or completely disregarded, which usually doesn't turn out so well. Either way, they can't be eliminated from any serious analysis of what makes things *work*.

For example, the force of *gravity*—I'm being literal here—reigns supreme in all things, in all places, for all time. It doesn't matter where you are or what belief system prevails ... what goes up must come down, and if you get in the way of a falling object you better have a catcher's mitt or a helmet. Other forces, both physical and relational, are equally as nonnegotiable, yet just as *manageable* as gravity: The power of love, the consequences of discipline and control, the influences of attention and apathy, parenting skills, the grace of charity, and the defining natures of fear, cowardice, and courage. These are forces of human dynamics that define both the principles and the outcomes of successful relationships and communities. They are every bit as constant and reliable, if not as precise, as the physical forces that rule our existence. Any psychological, sociological, or political view—which is the context of pretty much everything we *write*—must embrace these dynamics and honor their contexts in order to plow new ground or be even remotely effective.

The literary forces—I like to think of them as *physics*, in the same context as *gravity*—cannot be minimized or ignored. If you do ignore them, either on purpose or inadvertently, consequences ensue. Scary stuff. As in, the story won't work very well. But, as with other natural forces, they can also be *harnessed and applied* toward achieving a desired outcome. These literary physics are the engine and the wings of storytelling. Glide mode doesn't work very well in our trade; sooner or later the story will fall out of the sky before it reaches a landing strip.

And if it has no intended destination, that's the biggest mistake of all.

Some writers develop stories in a complete vacuum, in context to *nothing*—no principles, no expectations. They just sit down and spill it onto the page. (I've seen writing teachers who advocate this as a process, but they need to add that once spilled, you need to do a lot of cleaning up.) They then wonder why it doesn't work, and why it takes so long before it does.

That's the problem this book seeks to address, and solve. It's the "*there are no rules*" mind-set I am out to shift toward a higher level of comprehension. I seek to rewrite that cliché, which is actually a bit complicated. The difference between "rules" and "principles" is key to this understanding. By either name, they are the universal underlying story forces or physics that will affect your story one way or another, whether you like them or not, or whether you're aware of them or not.

You can harness those forces for literary good rather than leaving your story to chance or to the unproductive and invalid belief systems that have been your undoing so far.

Writers with some miles behind them are keenly aware of the forces they are working with. Sometimes newer writers fail to recognize the sheer power of *story physics* and how they come to bear on the work. They don't recognize that story physics enter the equation the very moment a story idea is hatched. Sure, they've heard of them before in different contexts—it's all just more writing conference noise from presenters nobody's heard of—but when they get back into the solitude of their writing spaces they tend to plow into their story trusting that somehow those forces will align naturally, organically.

It is, of course, possible that such forces could align naturally, but highly unlikely. Statistics prove this: Just look at the inventory in your nearest bookstore (if you can still find one standing) and count the number of titles you actually recognize. Now multiply that number by a thousand, and you're close to the number of *unpublished* books created in only the last few years that didn't even make it onto the shelf.

It's as simple as this: If the story idea and concept are, at their most basic level, bland or unoriginal or nonrelevant, then no matter how well you write the narrative the odds are stacked against it. You really can't make chicken droppings into chicken salad in this business. And too often our initial ideas, the ones we write in context to, *are* mundane to the point of being chicken droppings. But if you're willing to let some things go, you really can change them into chicken salad.

Story physics is the means of doing so.

Once you realize the risk of writing blindly (not to be confused with *organically*, which is a viable process, provided you accept the whole messy enchilada of it), and recognize the upside when you write *in context to something*, your entire writing experience will shift into a higher, faster gear.

My first writing book, *Story Engineering: Mastering the Six Core Competencies of Successful Writing*, is an introduction and overview of a powerful tool chest, presenting a fresh, criteria-based context for storytelling. *This* book focuses on the underlying powers that those tools leverage. Chapter 22 reviews the core competencies in a way that connects them to story physics, and Chapters 23 and 24 use two recent iconic bestsellers to bring it all home. If you haven't read the bestsellers, I highly recommend you rent the DVDs before diving into these sections, which contain serious and freshly reconveyed content.

This text is intended to be experienced as a discussion, with the tonality of a lively writing conference lecture. That's deliberate—it's an instructional modality based on the physics of adult learning—as is my abundant wordiness, which is fueled by my passion for this topic. I'll warn you in advance that I'm like a workshop instructor on too much caffeine. Maybe you've already heard it all, but I'm confident you haven't heard or explored it like *this*.

Sometimes truth and insight don't resonate at the first pass. The writing discussion is riddled with rhetoric and the obvious, as well as massive icebergs of pure gold. In this book I'll give you many looks and perspectives, many contexts, and abundant opportunities for a moment of Epiphany to descend. The inherent power of story physics is always there, waiting to be found and applied, but sometimes hidden in the obvious. When you do find it, when you embrace it, chances are you've found your best story, too.

Let the search for story begin. And may the power of story *physics* become your muse.

Larry Brooks
www.storyfix.com

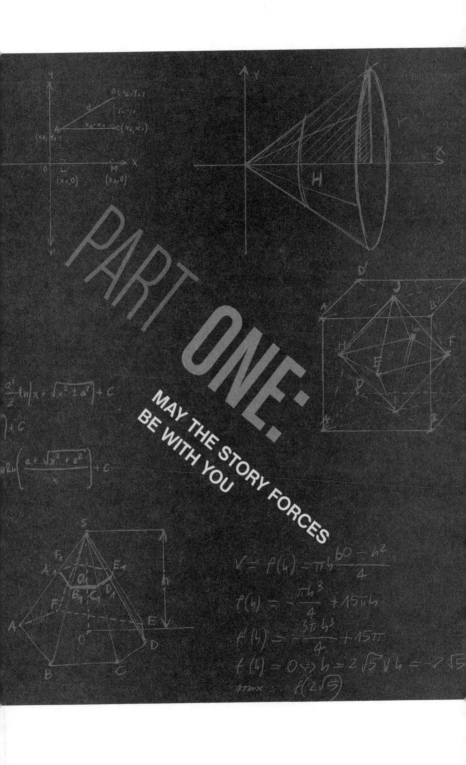

PART ONE:

MAY THE STORY FORCES
BE WITH YOU

THE SEARCH FOR STORY
WHEREIN WE EMBRACE THE PAIN AND CHAOS.

Every writer, every time, has to *find* their story before they can hope to get it right. If they stamp "final draft" on a story that hasn't truly found its highest and best self, something is left on the table that could have made the difference between success and failure.

Sometimes the story is lost at square one. It never stood a chance because you can't execute a weak idea into a strong story without making it into something else. The writer latches onto it like a conspiracy theory and can't quite translate his own attraction to it in a way that others will accept with equal clarity or zeal.

This story search-and-discovery mission takes many forms, from brainstorming and test flying to planning and outlining, to organic drafting (in effect, searching *as you go*). The search is a key part of the story development process—in essence it *is* the story development process—and yet, framed as a *search*, it's taken for granted by some and totally ignored by others. Not every choice we make within our stories is the *best* possible choice available. As you execute these creative decisions, they will define a path toward what comes next, creating a domino effect of consequences. Choose well, and your path will be prosperous. Make a bad choice or a wrong turn, or make a less than *optimal* choice for a given story beat, and the rest suffers for it. Such wrong turns can lead you to the precipice of a cliff.

And thus this is how and why manuscripts get rejected.

Before you can succeed in the search for story, however you go about it, you must grasp what's at stake, either intuitively or in context to something you've learned. This is true for story points within the draft itself, and as a critical step in the overall development of your narrative *strategy.*

Especially the strategy.

Because everything is at stake. Everything. No matter what your creative process. All writing processes, by definition, strive for the same things, and at the end we are left with outcomes that are totally defined by the physics—*forces*—of storytelling that the author has put into play.

The *search for story* is the quest for, and the application of, the essence and application of universal story *physics*—forces that lead to reader perception and response—within the context of your intended narrative sequence. You can *optimize* these forces by knowing what needs to be put in play within the narrative—and where—so the story can offer its inherent maximum value and impact. Just like a cook selecting the right ingredients and a surgeon selecting the right blade. To embark on a successful search for story, you can't settle for story elements and moments that could be made more effective and powerful by taking the underlying *story physics* to a higher level.

It's like playing a sport. The faster you run, the harder you hit, the more accurate you are—in other words, the *physics* of athletics—the better you will play the game. This doesn't negate or otherwise undervalue skill and intuitive in-the-moment judgment, but you can't argue that optimized physics don't empower that instinctual sensibility to a higher level. If you or I were to hit a golf ball on the nose, it might put us within a nine iron of a short par four. If a professional hits it on the nose, a birdie putt is the likely outcome. The reason is pure physics: club speed applied with optimal leverage and accuracy. The swing may look the same to the casual observer, but it's not. The physics are different.

Physics—in sports and in storytelling—are what separate professionals from the aspiring masses.

The *optimization* of story physics is precisely what successful authors accomplish. Because it's not a precise science, it's safer to say that the pros deliver the power of story physics at a consistently higher *level*, especially relative to dramatic tension and character empathy (the degree to which the reader will root for the hero). Great authors tend to nail those things. Even if they claim not to understand how it's done and they say that they just sit down and bang it out, draft by draft, they are utilizing physics. For many writers, drafting is their *process*, their mode of story search empowered by their instincts and story sense, sometimes referred to as *talent*. An understanding of the depth and nature of the search for story isn't a ticket to the bestseller list, but the presence of artfully rendered story physics—*craft*, however rendered—just might be.

The good news is that this doesn't have to be a guessing game or a blind shot in the dark, or even something that depends on *talent*. Knowing *what* to look for, what to land on—the specific essences of story physics, which become the *criteria* by which you vet the available creative options—is a huge step toward what others, reviewers included, will likely label as *talent*.

Talent is very much like luck. You get in line for it through craft and perseverance. And craft always leads to what you need to make it happen: story physics.

AN IDEA DOES NOT A STORY MAKE

Too many writers try to write their *ideas*. This is like trying to make wine out of a grape by simply squeezing the juice into a glass. It doesn't work, even if the glass is Riedel crystal. They begin with the seed of a story, and that becomes (too soon) the basis for a draft. Sadly, those writers *settle* for that story without considering better options along the way, without discovering a more compelling *concept* that arises from the initial idea, and without a contextual standard by which to judge their decisions. These writers fail to *evolve* their idea *into* a concept, one that kicks the door to better story physics wide open. A killer concept is a great idea on steroids, complete with facial hair and muscles, because it represents the *evolution* of an idea into a compelling dramatic story platform. And there are many ways to get it done.

An idea for a love story in a bleak futuristic society? Not bad. Having it play out within the arena of a staged death match to avenge a decades-old political uprising? That's way better. (If that sounds familiar, you're gonna like Chapter 24.)

Simply hatching an *idea* for a story is not the part and parcel of an effective *search* for story. If you start drafting from an undeveloped idea, you may or may not land on creative choices—story points, milestones, twists, context, and subtext—that deliver *optimized* story physics. If you do land on them at that level, it'll be out of context to a *whole* that is an extension of an empowered concept. It'll be a chunk of Godiva sitting atop a soft-serve yogurt sugar cone.

When you evolve the idea into a bigger, more *compelling* concept from the opening bell, using the strength of your story physics as the criteria for your creative choices, then you are in essence building narrative power and nuance into your story before you even write it. Or, if you're a drafter, *as* you write it, using that empowered concept as context.

An idea is merely the first step in a long, complex, and evolving creative journey. If that step is less than stellar (optimized), then the whole thing is already in trouble, or at least compromised to some degree, because you're already trying to make the proverbial sow's ear, albeit a pretty one, into a literary silk purse. It's like planning to be a surgeon but deciding to enter the job market after community college—the idea (become a surgeon) was great and noble, but the strategy (skip the medical degree and go to Ghana to practice) was flawed and fatal.

It's obvious when stated in a simple analogy. But you'd be shocked to see how often well-intended writers do just this. They begin with mediocre (or worse) ideas, to which they attach the tonality and machinations of a *this-is-really-important* cache and then render it with solid mechanics ... and then wonder why it gets sent back to them with a form letter.

It takes but one step to fall off a cliff. And sometimes that step is the first one in this journey.

At the end of the day, a story is much *more* than a single *idea*.

A story is composed of four major working parts: concept, character, theme, and structure (sequence of exposition), each with a separate and critical narrative context and mission. These specific contexts—you mess with them at your peril—may or may not arise simply from the idea itself, and each is absolutely powered by and ultimately judged according to the effectiveness of the story physics applied.

A story is *executed* through narrative scenes, which are composed of paragraphs and sentences (one's writing *voice* or style). Scenes are where story physics actually manifest on the page, either directly or with veiled cleverness, evolving from intention to execution. If a scene works, it's due to the level of story physics applied. If it drags, if it contributes little to the story, the physics have been compromised.

Right here at square one, the idea stage itself, is where we are confronting story physics in a meaningful way. Physics drive not only the scenes within a story, but the entire landscape and potential of the story itself at its earliest and highest level. Which is to say—and this is a bubble burster for some—that not all ideas are ripe grist for a robust story, and not all great stories arise from an initially compelling idea. It's always a dance between those two extremes, with *concept* playing the music and *story physics* determining volume and pitch.

TAPPING INTO THE INHERENT POTENTIAL OF CONFLICT

If your story doesn't offer *conflict*—and some "ideas" are better suited to conflict than others—then it's not really a story at all. A story about your summer vacation, for example, is an *idea* that isn't inherently dramatic. It has no conflict, per se. It's not a *concept* yet. You have to *add* something to it to *make* it a concept, which is precisely what you *should* do, and what you *must* do if the story is ever going to work. On the other hand, a story about a summer vacation in which your hero is kidnapped by crazy Italian tourists seeking to ransom her back to her employer, which is the CIA … now that's a *concept*, fraught with potential drama, tension, stakes, and the promise of a terrific vicarious ride. Make one of those tourists a woman who falls in love with you, a KGB agent perhaps, and you have a subplot on your hands, too. Make your hero the lesbian daughter of an ultra right-wing Senator, who got her the job to take her away from a life as a pole dancer, and suddenly you have theme, as well.

It's a delicious, siren-infested trap. Ideas that involve "the search for self" or the "search for meaning" are often written from this drama-devoid, naturally episodic genesis, without attention to any potentially unfolding dramatic tension that would elevate it into a *concept*. Character-driven material is good, but what drives the character should be full of conflict and drama and stakes. And *that* comes from plot … which is entirely driven by story physics.

Such is the grist and the nuance we are searching for.

Great storytelling through the search for story—the search for story *physics*—is all about avoiding the pursuit of weak ideas, about discovering rich and fertile concepts, characters, themes, and journeys that spring from the original idea to assume center stage. Each of those outcomes is a choice the author makes, and the creative options that make that choice into a *story* can be explored, vetted, tested, and optimized.

I've lived this. My third novel, *Serpent's Dance*, began as a baseball story about a guy who had his shot, blew it, went back to real life, discovered himself in a way that illuminated the source of his failures, and then went back to try again. (This was long before *The Rookie*, a film written by my friend Mike Rich, came out to critical acclaim.) I sent this idea to my editor at Penguin, who wasn't crazy about it. "Baseball stories don't work," he said (an opinion that is continually proven misguided). We worked through the idea, rather than discarding it, adding, shifting, playing "what if?" with it. The story that emerged doesn't have a baseball anywhere in sight. In fact, the hero is a woman, and the McGuffin is a software scam involving a secret plot by virus protection software companies to actually create and distribute the very viruses their products claim to protect users from.

We searched, we vetted, we trashed some stuff, we found a flow, and a new and better story emerged. What if I had written the baseball story, without this vetting? Hard to say, but I can say for a fact that the novel my editor and I did create from an original idea, one that ended up being a much richer and more relevant concept, was successful, and, in fact, is being republished this year.

We stand on the edge of a cliff, alone with our ideas. When we love them, we have trouble seeing how other people might possibly find them less than engaging. Hey, it was our summer vacation after all, and it was wonderful. We need a tool to elevate our ideas toward concept and story, some benchmarks, to help us search and decide.

Those benchmarks exist … in the form of story physics.

THE SHIFT TOWARD STORY PHYSICS
WHEREIN THE DEVIL ON YOUR SHOULDER, DRESSED LIKE A SIREN, SOUNDING A LOT LIKE EVERY WRITER YOU KNOW, IS SADLY SHAKING HIS HEAD.

Change is hard. And life is nothing if not an exercise in change.

There is a paradox out there, and it's seductive. This story physics stuff is so obvious, once you see it. And yet, so *not* a part of the writing conversation that defines the culture of writing conferences and on-line writing sites and critique groups. The trick, the goal, is something that every success story has embraced in some way: You need to stop listening to the belief systems and opinions of others and decide for yourself what is true. What works for *you*. You must determine how you will integrate it into who you are and how you write.

Just know that the *best* path for you might not be the easy way, the old way, or the way of your writing peers.

That choice is what this is about. Story physics are *true*. I'm not telling you what you should believe or how to write—in which case I'd be just another voice on your shoulder—but rather, I'm *showing* you the power of story physics so you can decide for yourself how best to find and apply them. Story physics are eternal, universal, impersonal. They will never let you down, though they might squash you or leave you hanging if you're not paying attention. Story physics are like love in that regard: Once you see it, you can't un-see it. Once you know, the choices relative to outcome become yours to make, rather than a well-intended but uninformed roll of the dice.

If your old beliefs and programs aren't working for you—in writing and in love—two things are likely true: You should consider changing something ... and, with awareness, the reason will no longer be a mystery.

I recall a novel I found a few years back—it actually was published in the late 1970s—in which the characters were, I kid you not, amoeba. The hero was a microorganism. Not exactly *Watership Down*, a modern classic featuring rabbits, which worked because the community of rabbits was easily parallel to our own sociology and was driven by dramatic tension and empathy for the rabbit hero. The setting in this amoeba book was, well, a place where microorganisms live. The bad guy was, you guessed it, an evil microorganism, what those of us with vertebrae might call a germ. Clearly, the author wanted to wax eloquent about the science of it all, and clearly, based on results, it didn't work as a dramatic narrative, at least outside of the faculty lounge.

Why? Because just about every facet of story physics was compromised, beginning with the idea itself. The story that sprang from it wasn't dramatically compelling. We had no empathy for the hero because nobody can relate to an amoeba, a character who has no feelings or human qualities (and to imbue them with such would have rendered the story a child's fantasy; no, this author wanted us to take this *seriously*). Pacing didn't matter, because it was hard to care what happened next. There was no vicarious journey, no stakes, no way to relate to the experience of the hero, much less root for ... *it*? It wouldn't matter if he wrote it with the eloquence of Shakespeare in a grad school biochemistry class. It just was never gonna work. It was a one-horse, one-joke effort. An *idea* without a concept. Novels like that don't perform in today's market.

And yet, to be fair, this novel was actually published, and by a major New York house. Which goes to show that William Goldman was right when he wrote about the business of storytelling: "Nobody knows anything." Which means we need to rely on something that is nonnegotiable: story physics.

I see a lot of stories in my work as a story coach. Most are not quite as out there as the amoeba novel, but some rely on conceptual centerpieces that don't create an opportunity for the elements of story physics to contribute. Remember, this is commercial storytelling we're talking about, the quest for a contract and an audience, and once we sign up for *that*, we need to look at a bigger picture than our own quirky fascinations.

Even cool ideas and concepts tank when the story physics aren't right.

For example, a story about medieval knights battling for real estate in twelfth-century Ireland .... This has potential and at least the hint of dramatic tension. But until the author adds story physics that turn the idea into a *concept*—a compelling hero with a problem (maybe he's Bono's distant ultra-great grandfather), stakes, great pacing, and a ride for the reader (where all of those accurate and colorful details appear)—all of it amounts to little more than a historical travelogue. I've seen it a dozen times in the past couple years: Authors who are excited about a theme, an arena, a time, and a place (especially in historical fiction, sci-fi, and fantasy) write their stories *about* that, and *just* that. Dramatic tension becomes subordinated to setting. Characters are there simply to be our eyes and ears as they wander about this cool setting. They underplay the story physics.

An effective story is about a hero with a problem and a resultant quest, with something at stake, with opposition standing in the way. It unfolds with compelling pace and exposition, resulting in empathy for the hero and a vicarious experience for the reader. Beyond the appeal of twelfth-century Ireland, all of these elements must come into play early, and that's right where these authors come up short.

A story is about a hero who does something.

It's *not*, at its highest level, about a time or a place or a thematic idea, or even a situation. Those are important yet peripheral issues, they are elements of staging that don't work in the absence of properly applied story physics, rendered through a professional level of execution via the Six Core Competencies of successful writing (see Chapter 22).

You know that old *silk purse out of a sow's ear* saying? The same is true of our fiction. The search for story is where one discovers if they are working with silk or the disembodied lobes of a dead pig. Story physics, when applied as *criteria* within that search, allow you to recognize whether you have an idea or a story, or if your idea can *become* a story.

Nobody gets to sidestep this truth.

Some writers claim they don't *need* to pay attention to those pesky fundamental principles and storytelling physics. Some of them come to my workshops. And sometimes they say stuff like this:

> "Don't overthink it, just sit down and do it, let the story flow, trust your instinct, do whatever the hell you want, keep working on it and it'll turn out like it's supposed to. There are no rules."

Semantics. One writer's "rules" become another's craft. But it's dangerous advice, because it assumes you already know what you need to know to succeed in doing it this way. That your story instincts are keen and evolved. Too often it results in stories that don't work so well, or never get finished at all. I hear from writers all the time who, like converted zealots from a cult, lament the years they spent believing that this was the preferred way to write.

It's interesting to know that what is obvious in other avocations and crafts isn't so obvious when it comes to writing stories. You wouldn't design an airplane without wings simply because you didn't think to or you don't happen to care for wings or you wonder what would happen to an airplane without wings or you want to prove your aeronautical engineering professor wrong.

Physics are always there. Your story can't fly without them.

Any contrary view is rhetoric colliding with naïveté spiced with a dash of attitude. It's an effort to push one's preferred writing paradigm—the easy comfort of just winging it—back to the forefront (which, when it actually works, already includes story physics in abundance, wielding these forces under another name). Is gravity a *rule*, or is it a universal *principle*? Again, semantics. "No running in the pool area …"—that's a *rule*. And perhaps ironically, like many rules, it is rooted in *physics*: If you slip, you'll likely crack your head open. Because of *gravity*.

Behind most rules and guidelines, even offensive ones, *physics* are quietly cruising between the lines to create consequences that stem from our choices. Writers are free to choose any process and form they wish, but the physics of effective storytelling are always waiting to either lift you up or carry your manuscript out on a stretcher.

Not long ago I flew into Salt Lake to give a keynote and a workshop at a writing conference. The young writer who picked me up at the airport was curious about my book (*Story Engineering*), which is about the *application* of story physics through process and criteria-driven dramatic *architecture* (a very engineering-friendly word, indeed). In the course of our conversation he told me that one of the writers who would be attending the conference, an older fellow who had been writing for years, said my book was unnecessary, that it just complicated what should be obvious, that there are only three things a writer needs to ultimately know—the beginning, the middle, and the end— and the rest is just more hot air. A *three-hots-and-a-cot* kind of guy.

I asked how many books this fellow had published. The answer was *none*.

Interesting. While I have certainly run into writers who line up behind this simplistic and sadly limiting belief system, none of them—zero—have been published. Even successful authors who claim they write by the seat of their pants manage to stumble upon (or evolve toward) story physics and put them into play, and if they do it often enough, they become names you may recognize.

Coincidence? I think not.

The forces of story physics don't care if you recognize them or not. Like gravity and sunlight and air temperature, they just are. Mess with them, or ignore them, at your own peril.

TO SEARCH FOR PHYSICS, OR NOT TO SEARCH FOR PHYSICS

This isn't the question you should be asking yourself. Because story physics—synonymous with story *forces*—are universal storytelling *truths*. You are always searching for your story as you develop it, however you develop it. The key, then, is not so much about *how* you search, but *what* you are searching *for*.

Can you recognize a kernel of gold when you see it, or do you settle for pretty rocks that fit nicely, perhaps conveniently, into a mosaic?

When a successful story does spring forth from a vacuum, meaning the writer wasn't worrying about story physics and, writing organically, just came up with stuff that seems to work at the time (and while it does happen that way, those books usually take *years* to write and rewrite), it isn't a refutation of the veracity of this writing truth. Rather, the writer doesn't recognize or value what has happened—specifically, *how* it happened—much like a miner who unearths something of value that he wasn't digging for. He chose the location and began to dig ... and dig ... until he actually found something of value. Perhaps such writers aren't aware that they had been engaged in a search for story at all. To them, it was all just writing, mining for gold within the idea itself. And even then—especially then—you can be sure that those story physics the writer wasn't acknowledging managed to instinctually align and ignite the story at its core, usually after multiple drafts and perhaps years of honing her craft.

You can test this.

Sit down and write a story without compelling dramatic tension. Which is to say, a story without the forces of story physics, of which dramatic tension is just one.

Write a story without a hero, or a hero who is not proactively heroic, a hero without a compelling problem to solve or an urgent journey to take, a hero who is not naturally empathetic and thus is not easy to root for. Now you're ignoring two of the essential forces of an effective story. Try to write a story with main players who are without emotional resonance, lacking a narrative with compelling pace and a story arc with subtext or thematic depth, with exposition that displays a less than vivid and engaging voice. Write it any way you want, including two hundred pages of character background before anything happens. Go ahead, ignore anything and everything you've heard about what works.

These, by the way, are things that get you rejected. For a *reason*. A few may ring familiar, and if so, it's not because the agent or editor doesn't get it. It's because they *do* get it—they know what makes a story tick, and they recognize it when it's there, just as they miss it when it's not.

They are all issues of *story physics*, and they can be sought after and applied. They can be searched for, discovered, vetted, and chosen by the author, either before writing a draft or while she is writing. And because our story choices are all matters of degree and imprecision, one's first impulse isn't always the optimal choice at all.

I've seen so many manuscripts that sprang from the intention to portray a protagonist who is lost in the world, who needs to find herself. And then, using that idea instead of a physics-seizing concept that evolves *from* it, they write an episodic, diary-like "story" about the hero's life, how he doesn't fit in, and then one day ... he does. They've written a story without dramatic tension, without a plot, without a hero's quest and problem and goal, without external antagonistic pressure (also dramatic tension), and without stakes that readers can identify with.

The original intention is honorable. But it wasn't a concept. It was a desired thematic *subtext*, perhaps a character arc stemming from the hero's inner landscape. But until you add those other elements of story physics—until you give this character something to *do*, which soon becomes a *plot*—it's not a story at all. Or at least not a publishable one.

Even Holden Caufield had something to *do*.

The story about the frisky amoeba who wanted to get out and explore another brain cell? The guy wrote like a poet. And it didn't work.

It never stood a chance, at least with readers. The only certainty is that two people liked it—an agent and an editor—probably because they were intrigued, like the author, by the idea. This isn't an exact science. I don't know about you, but I don't like those odds. Better to write a story that has everything going for it, rather than an idea that stands alone with nothing to turn into.

With fiction, art without craft isn't enough. Craft without art can sneak through, but you're more likely to see your name in print if you bring both to the party.

Paste this over your writing desk:

A story isn't just about something ... a time, a place, a situation, a theme ... but rather, a story is about something *happening*.

Consider this absolutely reliable paradox: A story *can't* work if certain fundamental principles and physics are weak or missing, yet it only *might* work if they *are* in play. You get to choose which game you're playing.

It's like an audition for a Broadway play. Everybody who shows up can sing and dance. Those are the physics of that particular craft. But only a few get a part. Possessing a solid grasp of the physics is merely the ante-in to a professional level of craft.

There is no reason to audition without these physics on display. Because the person who gets the part will not only possess them, they will have mastered them.

That is our goal: to understand and master the craft of force-driven storytelling. To select concepts and design stories from those concepts that allow for *optimized* story physics, which leads to memorable reading experiences.

3

THE THREE PHASES OF STORY DEVELOPMENT
WHEREIN WE BRING ORDER TO WHAT MANY EXPERIENCE AS CHAOS.

Do you think you can out-write John Grisham?

How about James Patterson? Nora Roberts? Maybe that fortunate young lady who wrote *Fifty Shades of Grey*? Do you think the usual suspects on the bestseller lists are overrated, or at least simply *lucky* to be there? That you can do what they do, maybe even better than they can? Do you suspect something else is going on here besides the stories they tell, like the leveraging of a brand name for the marketing of the mediocre?

Many writers do believe these things. It's an interesting little conceit that is somewhat unique to writers. Few of us believe we could nail an open field tackle of Reggie Bush, that we could go toe to toe with Josh Groban on a stage, or that we could open a gallery with our watercolors and ceramic glass. And yet, we read the latest bestsellers and, while perhaps gripped and moved by those stories, we remain foggy on *how* that happened, when those books seem so smooth and easy—so *simple*. How could this happen for a book that doesn't seem all that challenging when it hasn't yet happened for *your* book?

It actually *is* easy. You have six basic realms of story physics to work with, and six tools to use in doing so. But it's *not* simple. Not even close to simple. In fact, do the math: With that many variables in play, and with any number of levels of application within each, there is virtually an infinite number of potential outcomes possible. That's the paradox we must live with as writers.

Writing an effective story looks so easy, especially when executed by those brand names. But it wasn't easy for them to write, so don't be tempted to confuse this with a story being easy to *read*. Luck is a lightning bolt that only strikes once (usually), while repeated success is the product of a learning curve and a whole lot of skill in juggling those twelve variables of physics and craft. Make no mistake, the writers you envy didn't just stumble upon something. Rather, at the end of their process they were in command of certain storytelling *forces* that rendered their stories effective, forces that are a product of a sequence of events and milestones that are part of a fundamental architectural storytelling model. The power of those stories is *cause*, not effect. It was summoned forth from within the inherent parameters of the idea itself. It doesn't matter *how* they wrote it—process is all over the map among those who are famous enough to get asked about it—but rather, how their stories seized the inherent power of story physics.

Nothing about a good story is random, accidental, fortunate, or mysterious. Many one-hit wonders and more than a few of the books from household names arrived at the editor's desk in need of help, the delivery of which returned them back to the energy-centric heart of that architectural model. Everything about a successful story falls within the sphere of—and the possibilities within—*craft*. Story forces, or the lack thereof, come to bear upon the power of story whether the writer understands them or not. And in the case of first-time writers, if you don't nail them, editors won't rescue you, they'll reject you.

Story forces are accessed and optimized by authors in a certain way, through focuses brought to bear in a certain order. The more you know about them, the sooner you'll put them into play.

THE THREE LAYERS OF
THE STORY DEVELOPMENT PROCESS

Sometimes these phases of the process occur concurrently, sometimes they are very segregated, but they always unfold in this order:

1. The **SEARCH** for the story, based on an initial spark of an idea, that evolves into a concept and then a story sequence.

2. The **DESIGN** of that story.

3. The **EXECUTION** and polishing of the story into a final draft.

Search ... Design ... Execution

The bulk of the story discovery process—the search for and the vetting of story points, contexts, and subtexts—resides within step 1 above. The search actually continues in step 2 because new ideas don't care where you are in the process, and good design almost always tweaks the original vision through a shaping and honing process. By the time you deem a draft to be a polish away from finished, here's hoping you've completed a thorough story search, and that your design will hold up under scrutiny.

That's the sequence of every story's creation, even if the writer doesn't see it that way, or even if he doesn't do it in that order. You can actually back into an idea—a new and better idea—through writing a draft (what organic writers claim to be the holy grail), but what's really going on is the first idea is yielding to something more effective, which was inspired by a continuing search (perhaps subconsciously) on the writer's part because they sense they need more.

More story physics.

Maybe that's it, that's the problem right there. This could be what stops some books from being published. You start out by heading for one thing, discover you'd rather go toward something *else*, and yet fail to go back and fix those chapters that, it turns out, didn't know where they were going in that moment.

The draft that works, the optimal draft, will be written *from the outset* in context to an idea and a resultant concept that has sufficiently powerful story physics to deliver to the story. Not from a draft that starts out as one thing and morphs into another. The draft you buy and read will be a revision of a draft that wasn't sure.

It's very empowering to recognize when you are, in fact, still engaged in the search for your story. This is true even for drafters ... perhaps *especially* for drafters. This realization allows you to try, vet, discard, and embellish certain story beats, all as part of the search process, and as a value-adding (rather than restarting) aspect of the design phase. It prevents you from *settling* or swallowing a fatal pill disguised as a vitamin. When the seed of a story beat feels right, when it feels *better* than one that already occupies that space, this process of search has just paid dividends.

Maybe your prose indeed outshines that of those rich and famous authors. Maybe that best-selling story seems shallow or contrived, at least to you. But maybe your prose and your review of their work isn't the point. The real question is this: Do your stories harness the power of storytelling at its most basic, physics-driven level? Have you searched for them, vetted them, and decided upon them in context to what you know about the forces of storytelling? Or have you settled, made your choices based on where you *are* in the story, rather than via an informed vision for where you should be?

It can happen, *if* you know what those storytelling powers (physics) are, and how to apply them. You search for and discover them in the first phase, design them into an unfolding sequence in the second phase, and execute them in the third phase.

All of this happens either through a series of drafts (known as *pantsing*, for *seat-of-the-pants* storytelling), story planning, or a combination of both. All share the same criteria in terms of outcome, and all require the same appreciation for the inherent storytelling forces at your disposal.

This isn't a call for outlining or even an endorsement of it as a process (which I do endorse, by the way). Drafting can work just as well ... when done right. While drafters don't like hearing it, the fact remains that this is the steeper path, because the search is engaged within the draft itself. It's like taking off in an airplane and then trying to file a flight plan. Of the many manuscripts I see that have major conceptual and structural problems, the vast majority come from seat-of-the-pants drafters (unofficially known as "pantsers") who got lost along the way.

Story physics don't play favorites, and they don't care how you write. They're simply forces that determine the outcome of *what* you write.

The means by which a writer engages in step 1 and step 2 can look almost identical in every way: You are *drafting* until you get it right … or you are *planning* until you get it right. "Right," in both cases, doesn't arrive until you find the story that works best as a result of optimizing the inherent forces/physics. When you get *that* right within a draft—no matter what number it is—it will stand a chance.

But right there, at the difference between a planning draft and a final draft, is a fork in the road, one the enlightened writer recognizes. If you know you're in a *search* phase—again, either in a draft or within an outlining/planning process—each story beat is up for grabs. When a better idea dawns, you go back and rebuild the draft/outline in context to that better idea. That's the essence of the search for story: to deliver better story beats (moments) to the page.

If you settle for your first idea, generated from within the natural and sometimes ecstatic frenzy of pouring out words, or if you simply leap from one idea to the next organically, without holding them under the scrutinizing light of context (story physics and story architecture), you may be missing an opportunity to add value.

Or, you may be reading a rejection letter soon.

What *is* a better idea?

A better idea is one that ratchets up the level of the story physics—intensity, clarity, or originality—in play at a given moment. Some examples: A stronger concept leading to more tension, conflict, and stakes; a more compelling hero and a scarier antagonist; a richer theme and a more dramatic subtext within which to showcase it; a more vivid and vicariously rich hero's journey, in pursuit of a worthier goal with more meaningful consequences; a better first plot point (one that leverages everything to a higher level just when it's needed most); better and more compelling story milestones; more effective scenes.

When you make a change in a story, when you revise—either during the outlining phase or during a draft—you are, in fact, harnessing the power of story physics. Because if it wasn't a better idea you wouldn't opt for it, and story physics is always *why* it's better.

If you can actually *optimize* each of the elements and essences of story physics during your first draft, without an outline to use as a vetting mechanism, then congratulations, you are truly gifted and a bona fide literary force to be reckoned with. But if you can't, then recognize that the opportunity for these upgrades exists no matter what your process and no matter where you are within it, either through a constantly evolving story *beat sheet* or through a series of drafts (which, in essence, is a long-form story beat sheet) that lead you to the discovery of better ideas and clearer identification of weaknesses.

What we're talking about here is natural law.

And there are valuable lessons to be learned from it: While fundamental craft is the ante-in, it is the presence of differentiating *power*, the pure brute storytelling *force*, that separates good from great, published from unpublished. You can jump from an airplane with any ol' parachute strapped to your back, but the better the physics applied to the design and creation of that parachute, the safer and smoother your descent. In the case of our stories, the design and execution responsibility belongs solely to us—there are no factory-sealed products on a shelf for us to strap on, but only design *principles* showing us how to stay alive—and we are the ones making a leap into the abyss, where physics are in full and unrelenting command of the outcome.

As we witness natural law in avocations other than writing, we see that effort, knowledge, and all the practice in the world cannot always make up for a lack of strength, speed, or a natural gift, or even a falling ladder. Few are born with *the gift*. Success is almost always the result of the building of skill and experience upon a base of inherent physics, sometimes learned and acquired over years. Many of the players who get cut from the team are as fast and strong as the athletes who end up with the paycheck, but rest assured, nobody gets invited to the tryout unless some level of those physics is in evidence.

In writing, a natural *gift* is not required. The only requirement is to *understand*, and then to act upon that understanding. As writers, our realities aren't defined by *natural* talents, even though some writers appear to be "born storytellers." In fact, there may not be such a thing as a natural writing gift. That *knack for words* you've been bragging about? Not worth a plug nickel in the publishing business if your sense of story is lacking.

This always has been, and always will be, a *learned* craft.

Most overnight successes are years, even decades in the making.

In his book *Outliers* (2008, Little Brown & Company), Malcolm Gladwell postulates that great success in any skill-, art-, or knowledge-based undertaking requires at least ten thousand hours of practice and study, trial and error, failure and success. Do the math: That's a bunch of years no matter how many hours per day you sit in front of a screen. Writing fiction is perhaps as vivid an example of Gladwell's hypothesis as any.

Your process doesn't define your outcome.

"Oh, I'm sorry my story isn't better, but that's my process so that's what we get." I've actually heard that from writers who claim they can't find their story beats any other way. Their process defines their outcome. Some people can lose weight simply by looking at a treadmill, while others simply don't know how to use a treadmill. Both are processes. And process is something we all need to choose. Hopefully, we pick the right one for us.

Your process may define the timeline and the number of ink-jet cartridges required to get there, but the requisite story forces that *need to be in play* at the end of the process are the same no matter how you go about it; i.e., whether you blueprint every story beat or confront every blank page without a clue as to what should come next (and thus have the assurance of a massive revision process). And thus you have to do it over and over until you get it right. With either extreme, the identification and harnessing of those forces is your goal. It is a goal more efficiently and effectively attained when the search for the vehicle itself—the story—is an empowered one.

That's the *search for story*. To know what *should* come next, based on what is called forth from the story forces you are wielding. You are searching for story beats that deliver the most powerful and appropriate level of story physics possible.

At the highest level, there are six forces of story physics.

They're presented and broken down for you in the next chapter. You now have context for them, and you've seen how essential they are to effective storytelling and how they are the *point* of any writing process.

Because they break down into substrata, it could be successfully argued that more than six exist. These aren't *core competencies* (which could be confusing at a glance, because there are six essential core competencies involved in storytelling, each of which uses multiple elements of story physics; see Chapter 22) as much as they are the empowering forces behind them, the very things that make the Six Core Competencies effective and necessary. Every successful story has some combination of these forces going for it, no matter how they find their way onto the page. They are always available, always ours to leverage.

4
STORY PHYSICS ... DEFINED
WHEREIN WE GET TO CHOOSE HOW WELL OUR STORIES WILL WORK.

Story physics aren't the *recipe* for a story. Rather, they are the qualitative nature of the *ingredients* that comprise the recipe. Nor are they the *tools* used to create a story (those are available in Chapter 22). Rather, they are the *forces* that those tools apply and leverage.

Mild, medium, or hot ... we get to choose.

Let's take that analogy a step further. Equate the writing of a book to a lavish meal: multiple courses, different flavors, all aligning with a theme. It will require tools—pots, pans, a stove, a butter knife—to prepare. It will require a basic recipe and some sensibility of cooking as a craft (note to self: don't serve steak that's as hard as a hockey puck). It will be composed of various ingredients, each with a different role that will add to the outcome. The courses should be served in a specific order, in certain combinations, and both the ingredients and the recipes need to align with their assigned roles in the dining experience (a little Tabasco in the dessert isn't gonna work).

The cook buys the ingredients from the store, and then uses the tools that are on hand, the tools she's comfortable with. She uses frozen ingredients or discounted items with impending "sell by" dates on the packages. She might use the house brand, instead of the expensive stuff. Rather than whip up sauces and spices personally, the cook opens a jar and just pours.

A true professional *chef*—someone on a different level than a *cook*—thinks otherwise, even with the same recipe in hand. A chef grows her own spices, harvesting only the perfect specimens. She shops at an elite butcher and visits farmers' markets for the freshest fruits and vegetables. She frequents a special bakery that has never let her down. She understands the nuances between a product grown in Italy and one grown in Kansas. She uses elite, professional-quality tools, chosen through the context of her training and experience.

She's into flavor, texture, freshness, and color.

Same recipe. Same food. But the chef doesn't settle, because intensity of taste, nuance, and plate appeal matter. The chef understands the *physics* of what will result in a stellar dining experience, and she doesn't serve anything less than optimized ingredients prepared with professional tools. She doesn't mess with nature in that regard, even though she may make the recipe her own.

Physics are nature *applied* to a goal. The physics of cooking are similar to the physics of storytelling: Better ingredients and better tools, applied to a proven recipe that allows you to season to taste, lead to a better result.

The difference between a cook and a chef is this: The chef honors the recipe, but adds her signature to it. The chef respects the physics of preparing a meal, even beyond the selection of ingredients (meat must be cooked for a certain amount of time, spices must be used within a range between too little and too much, some dishes are served hot, others cold, others at room temperature) and doesn't settle for sirloin when filet mignon is the intention. These are issues of *physics*. They aren't *rules*—chefs hate rules—but they *are* truth and consequence. Nature. It is this combination of recognizing quality ingredients and applying them within the context of governing physics and the liberating limitations of the tools of preparation and the nuances of the recipe that make for a great dining experience. Compromise to any of these elements puts the dinner at risk.

So, too, do professional writers get to choose what ingredients they use, and how they are combined and prepared. Degree, nuance, and timing are ours to craft, even when the recipe is nonnegotiable, which it sometimes is, at least contextually. Those choices can dictate success or the need to toss the whole thing in the trash and start over.

There are six key elements of story physics.

Six *literary forces* that, when used as criteria for narrative choices—as both qualitative and quantitative criteria and benchmarks for vetting story choices—result in a more *effective* story that seizes the inherent power of the available physics. Six forces that, when allowed to simply manifest organically within the flow of drafting, even though better choices may exist, may actually *limit* the story's ability to reach its fullest potential. This can happen when the writer accepts the first thing that pops into her head for a particular story beat, manifesting in the moment of creation. Or worse, when she *forces* a beat into being—also known as trying to write yourself out of a corner—thus pointing the story down a path that may or may not be the best course, the most optimized sequence of beats. In other words, leading you to more inescapable narrative corners.

Here's an example of choosing the right spice for your story: You give your hero an everyday job because he's an everyday guy—in other words, you give him a *boring* job—when any number of compelling jobs would better serve both characterization and plot. Why? Because it was—or is—*your* job, and you know it well. Somewhere in your writing past you've been told to *write what you know*—solid advice, but not always the best advice—so this leads you to unvetted choices in this regard.

Maybe *your* job fascinates you, but is it inherently compelling to others? Unless the plot depends on the hero's occupation, in which case the plot defines it, then this is an opportunity to contribute to characterization and context by way of injecting something interesting into the mix. Something that possesses stronger story physics. Politically correct or not, a person's career says something about his overall character: A person who is an embalmer or a career fast food worker is viewed differently than, say, a musician or a tax accountant. It's not a matter of judgment, but rather one of compelling details versus details that don't contribute one iota. Compelling—*interesting*—is always better, unless you really do want to paint your character as, well … vanilla.

I submit to you that there is always a creative choice at your disposal that will contribute to the story. Sometimes you just have to search for it, rather than accept the first thing that pops into your head.

Story physics are six forces—realms, essences, powers, leverages—that define the story experience. They will determine whether your novel is stimulating or boring, exciting or flat, surprising or obvious, sexy or vanilla, all through the inherent power of their very natures and their connection to common human urges and empathies, as well as their *degree of intensity* in context to how they are used. And always, they are something over which we have complete control.

Readers want to care, to feel. They want to learn, wonder, thrill, marvel ... to seek answers, be surprised, be frightened and concerned, to root for and empathize with something or somebody, and finally, to be some combination of satisfied, dumbfounded, shocked, delighted, and completely glad to have invested time in this story. Story physics—the choice and leveraging thereof—are the means by which it happens.

Readers lose themselves in novels and films in two seemingly contradictory ways and for two paradoxically opposed reasons: They want to escape the mundane, the real ... and they want to see life shredded into meaningful subsets. They want to live another life for a few hours. It is our job to make that life rich, exciting, and meaningful, the very antithesis of boring.

Story physics make these reader outcomes *happen*. From the initial idea forward, they are yours to wield. The leveraging of physics, through the writer's choices, can elevate the initial idea itself, turning good into great, changing vanilla into triple chocolate thunder. Story physics are the *fuel* for the fire in your story. You need to find the best fuel instead of the easiest and nearest, to search out and grab the quickest to ignite, the longest and brightest burning. Why use a match when an explosion would be better? You need premium gasoline on your fire, not the leftover grease from yesterday's fish fry.

One of the main reasons stories get rejected is that the author didn't reach deep enough or high enough (which are not contradictory terms).

Writer, meet story physics, a group of powerful essences that, once understood, are destined to become your new best friends. Whether you've realized it or not, they are already at play in the stories you write. Only now, you can tell them what to do instead of leaving them to run amok or exit the building altogether.

1. A COMPELLING NARRATIVE PREMISE, QUESTION, OR PROMISE

You begin with an idea. An idea can be so nonspecific that it barely qualifies as an idea ("I want to write a love story"), or it can arrive as an entire *implied* story told in one line or phrase ("I want to write about the 1980 U.S. Olympic Hockey team"). At some point the idea needs to grow into a concept, something that sets the stage for an unfolding dramatic arc driven by an unfolding character arc. When an idea implies or introduces conflict, it has passed into the realm of the *concept*.

Even that hockey team idea is without concept.

Every story needs a concept. You can't write "an idea" as a successful story *until* it becomes a concept.

But not all concepts are alike. Some concepts that perfectly fit the criteria—they define or imply conflict and pose a dramatic question—aren't very powerful in terms of story physics. "A love story between a man and a goat" is a concept but not one that optimizes the inherent power of this element of story physics. You'd have to bring a lot more to it for that to happen—"a love story between a Muslim and a Republican," for example—whereas a solid concept is immediately compelling, even before it's written.

That doesn't mean you can't add something to *make* an idea work, but it also doesn't mean that you should *settle* for it or try to make it work through the writing process, also known as the search for story. In this example, the search for story, at its most elementary level is, in fact, a search for a stronger and deeper concept. If the idea is inherently flat, unoriginal, or otherwise uninteresting, and if the concept that arises from it is described the same way, it's that much harder to add story elements that elevate it.

We're talking about a *compelling* concept that rises on its own merits (raising the Titanic from the ocean floor; the plight of black maids in Jackson, Mississippi, in 1962; a young girl thrust into a fight for her life in a cruel dystopian society's rite of dominance and control). Begin your story development with a concept that asks dramatic questions—questions that, by their very nature, promise answers that are compelling, interesting, and rewarding.

Taking nothing away from Dan Brown, but there are a few thousand writers out there who could have tackled the same idea and combination of elements he used in *The Da Vinci Code* and written a good book or screenplay. How so?

Because the concept and the myriad themes were absolutely stunning in their boldness and would be in pretty much any competent writer's hands. (Though, to be clear, execution remains a required part of the process and is, in fact, one of the essences of story physics, in addition to being broken into two of the Six Core Competencies; see Chapter 22 for more on that issue.) Such conceptualization has little to do with prosaic *talent*, although you *could* argue that one's ability to recognize a compelling concept is, in fact, a sort of talent, though it's one that can be cultivated through an understanding of the story physics involved, paired with a killer imagination. But conceptualization has *everything* to do with differentiating the inherent *power* of one idea/concept versus another idea/concept, and then knowing how to develop and execute it.

And for *that*, Dan Brown is to be admired. He seized the inherent power of an idea (which could have been any number of things) that quite naturally evolved into a killer concept—or in this case, a set of concepts that melded into one driving narrative—which was then executed with a keen sense of design and symmetry. The resulting story was elevated via two of the Six Core Competencies—concept and theme—to an astoundingly effective level. The result was book-selling history.

A lot of writers, speaking as readers, say they didn't care for the book. Though we're all entitled to our opinions, in many cases, that view has as much to do with personal belief systems, ignorance, and downright jealousy as it does with literary sensibility. For every commercial blockbuster that has a plot—and they *all* have a plot—there's inevitable noise from writers who don't write those kinds of books and feel that an injustice has transpired.

No, story physics are what have just transpired.

From the very moment of a story's conception, writers can begin searching for story beats that offer strong story physics. You can ask yourself what's interesting about this idea and what could make it more interesting. How will it lead to *conflict* for a *hero*? Does it result in a spine that can be unspooled with deliberate pacing? Will it cause the reader to feel something? If it doesn't do these things, recast it from a more conceptual context and see what happens.

As writers, we should accept that not all ideas—even our own—are interesting in and of themselves. We should ask what we're going to bring to the idea to elevate it.

Elevate it to what? To the level of a *concept*.

Once elevated, what questions arise from your concept? What are the expositional answers (the narrative) you will deliver in your sequence of scenes and story beats? What is inherently compelling and wonderful about them?

Going back to an earlier example, "a historical novel about twelfth-century Ireland" is an *idea* that isn't inherently interesting beyond the landscape and sociology. It's not a concept yet. Standing alone, it's not enough to carry the story. What conceptual questions does this ask beyond, "Okay, Ireland is pretty cool, so how can I show it being cool?" Make no mistake: To begin writing a draft with *only* that idea in play is merely a starting point in the *search* for a story.

This can be particularly challenging in genre fiction. A mystery is essentially a story about a murder in need of solving. A romance is about two people falling in love. The compelling questions, then, are things you must add to that genre-defining requisite concept. You do this by using all the available story physics to flesh out the idea: a compelling setting, a formidable obstacle, an empathetic hero, and something new and energizing, followed by stellar execution.

Judge your concept against these benchmarks: What does your concept imply, promise, or otherwise begin to define in terms of an unfolding story driven by dramatic tension? What might a hero want within this concept, and why, and what opposes that desire? The right concept will lead you to this; if it doesn't, chances are you haven't tapped into the power of this particular essence of story physics.

Going back to the beginning of this discussion … I mentioned the word *premise*. The first element of story physics is a *compelling premise*.

There are differences between an idea, a concept, and a premise. Some consider this nitpicking, but for writers looking for an edge, it's a useful differentiation. Just as an idea without a resulting concept is still a blank page, a concept without a premise is less of a story than one *with* a compelling premise.

Concept is focused on the potential for dramatic tension. *Premise* happens when you add a *character* to the mix.

So, in the case of *The Da Vinci Code*, it could break down like this:

> **IDEA:** *A story about religious veracity based on certain myths that exist to this day, including Leonardo Da Vinci's supposed membership in a secret sect.* (That's a strong idea, in that it already leans to the conceptual side, because it implies conflict by challenging widely held belief systems. A more simplistic idea might have been: *A story about the veracity of the church.* Or *a story about the Holy Grail.* Or about three dozen other potential starting points … Dan Brown isn't returning my calls to clarify.)

> **CONCEPT:** *What if Christ didn't actually perish on the cross, and the church buried the truth to ensure their authority and has since been killing people who come close to finding out the truth using a secret sect of assassins that has survived the centuries?* (Notice there are no characters here, just drama and tension.)

> **PREMISE:** *A story about a symbologist called in to interpret clues at a murder scene, leading him to the discovery of connections that involve larger powers and put his life in jeopardy as he gets nearer and nearer to the truth and the people responsible*

for it, who happen to reside at the highest levels of the Catholic church itself. This premise is character focused, with an equal dose of drama and powerful themes.

Idea leads to concept, and concept then leads to *premise*. Evolution is involved in both. Character—the essence that transforms concept into premise—is at the forefront of storytelling, neck and neck with conflict in the race for the most empowering aspect of the craft. So it's not really a story until concept is married to character. Even if your idea is simply a character (my first novel began that way), you need to make a concept out of it, and when it begins to lead somewhere, that slug line is called a *premise*.

A story about living through the Great Depression ... that's an *idea*. A story about surviving the Depression by stealing food from others ... that's a *concept*. A story about a young boy who learns the truth about how his parents survived the Depression ... that's a *premise*.

The first element of story physics is a *compelling premise* for a story. This is rooted in a familiar cliché: You can't make a silk purse out of a sow's ear. Make sure your premise is pure silk and you'll have a better shot at filling the resultant purse with some coin at the end of the day.

2. DRAMATIC TENSION

This is simple, universal, and eternal: Your story has to have a *hero* (a protagonist who ultimately resolves the story). You, the author, have to give that hero something to *do* in the form of a need, a challenge, a problem to solve, a goal to reach, or a quest. And then you need to put *obstacles* in the way of the hero's pursuit of a solution or the desired outcome. The impending collision of the hero's goal and those obstacles is *dramatic tension*, which arises from *conflict*. It poses the question: What will happen here? Then, right behind it, the stage is set for the next critical question: And why should I care?

If you were forced to identify one word, and one word only that is the front-runner for the most essential essence in all fiction, it would be *conflict*. No conflict, no story.

As you search for your story, this should be the driving essence that you apply to almost all of your creative choices. How does every scene, and every moment within every scene, serve the building or manifestation and exposition of *conflict*?

Why is conflict so essential? Because conflict is, either directly or indirectly, the stuff that generates *dramatic tension*, which is one of the essential forces of story physics.

Character-driven writers try to challenge this all the time, and it never works. Even if the conflict is internal and subtle, it needs to be present and act as a catalyst in the story. Ironically, those same writers who decry conflict in general rely on it as the source of dramatic tension—which is nonnegotiable—in their stories by virtue of an *inner* conflict within their characters. The more internal and subtle it is, the more the other story elements and physics need to be put into effective play. That said, external conflict, however less-than-thrilling, also needs to be present or the story plays like the transcript from a marriage counseling session.

Every single scene after your First Plot Point (see Chapter 22) should exhibit some dramatic tension to some variable degree, at least contextually. Every single scene before your First Plot Point should contribute to the *setup* of that dynamic, either through foreshadowing, hero backstory and present context, the establishment of stakes, or the ramp-up to the First Plot Point story turn.

What makes this work—the physics behind it—are the *stakes* you've established for the hero, often expressed as a dramatic question: Will the hero get the girl? Will the girl get the hero? Will the city be saved? Will justice be done? Stakes are the *why* that drive a story, the motivation for characters to want what they want and do what they do. What could be won or lost? What are the consequences of success or failure? If you can harness these conflict-driven physics by making the reader care based solely on those stakes—which also leads you to another of the six essential elements of story physics—then your story will very likely work, and work well.

The Hunger Games (see Chapter 24) wasn't just about a girl and a dystopian society that, in a frightening way, reminds us of ourselves.

That was the concept, one that wasn't fully developed until *conflict* and *premise* were added.

The story's architecture was driven, almost exclusively, by dramatic tension arising from *external* conflict (though Katniss has her fair share of internal conflict as well). She is sent to a place where everybody is trying to kill her ... conflict doesn't get more external than that. Evil puppet masters are trying to torment her for the amusement of the audience before she's killed. Injury and nature get in the way of safety. Friendship challenges survival. Her internal resistance to love and her confusion over her feelings—the internal conflict in this story—threaten her ability to survive in this externally dangerous situation.

In *The Help* (see Chapter 23), conflict takes the form of social norms and belief systems, which underpin the behavior of zealots and cowards, allowing true heroism and character to emerge. It is a vicarious ride (we feel like we're right there in 1962 Jackson, Mississippi) fueled by empathy and a true desire to see the dramatic tension through to a satisfying conclusion. In other words, story physics are present, and three of the six are used in that one descriptive sentence alone. *The Help* demonstrates how story physics integrate to create a sum in excess of the parts.

You could say (and we often do early in the story search phase, before we realize that it needs more juice) that such a story is *about* setting or theme. Yes, *The Help* is a story dealing with racial norms and the plight of domestic help in 1962 Jackson, Mississippi. But that description of what the story is "about" only works in elevators and e-mails, since it provides none of the structural dramatic grist that tells the real story, or more important, gives the writer something to actually write about in a true *story* sense. Without Skeeter and her book project, without that nasty pie, the story would play like a freshman sociology report. It is the dramatic tension that makes *The Help* work, in combination with brilliant conceptual and thematic narratives. And if you've been paying attention, you may notice that the first two elements of story physics defined here reside at the heart of why this story works. Even if the other elements were executed with mediocrity (which isn't the case), *The Help* would have stood a chance at success by virtue of these two story forces alone.

3. EXPOSITIONAL PACING

As I was writing this, my wife was reading John Irving's book, *In One Person*. After the first few pages she turned to me and said, "You gotta read this, he hasn't lost a thing, gorgeous prose." Of course. He's John Irving, the wrestler with the poet's eye for lyric moments and a screenwriting Oscar on his mantle, based on his bestseller, *The Cider House Rules*. And prose is one of the Six Core Competencies, so my wife was bound to notice.

A few days later she was reading a magazine instead of the book, which sat on her nightstand with a bookmark inserted about halfway through. When I asked about this, she said, "I think Irving's lost it. Or he's unburdening some inner demon, and that demon is kinda boring." I asked her to expand on that. She told me that the story rambled, that there was no direction, no real conflict-driven plot, that "it's all inner dialogue, all character." I then asked, somewhat rhetorically, if that was a bad thing. She answered, "It is if I no longer want to read the damn thing."

Well, he's John Irving. He gets to do that. Just like Stephen King gets to write 1,000-page behemoth novels that could be cut down to 450 pages if anybody had the balls to edit the guy. Same with Jonathan Franzen, the reigning sex idol of intelligentsia-obsessed literati. I bought both of his books, thinking I should and could learn something from one of the best-reviewed authors of the past ten years (reviewers being among the intelligentsia-obsessed demographic), but I couldn't finish either of them. There's a place for stories like those, but let's be clear: They're not for everybody. And they're not models for *commercial* fiction at its best, despite their numbers (which I would bet include a higher-than-normal proportion of incomplete reads). As a writer, you need to know precisely what audience you are writing for. And you need to give them what they expect and want. The more genre-rooted your story, the more essential this is.

The problem with Irving and Franzen's books—for me, and for a lot of people who jumped on the bandwagon because of some inner guilt about needing to *read up* instead of pandering to our more commercial literary appetites—is an issue of story physics. Or the lack thereof. These authors don't really optimize dramatic tension, and they don't offer a terribly compelling central premise. What they do offer is a deep dive into character, which is extremely difficult to do in such a way that it rivets the reader to the pages. Which didn't happen for me, my wife, or anyone else who will fess up.

No disrespect, those guys are genius writers. That's part of the problem: The rest of us *aren't*.

Dramatic tension and compelling premise aside, there's another opportunity that isn't seized by the works of the authors I've just mentioned. They adopt a languid *pace*, or no pace at all. Franzen's work, in particular, reads like a still photograph to which he gives highly pixilated interpretation. Nelson Demille and Michael Connelly and Dennis Lehane and Nora Roberts (each of whom are on occasion every bit as literate and poignant in their prose as Irving and Franzen), on the other hand, are all about artful *pace*. Their novels jump quickly into dramatic tension, grab us with empathy for the hero, and then hit the gas, and the story accelerates from there. No freeze-frame vivisections for these authors, which makes them a joy to read, instead of a chore.

Pacing is totally within the author's control. The best pacing is executed in context to the core competency of structural architecture, which calls for the story to fall into four sequential parts of roughly the same length, each with a different contextual mission, each separated by major story milestones that also have a distinct mission to accomplish within the narrative (see Chapter 22). The mission of the four parts and their separating milestone beats is, at its highest level, the optimization of *pace*.

The Part One setup of the story is where pacing takes a backseat to introducing hero, a world view, the stakes, and the impending machinations that will reveal themselves at the First Plot Point. This scene—and it is arguably the most important moment in a story—is what separates Part One from Part Two. Once you are into Part Two, however, you should proactively look for ways to move the story forward. The hero now has a problem to solve and/or a journey or quest to undertake, and the context of this second quartile is to show us the hero's *response* to this new state, which was launched (or, if it was put in play earlier, then fully launched and informed here) at the First Plot Point.

Part Three accelerates the story even more, adding pressure and stakes to the hero's proactive *attack* on the problem, moving into this contextual mode from Part Two's *response* context. Part Four really hits the gas and cranks up the heat (dramatic tension), with converging story arcs and character motivations, setting the stage for your hero to be the proactive catalyst for the story's resolution in Part Four.

Once again, *The Hunger Games* provides a clinic in pacing. The story starts fast, with Katniss volunteering to be the tribute from her district. She travels to the Capitol and begins to train, bringing her closer and closer to the Games and further accelerating the pace.

But in this story, Katniss's relationship with Peeta is the character-driven part of this dramatic tension, and it begins to accelerate in Part Two. Peeta makes his affection for Katniss public, and their sponsor, Haymitch, endorses this as a brilliant survival strategy. This relationship is a new wrinkle, and it accelerates the pace. Then, during the initial part of the Games, Peeta appears to betray her, thus further heightening dramatic tension and once again accelerating the pace.

As you experience this story, notice how it moves faster and faster as it progresses, even after a quick start. This is pacing at its finest, even within the context of a first-person inner dialogue as the narrative voice.

At any given moment in your story, consider how each scene or moment is contributing to pace. Depending on where you are in the story, you can then assess whether you're pushing the physics or if the story is on pause or even going backward when it should be pressing forward.

The last thing you want is for the reader to feel like the story had better pick up fast, that nothing's happening, and that he's beginning to get bored. Pacing is a learned sensibility, one not naturally transferred from one's sensibilities as a reader to those of a writer, which is unfortunately a default context from which some writers do their work. The story instincts we acquire as *readers* often fail us when staring at the blank page of a story of our own creation.

One of the most common faults of poorly paced stories is the lack of a central spine that serves as the energy source for dramatic tension. In other words, *episodic* stories that are more about a time and a place, where the hero simply goes from adventure to adventure without each event connecting to a core story that moves forward and gradually— and in spots, not so gradually—growing and shifting and intensifying, becoming at once clearer and more dramatic. Life stories, in the form of novels or screenplays, are often guilty of this, and the only way this really works is if the life in question—like J. Edgar Hoover or Abraham Lincoln, whose lives have both been made into movies—is already something readers are interested in.

The solution resides in combining some element of dramatic tension that spans the *entire* book, and then being downright strategic about how the story grows and reveals more of itself. In *The Hunger Games*, for example, the Big Dramatic Question regarding Katniss's survival is always looming. But along the way there are other little dramas that play out and are resolved, and each of them takes us deeper into the story and closer to the Big Picture resolution.

If you're not moving forward, you're dying. That's an axiom in life, and it's just as true in fiction.

4. HERO EMPATHY

From Day One of our writing education, the notion that our stories are about a *character* or *hero* has been pounded into our heads. Sometimes this is positioned as the supreme *mission* of storytelling, that fiction is *all* about characterization and that our readers need to *like* our hero.

True, and not true. It's a bit of a paradox, but in a good way.

Our stories require *both* a compelling protagonist and a compelling premise. When it all works, one begets the other. Characters need a stage and something to *do*. Without conflict and dramatic tension, what they do becomes episodic. Busywork. Another slice-of-life vignette. But when they have a significant and dramatic goal, something to find, achieve, flee from, or survive, the characters have a bigger stage upon which to strut their stuff and reveal their facets to an extent that your college lit professor feels vindicated in his character-centric rhetoric.

There is a difference between observing and analyzing a character and emotionally participating with and rooting for a character. The latter two are orders of magnitude and are more powerful as a storytelling strategy. To apply this strategy, you need to give your character a quest, a journey to take, a problem to solve, a goal to strive for. In other words, a *plot*.

It's a myth that the reader must *like* your hero. It's good if it serves your story, but not always necessary. Antiheroes are everywhere these days (Bruce Willis makes a living off them). What isn't a myth is this: The reader must *root* for the hero. The same goes with an antihero's goals within the story quest, though this is not an absolute, as some successful stories are about the protagonist's decline and fall. This connects to other elements of story physics because it demands that the author put the hero into a situation (dramatic tension) that is pressured by stakes and conflict, and thus asks us to feel his pain or hope or whatever, and to root for him along the way.

So how do we make *that* happen?

By creating *empathy* for the hero's situation, plight, need, and quest, all in context to that which opposes him. When we put our heroes on a path toward something and give them something to do, with stakes attached, readers *feel* it. They get into it. Readers should *feel* the dramatic tension in a story as if they are right in the middle of it. Not just because it's scary, but because they can easily relate to the emotions and stakes of the situation, the very thing the hero is feeling in those moments. They come along for the ride, understand the predicament, experience the fear and the hope and the frustration. They empathize, and thus, they *root* for your hero.

Stakes are the means to creating this empathy. When the reader can *feel* the stakes and what might be won or lost, you've hooked them.

STORY PHYSICS

You can make them feel it by clearly showing the *consequences* and price of success or failure and its ultimate effect on everyone involved.

Read a Michael Connelly novel and you'll see this at work. There's more going on than a whodunit proposition to solve. The best mysteries always give the reader a sense of the stakes. There is *power* behind the crime and the need for justice. We relate to the victims, and we relate to the detective or the protagonist acting as investigator. We don't merely recognize the stakes, we *feel* them. We *empathize* with Connelly's heroes and his victims, because he touches us in ways that cut to the core of our humanity. This is why he owns his genre.

The romance genre is nothing if not focused on hero empathy. If the reader doesn't feel the heat and chemistry, if the heroine's longing and inner demons aren't relatable, then the story won't work as well as it otherwise might. Successful romance writers focus on manipulating the reader into empathizing with the hero—in romance they still engender this, because there is always a hero and a heroine, but the true hero status is variable, because women love their bad boys, after all—and thus provide a vicarious ride along the way (yet another element of story physics).

The Hunger Games again demonstrates this element of story physics at a stellar level. We relate to Katniss (especially if you are a teenaged girl, a demographic that represents a high percentage of those thirty million book buyers). We can easily understand what she is going through, even though Katniss's reality resides far beyond our own. We can imagine it in visceral detail: the utter terror, the hopelessness, the sense of impending doom, the will to survive, the sting of betrayal (when it appears that Peeta has switched teams), the compromises that are forced upon us. The author, through her choice of narrative voice (first person present), takes us deep into the psyche and thoughts of her protagonist, and the result is an easy leap from our reading chair right into Katniss's skin.

That's *hero empathy* at work. Notice how it feeds off dramatic tension, which manifests from a compelling premise, a premise that is *equal* parts conflict and character.

5. A VICARIOUS READING EXPERIENCE

Staying with *The Hunger Games* for a moment, we not only feel *for* Katniss (hero empathy), we feel *with* her (vicarious experience). This is a subtle but critical differentiation that the enlightened writer can leverage. The reader gets to *be there* with Katniss in the midst of the Games.

My step-granddaughter (yeah, I'm that old) read the book twice and saw the movie three times. I asked her why, and her first answer was, "Because it's so cool." Being an old fart, I pushed back, offering that kids killing kids isn't really cool at all, that it's kind of dark. After wrestling with this, we landed on what drew her to this story: the feeling of being alone and in charge of your own survival, a kid being empowered, and experiencing what it would be like to live that nightmare (she admitted that much) with death always on your heels. She felt it. And that's what made this story one of the best-selling series of the last decade, right up there with Harry Potter. Which, by the way, leveraged vicarious reader experience just as brilliantly.

Remember *Top Gun*, the 1986 film starring Tom Cruise as a maverick F-14 fighter pilot? (I've been criticized for using this story as an example, but literary snobbism aside—*Top Gun* being a bit of a guilty pleasure—you can't argue that the film worked for this very reason.) It was a blockbuster, not critically acclaimed, but certainly successful in terms of box office receipts. I was among the folks who paid to see it multiple times, and then bought the DVD, which I still put on from time to time.

But why? Not because of the great writing or the stellar acting (which was fine, especially Goose), or the soundtrack (which was killer). No, it was something else.

It was those fighter jets. That aircraft carrier. The training regimen. The camaraderie of pilots. The film presents a ride (almost literally), a lift, a life experience I'll never get to actually have. It's the *vicarious experience Top Gun* delivers that makes it work, which only tangentially connects to the power of the story being told, which in this case isn't particularly interesting. The love story could have taken place within any environmental context. We weren't rooting for Maverick and Charlie as much as we were rooting for Maverick to get back into the cockpit.

Vicarious experience is a powerful but rarely discussed element of story physics. It is something separate from, yet closely aligned with, *hero empathy*, which asks us to make our readers feel the emotions and state of mind of the hero, and thus, root for her or him. Vicarious experience, while certainly elevated through a high level of hero empathy, is different. It allows the reader to feel *the sensations of a given moment*, to experience being there, going through the moments and existing in the situations that are presented in the story world, in a way that transcends simply reading *about* it. The reader becomes a part of it all.

When you can make the readers root for the hero because they can feel what it would be like to *be* the hero, *and* transport the readers to another time and place and live the journey for themselves, vicariously, you've just optimized two key elements of story physics.

Remember *Avatar*? I submit to you that the reason you went back to see it in 3-D had little to do with the story. It was because you were transported to another world, in another time, and you were able to *feel* that experience. To fly on the back of a dragon. You may or may not have empathized with the hero (not so much the second time), but that's a different set of physics. *Avatar* was, for all intents and purposes, more about *you* than it was those digitally generated characters.

You don't need an action story or a science fiction premise to put vicarious experience to work. Have you ever wondered why television's *The Bachelor* attracts tens of millions of viewers each season? Not for the characters, at least beyond a mild degree of empathy. More likely, it's because you get to recall the sensation of new romance, of falling in love, and of battling yourself and other suitors for the attention of someone else. You get to fall in love again, to take that ride for yourself … vicariously.

A few years ago Royal Caribbean cruise lines held a contest in which entrants were asked to submit a fifty-word essay, including a tagline, about the experience of cruising. There were fifteen thousand entrants, and there was only one grand prize winner, who would be awarded a free cruise for four.

I love cruising. Absolutely love it. So I took a swing.

Well, I won. Took the Grand Prize over fifteen thousand other entries. My tagline? "*Fall in love again.*"

This was followed with forty-six other words describing what that particular concept might look like on the deck of *Explorer of the Seas*, a 140-ton floating honeymoon. The bad news was … I didn't read the fine print, which stated that "professional writers may not enter." I had twenty-five years of copywriting experience and four published novels under my belt, so there was no appealing to the judges. They sent me a robe and a logoed hat with their condolences. And somebody else took the free cruise.

Vicarious experience drove all of it. The tagline, the copy, and the fact that the judges liked it best out of a stadium full of entries. The next vicarious experience I offer here: Imagine how *that* felt, if you were me.

Kathryn Stockett took us back to 1962 Jackson, Mississippi, in *The Help*. We were vicariously there. That feeling, that force, resides next to but separate from our affection and empathy for the characters and our outrage at the values that suppressed them. The vicarious experience was a big part of the draw in both the book and the film.

The combination of hero empathy and vicarious experience becomes a whole that greatly exceeds the sum of those two parts. They are like a spark and a pile of dried wood: The ensuing explosion of energy is far more than either could generate alone.

6. NARRATIVE STRATEGY

The word *narrative* means "story." While "writing voice" is one of the Six Core Competencies of successful writing (see Chapter 22), this isn't what I'm referring to here using the term "narrative *strategy*." Nor am I referring to the floor plan or structure of the story (also covered in Chapter 22). Rather, "narrative strategy" refers to how you tell the story in terms of point of view, framing devices, and other creative approaches.

This may stretch the classic definition of physics, but I think in our case it applies. Consider a human body: beautiful, all the requisite parts in place, with perfect features and muscularity and great hair ... but it's not *alive* ... until it is. That life force is pure physics. It doesn't really live life in a compelling way, until it does, through feeling and experiencing. None of the other features of human beings matter until the parts, beautiful as they are, are brought to life. A brilliant narrative strategy brings life to a story that might otherwise not resonate as well.

What do I mean by *point of view*? In *The Help*, Kathryn Stockett told the story through three first-person narrators, each of which had equal claim to the title of protagonist. That was a *strategic* choice on her part, and the story soared because of it.

What do I mean by a framing device? This is when one character seeks out the story from another, is literally told the story that we came to hear. *Life of Pi* was written that way, presenting us with a writer interviewing the modern-day survivor of a disaster at sea, which we see in a series of flashbacks driven by the interviewee's narrative. The movie version of *Interview with the Vampire* was written that way, with Christian Slater as the story-seeking journalist. The recent film *Anna Karenina* was told through the façade of a surreal stage play, with the point of view switching between surreality and realism seamlessly.

How you will tell your story is as critical as *what* story you will tell. And the reason we get creative with that choice has everything to do with story physics.

Story physics are like one's personality traits and inner character. You have to *do* something with them before you can make a difference, before you can experience the consequences of your actions or your intentions. You can work on your personality, you can search for it and practice, but in the end none of that matters until you take it out in public.

And yet, even when you do things right, the results are still up for grabs. The extraordinary remains elusive. To have an extraordinary result—a goal we all share when we set out to write a story—we must do something extraordinary, beyond the norm. Truly, we are seeking to make our whole story a sum in excess of its parts. That's what narrative *strategy* is about … nailing it, elevating it, injecting something indefinable and unique into the mix.

A lot can go wrong with a story, even with these story physics on the tarmac ready to take off. The best airplane in the world, with the strongest engines and newest electronics and most comfortable interior, is just a heap of parts and potential until a competent pilot buckles in.

This one is "the X-Factor" of writing. It's hard to define, very much the product of experience. It's part writing voice, part wit, part pathos, part structural framework, part intangible. It's story *sense*. It's craft. It's our personal touch. It's the sum of our choices along the way.

Not all stories are high concept.

Nor are all stories terribly vicarious. They don't all deliver an experience you'd want to have. In fact, some of the best stories deliver an experience you'd never want to have. But when a story really works, you can't put it down. In these stories, compelling forces combine on the page to become a sum of specific elements that are in excess of their parts. If one of those elements is underwhelming, then stellar execution often compensates and lifts the story into effectiveness.

This is precisely how John Irving and Jonathan Franzen gained fame. It's not their concepts or the dramatic tension in their stories. It's a combination of other things, executed with stellar skill, nuance, and sensibility. If you want to write stories like theirs, with languid pace and thin tension, then you better be as good as they are in that regard. A tall order.

Meanwhile, if we're not that good, a whole bunch of story physics are waiting to help us out.

It's like the best plate of spaghetti you've ever tasted. Nothing special or original about it … it just *works*. And it's no accident. The fact that it works so well is a function of the physics of cooking spaghetti … sometimes the chef just *knows*.

And sometimes the best spaghetti is served on paper plates.

Keep these story forces—the physics of storytelling—front and center as you search for your story.

Don't latch onto ideas without attempting to optimize them. The forces of storytelling are too easy to take for granted. The moment you connect a character to impending conflict you will see story physics in play, but story physics are always a matter of degree, intensity, and compulsion, which are levels you can control.

Don't settle. Instead, seek to blow your readers out of the water.

WRITING IN CONTEXT TO ... SOMETHING

WHEREIN OUR STORIES OBEY MANY MASTERS ... OR NONE AT ALL.

Allow me to bottom-line this for you: The best, most empowering context for writing a story comes from an understanding of the basic essences of story physics just presented to you. They affect every decision you will make in your story. They are, quite literally, the wind beneath your literary wings. And if you want your story to fly, you need that wind to be working *for* you.

But other contexts are out there, some of them helpful, some of them singing a siren song. Some folks write with only an experiential grasp of story physics; they've seen them in action in stories they've read, sometimes without recognizing them as such, and they've heard them talked about with less precise terminology. Trying to harness them in this manner is like trying to cook a gourmet meal using only your experience as a dinner guest.

Storytelling and marriage have much in common.

To start with, they're both love affairs, or they should be. Thing is, your story doesn't talk back to you (it might be easier if it did). It doesn't cheat on you, either, and if *you* cheat there will be consequences, and your story will betray you. You're on your own to get along, to imbue the relationship with what it needs and take what it offers. The success of the relationship—and the story—is completely in your hands.

Allow me to leverage *that* analogy for a moment.

Relationships are hard. It becomes harder the longer we're in one, because time brings new challenges related to apathy, laziness, and boredom. To succeed at it, if we ever do, we must apply what we've learned and tested and adopted along the way.

Or not ... which is also *context*, for better or for worse.

It's challenging for a relationship cruising along on autopilot to be blissful. Autopilot doesn't factor in variables, and it won't safely get you through storms, emergency landings, or scheduled stops for maintenance. It's just coasting while you are paying attention to other things. A relationship on autopilot lacks passion, surprise, and a baseline sense of joy. It's a ticking bomb that will explode when an emergency light pops on.

Everybody—in marriage and in writing—brings *context*, for better or worse, to the relationship. Sometimes it's simply what you've learned about love from your parents (risky, that; the "Greatest Generation" wasn't so great in that regard). Or, maybe you've read all the books, taken some classes, had some counseling. Maybe you majored in human psychology in school. Sometimes you just feel your way through it, communicating with your partner as best you can to reach mutually acceptable settlements and goals.

Again, that last one doesn't work for writers, because the story doesn't talk back. It gives you no feedback. Agents and editors do, and then it's too late.

In a primary relationship, you wouldn't think of saying this:

> *Gee, this is hard and confusing, so stop telling me what does and doesn't make a marriage work. Stop breaking it down into its most basic levels and then talking about tools I can apply to the challenge, and stop telling me how to make my marriage stellar in a neighborhood full of separations and weekend visitations, which is just, I dunno, normal. It shouldn't be this frigging hard. Just let me wing it and make my own way,*

because all that psychological crap is just so darn confusing. I
mean, just look at the Joneses next door—they don't ever talk
about their relationship and they seem happy as hell.

Then again, maybe you *would* say this—too many folks do ... but that's another book about another problem.

This is what some writers feel when confronted with the depth of knowledge available about storytelling. They're advocating literary autopilot—which is a helluva lot easier, at least until something goes wrong—but beware, it's a recipe for frustration and a long apprenticeship full of multiple drafts.

We all get to choose what context we bring.

The relationship between storytelling physics (from the previous chapter) and storytelling tools (in Chapter 22) opens an intriguing and promising door of literary opportunity. It means we have *access* to those physics using something other than our gut instincts and our learning curves, both as readers and as writers. These things give us standards, benchmarks, expectations, and solutions. But like a nonpilot sitting in the left seat of the cockpit in an airplane, the tools won't work unless we understand how the machine *operates*. We need to know how and why a relationship exists between the machine itself and the physics that allow it to function. The designer of the airplane has to know this, while the pilot doesn't. She or he only needs to know what to do and when.

Here's an evolved insight: As authors, we are *both* designers and operators of our stories. We must know how to build them, and then we must know how to command them.

With writing, it's overly simplistic to ask, "Is this good enough?" A better question for self-editing is this: How do we *know* if it is good enough?

It's even more useful if we get more specific with these questions, directed at any given moment in the story:

- What is the dramatic tension at this moment, and overall?
- What dramatic question is in play at any given moment?

- Is the pacing right?
- What is my reader thinking and feeling at any given moment?
- Will my reader experience empathy for my hero and root for him or her on that path?
- Is my story delivering a vicarious experience, or is the reader kept at arm's length?
- Is the conceptual centerpiece of the whole thing going to be compelling to anybody besides me? Can I get outside myself and explain why?

MULTIPLE LAYERS OF CONTEXT

Context is everywhere. A writer needs to determine if the context he is applying to his work is empowering or not, self-discovered or absorbed from credible sources, clear or confusing, proactively present or completely missing from his own awareness. (One of the great gifts in a writer's journey is to realize that he doesn't know what he's doing.) Did you arrive at the decision to write a story through your blissful experience as a reader, perhaps after reading a particular genre or author? Did you secretly believe you could do better? How does your formal training—school, workshops, books, and so on—create context for your approach to storytelling? Have you rejected context because it's too hard? Because it violates what you signed up for, which is some mystical, soul-liberating process that is completely free from the dogma of structure and commercial expectation?

Is that you?

Maybe your context—your base of craft and knowledge—was gleaned simply by being an avid *reader* of stories. That's common, and it can instill a certain sensibility about story structure and nuance. But it also can be limiting, like thinking you can be your own lawyer because you've seen so many courtroom dramas. To switch metaphors, you can't learn to fly an airplane by sitting in coach. So much more is going on within a story, especially structurally and even strategically, than most readers recognize or are equipped to comprehend (the goal being to manipulate the reader's emotions, which is precisely what story physics allow you to do). Many readers just sit back and read, enjoying the ride without understanding what the writer has done, or how.

Regardless of the source of one's contextual basis in these regards, external contexts also apply directly to your story.

Like the marketplace, for example. What genre are you writing in? What books out there are similar—*too* similar—to your project? If you have an author brand and a following, either from previous books or your website, does your next project align with them? What politics and sociology might affect what you're doing? Are you trying to be commercial, or are you an artist who doesn't care what anybody thinks (both are viable, but let's be clear, they are *very* different, albeit powerful contexts).

Context also applies in a structural and mission-driven way *within* the stories we write. In fact, that context is the most critical of all, because it defines the author's ability to *optimize* the story. For example, a macrostory (sometimes referred to as the "A story"), has four parts and key milestones. The scenes that fill those parts must align with a microcontext of dramatic optimization. Both are mission-driven endeavors, with differing yet complementary contexts in play. Some of that might relate to a subplot (the "B story"), while some might simply serve as transitional exposition.

Life itself is nothing *other* than context.

The only things in the universe that exist in a vacuum are floating in outer space. And even *they* have context. Context is like oxygen: invisible, essential, and taken for granted. At least, until something goes wrong. It's also like gravity. Ignore it or mishandle it, and you will most likely crack your head open.

The search for story and the way you apply story physics are totally dependent upon context. The context of what you know about making a story effective—story physics—defines the outcome of your search, and thus, the destiny of your project.

THE CONTEXT OF STORYTELLING

At my workshops, I often ask the group a warm-up question: From what *context* are you writing your story? A sea of blank stares usually manifests before me.

It's not that they don't have answers, or that they don't understand the question, but rather because they've never thought about storytelling from this perspective.

A powerful list of contextual issues comes into play within the writing of a story. They can take the form of questions, which challenge writers to inventory what they are bringing to the task, and where they came from.

- **DO YOU UNDERSTAND THE FUNDAMENTALS OF BASIC DRAMATIC THEORY?** If so, what is the nature and evolution of the core conflict of your story? Is it internal or external in nature? What is its inherent tension? What is the arc of your character? The thematic landscape? The structural architecture? If these answers elude you, odds are you won't know what went wrong until someone tells you. And rest assured, they will.

- **DO YOU UNDERSTAND THE CONTEXTUAL DEMANDS OF THE GENRE YOU ARE WRITING IN?** How does it differ from other genres, and how does it create expectations from readers, agents, and publishers, and thus put a fence around your creative options?

- **DO YOU UNDERSTAND THE CONTEXT OF THE SIX CORE COMPETENCIES OF STORYTELLING?** Have you covered each base with equal emphasis and considered the inherent criteria defined under each? (See Chapter 22 for a primer on the Six Core Competencies.)

- **WHAT IS THE CONTEXT OF YOUR STORY'S ESSENCE?** Have you harnessed the inherent power of its setting through time and place? With voice? The use of subtext? Does your premise have an inherent appeal, or are you relying solely on your execution to make the story compelling?

- **DO YOU CLEARLY KNOW THE CORE STORY YOU ARE TELLING VERSUS A THEME OR A SETTING OR A CHARACTER BACKSTORY?** Trouble awaits if you don't, because each of those other focuses are void of dramatic tension. They are a stage upon which a story plays, but from the writer's standpoint, they are rarely the core of a valid "story."

It's alarming to realize how many writers can't define what a story even *is*. They are surprised to learn that the only essential elements are conflict and character, and yet, so much more is involved—like the story physics that make it *work*.

The answers to each of these critical questions connect to story physics—the very things you should be searching for as you develop your story. They provide the most empowering, directly applicable context for your writing.

In a world in which authors of journalism, essays, and school papers believe that *content* is king, as writers you need to understand this: In fiction, *context* actually wears the crown.

THE WAYS AND MEANS OF THE SEARCH FOR STORY

WHEREIN WE REALIZE THAT ALL WRITING ROADS LEAD TO ROME.

Within the Six Core Competencies model, only two realms of *execution* exist: scene writing and writing voice. The other four are elements, specific essences and benchmarks, each of which is driven by story physics. (See Chapter 22 for definitions and interrelationships of the Six Core Competencies.)

But when it comes time to put your hands on a keyboard and write a draft, no matter which draft you're on, it all comes down to one thing: scenes ... the infusion of story physics within each of those four elements.

STORY BEATS

The search for story is the identification of *story beats*—specific scenes and moments that present and integrate situations, dynamics, facts, lies, actions, and contexts that move the story *forward* while informing the characters, the reader, or both. Story beats deliver the maximum effectiveness possible within the context of your approach. In other words, shorter words, or story beats, seize the moment by *optimizing* the associated story physics.

But you know that by now. So let's go deeper and see how we can make this happen on the page.

A plot twist, a surprise moment … that's a *story beat*. When anything changes in a story, whenever something new (even if it doesn't change anything, even if it's a deliberate head fake) is presented, that's a story beat, too. The three major milestones (First Plot Point, Midpoint, Second Plot Point … see Chapter 22) are major story beats, as are the hook, the pinch points, and anything else that moves the story forward. It could legitimately be argued that every scene in a novel or screenplay is a story beat, which in application means that the author who *plans* is looking for major story points *first*, to serve as a framework for the entire narrative, and then filling in scenes—I like to think of these as *connective tissue*—between those milestones, each delivering lesser story beats.

Big or small, each scene needs to move the story forward. Each scene is the vehicle for the delivery of a story *beat.*

If your character goes on a first date and sparks fly, that's a story beat. But if on the way home (in the next scene) he calls his ex-girlfriend to confess he wants her back, that's also a story beat. Both moments move the story forward, in effect setting up whatever is to follow, even if that happens later in the story. When it does happen, it will be yet another story beat.

That said, any scene that *doesn't* offer a story beat is risky. If you accept that each scene should be written in context to a mission you've established for it (see Chapter 18), one that is in context to forwarding the narrative whole, then you also need to realize that a scene without a mission is like hitting the Pause button on your story. Not a good thing.

Of course, this doesn't mean that every story beat needs to be a world-ending confrontation or game-changing epiphany. Some scenes are worthy because they illustrate a reaction to something, or a moment of reflection, perhaps. Even a flashback. For example, the moment when "their eyes meet" in a love story can take many forms. The idea is to make that moment compelling and memorable while contributing to the characterization of the participants.

That's the nice thing about story structure: It doesn't *tell* you how to do anything, creatively and strategically, other than the context that needs to be in play, depending on where you are in the story. Structure provides a framework, a place to hang the picture, without telling you what the picture should be, other than in a contextual sense. You wouldn't hang a college graduation photo above the toilet … that's the learning curve and inherent sensibility an author needs to bring to the party, and it's why, even when principles of structure are honored, some stories work better than others. We live and die by our design choices.

When you honor the context defined by structure and make a good choice in the process, the chosen moment is *optimized* … a positive and powerful creative choice for that particular moment.

The best way to optimize a scene is to understand precisely what it needs to accomplish in order to contribute to exposition. In other words, you must find its *mission*. It's usually just one expositional piece of information, one mission—a twist, a layer, a piece of business, foreshadowing, etc.—one bit of narrative content that needs to be conveyed to the reader, delivered with characterization.

Filmmaker Quentin Tarantino is a master at optimizing moments through selecting specific elements of exposition that jack story physics through the theater ceiling. In the first scene of *Inglourious Basterds*, Tarantino knew what this mission was, almost certainly before he wrote it: to show the bad guy allowing a young girl to escape his grasp after cruelly killing her family. And—as is always true in any scene, and therefore is rarely the sole mission of scene—to contribute to characterization in the process. This opening scene—the opening hook—is critical to setting up the narrative, as the girl later returns to become the primary catalyst in the film. So many story physics are applied in that scene that the audience can't help but hate the bad guy, root for the girl, and feel the complete and utter terror of *being* there.

A scene can last a minute, or it can last five minutes or more in a film. In a novel it can be as short as a paragraph (though such a brief scene becomes one of several within a chapter), or it can go on for pages. Length doesn't imply the incorporation of multiple driving missions—ideally there should be one expositional mission in each scene, with characterization layered into it. Scenes in which nothing happens, where only scenery and asides and character layering are offered, become pace compromisers that haven't been optimized. You can only include a few of these, judiciously offered, in a story before you hobble the whole thing. When you know what a scene must accomplish—its narrative *mission*—the stage is set to create something compelling and memorable. Something that moves the story forward, or at least adds to the base upon which the story will grow.

Tarantino's opening scene lasts nine minutes. It shows the evil Nazi commandant (Christoph Waltz in an Oscar-winning performance) arriving with his goons at a farmhouse with a full display of soft manners that barely hide his deadly agenda, which he pursues with sadistic glee. He sits down with the landowner over a glass of milk—a deliberate and totally creepy creative choice—to engage in a subtext-riddled conversation, which is intercut with shots of the trembling family hiding directly beneath the floorboards. The tension builds like a burning fuse for nine excruciating minutes. Finally all hell breaks loose when the milk is gone, the family beneath the floorboards is machine-gunned down in cold blood, and the daughter escapes in a moment of hormonal hesitance that the commandant will later regret.

The physics of dramatic tension and character empathy are the products of choices, and nowhere is this truer than within scenes. This is driven by sensibilities that, while being prompted by the principles of structure, are hard to teach and even harder to acquire. The farmer and his daughters are sympathetic characters in the opening scene, so this is pure empathy in play, as well as vicarious experience. The writer's goal is getting the reader's head into *that* space.

THE TARGET CONTEXT
FOR EVERY SCENE YOU WRITE

This writing principle will never betray you. It was presented in Chapter 1, and it's worthy of reprise here:

The objective of storytelling, the point of it all, isn't merely to write about something. The highest goal of your storytelling is to write about something *happening*.

This guideline—a rather golden rule, actually—can and should be applied with art and variability, but it is never wrong or irrelevant. In Part One of a story (see Chapter 22), you can possibly get away with one or two short scenes that aren't about anything happening—little backfill narratives and observatory exposition—and if the ensuing story is dense with dramatic tension and pace, you might get away with one or two additional short scenes that defy this guideline, too.

But that's it. If you pepper your story with scenes in which nothing happens, where the reader perceives no forward movement in the exposition, your story will be at risk.

How does this happen to writers who mean well?

Sometimes your passion for a theme or a historical event can overwhelm your sense of story exposition. You can easily inject too much journalism without realizing that you've just put the story on hold, perhaps in multiple locations.

If you set out to write *about* a theme—love, history, justice, prejudice, religion, abuse of power, right to life, gay rights, or any other *issue*—then you really should skip pasting the above golden rule on your monitor (as previously recommended) and blow it up to a six-foot poster that you nail to the wall of your writing space. This principle is a bigger parachute for such writing types more than anyone else.

If your story physics are subordinated to your fascination with a particular theme or place or moment in history, if your story is more about *that* than it is about a character with a problem to solve and a goal to reach—in other words, if it's not about something *happening*, with opposition and stakes in play—then you are already in trouble.

When you can write about something *happening* and *still* make your story *about something*—by putting your story *within* the context of the time, place, or thematic petri dish you have in mind—then, and only then, will you have elevated your story to a level that someone, hopefully a reviewer, will call *art*. But you'll know it's more craft than anything else, because its genesis was gleaned from principle-driven storytelling rather than muse-informed storytelling.

In each and every scene of your story, ask yourself this: What is *happening* here, right now? How does it connect to what's come before, and how does it relate to and set up what will happen next, and thereafter?

You should begin every scene with *that* as your goal, but within the *context* of a strong thematic tapestry. Strive to evolve your story in a way that will allow it to explore the theme itself, not through analysis, a narrative breakdown, or an essay that you've slipped into your narrative. Aaron Sorkin can get away with this, but for the rest of us, those looking to break in, stay away from the temptation. Illuminate your themes *through the consequences* of what your characters choose, do, and feel.

So rather than asking (or answering, when asked) "What's this story *about*?" ask and answer *this* instead: "What *happens* in this story?" Once you have the answer, apply story physics to make it work.

When you know the difference between writing *about* something and writing about something *happening*, you'll have crossed a threshold that will empower your stories, and perhaps your writing career. Or at least get you into the game, because most of the manuscripts in the inbox are already lined up behind these principles.

The Great and Deep Trap
so many new writers fall into.

Here's the most common mistake—more like a dysfunctional belief system leading to an inefficient process—that I see in my work as a story coach: writers who don't write their stories in context to *something*, be it the principles of story architecture, a story plan, an ending they are shooting for, or *something* that becomes the very heart and soul of the story they are working on. *That* something *should* be the discovered story, even if the beats are not yet completely clear.

This trap is avoidable. And we all get to choose.

I'm not saying you must *plan*. Planning isn't a mandate, but it is a recommendation, and once you begin to understand the underlying physics, it is perhaps inevitable, at least to a degree. Even the staunchest of organic writers—ones who, in their interviews, claim to have no idea where their works-in-progress are headed—are quietly, perhaps unwittingly, engaging in some form of story planning in their heads. Because if they weren't doing so, at least during the draft they end up submitting, their stories wouldn't work.

PART TWO

THE OPTIMIZATION OF
STORY PHYSICS

IDEA VS. CONCEPT
WHEREIN WE ACKNOWLEDGE THAT THERE *IS* A DIFFERENCE, AND IT IS EVERYTHING.

Every spring, professional baseball players gather in Arizona and Florida for spring training. Every single day they drill on basic fundamentals: fitness, batting practice, game situations. And every day they improve.

This chapter is like that. We've discussed this topic before, but now we're going deeper, to a *professional* level of understanding. This is a potential deal breaker.

I had lunch recently with a writer friend who is awesome. She brought her lovely sister, and I brought my lovely and awesome wife—the prevailing awesomeness was almost overwhelming—and over omelets and gluten-free bread we had a grand time commiserating the experience of writing serious stories seriously.

Like most writers, my radar for "what if?" propositions is always rotating, and I got a hit when the conversation turned to the ladies room at one of the area's hottest bars, the kind where all the women look like they're on the opening episode of *The Bachelor* and all the men look like the buzz-cut, cheesy, golf-shirt-wearing guys whose reality television housewives are, for some reason, always chasing them down. It was their story, but it resonated with me as a potential *idea*.

At first blush it looked like a winner. There was a time when I might have actually gone home and started writing it. Because I believed that, if I did things properly, applied the right dramatic forces in just the right places with just the right touch, I could make any idea into a winner.

Hear this: You cannot make *any* idea into a winner, any more than you can make any kid into a professional athlete, any tune into a chart-topping hit, or any honest Joe into the President of the United States. An idea that doesn't have winning DNA needs to be morphed into one that does.

The good news is that DNA is ours to *breed* into the idea, by turning it into a *concept* with massively inherent potential.

The ladies talked about a woman who has served as the hostess in the ladies room at that famous local club for the past ten years. This woman was beloved by all who had washed their dainty hands or reapplied makeup there. I immediately pictured Viola Davis in an Olive Oyl pillbox hat, dishing out towels and smiles and sage advice for dollar tips.

Oh, the sights she must have seen in the room, the stories she must have heard. She, it was suggested, should write a book.

A book of anecdotes and lessons learned. An episodic book without an overarching plot, which I would have to totally dream up. (See how easy it is to be seduced by the belief that this type of story can become a *novel*?)

Not yet discouraged, I went in that direction.

A "what if?" descended on me: What if this woman heard something in that bathroom that she shouldn't have heard? What if she overheard whispers about someone in the bar who wasn't supposed to be there, doing things that shouldn't be done? And what if something happened later in the evening inside that bar, something bad, lighting a fuse toward the elimination of anyone who knew who might be at the center of it all?

Suddenly Viola Davis (I find myself always casting novels with stellar actors, even at the very first spark of inspiration) was the heroine running for her life while working to help the bumbling detectives find the bad guy before they found *her* in a dumpster.

I pitched the idea to the table, and resoundingly heard what most writers hear when they spout an off-the-cuff idea, especially to people who *aren't* writers (although one of the three is, in fact, a great writer): *Oh my God, you should write that! Really! That'd be so cool!*

It was breakfast, mind you. No alcohol involved.

Notice that while the initial idea energized them, it was the addition of a *concept* that got them out of their chairs.

We brainstormed for a while—always a fun exercise—taking it through the First Act to a proposed First Plot Point, at which time the food arrived and we turned our attentions elsewhere: to why some writers drink and others simply go mad. (Sadly, these sometimes seem to be the only two available options.)

But notice what happened here: The original idea was quickly subordinated to a conceptual *story* idea. I had no guarantee that the ladies would have been as enamored with the latter as they were with the former, which—wait for it—wasn't a *story* at all. It was just an idea. A door opening to a path that led to something *else*.

We had to turn the idea into a concept before it was worthy of consideration as a project. And that, dear writer friends, is precisely what you need to do *each and every time* an idea explodes in your brain, *before* you start writing something *from* that idea. Getting to the point where you can recognize this paradoxical moment is entirely the point of your writing journey.

This is the most common mistake I see: manuscripts based on ideas, rather than on concepts.

On the way home my wife asked me, "So, are you going to write that story?"

I didn't have to think about it. My answer was a firm, no-looking-back *no*. The reason had everything to do with story physics. They just weren't there for me.

Ideas are just that, and nothing more.

They are aromas, not foods. Promises, not deliveries. Seeds, not gardens.

Ideas acquire value when they point us to something more substantive than whodunit gratification, when they put you, the writer, into a place that transcends immediate gratification and allows you to go deep and wide.

Ideas should scare the crap out of you. Or, at least, they should excite you to the point of obsession. When you link a compelling "what if?" proposition to a deeper realm of time-tested passion ... *now* you're on to something.

That's the story you should write.

And while that first idea of the bathroom hostess did indeed lead to an idea about an innocent woman overhearing something dark, that idea was, for me, still void of anything magnetic or compelling enough to keep growing it. I had no real passion for the ladies room at this club, nor for the social dynamic that becomes the social arena of such a story, which was the story's original energy. I've never been inside a crowded ladies room full of preening cougars—and yeah, that sounds kinda interesting, I admit—but who am I to write this story?

If you happen to like it, have at it. It's all yours.

If I'd been harboring a *thing* for ladies restrooms ... maybe it could have flown. But no. Perhaps someone who does have that closeted fascination could have grown that idea into something workable.

Great stories demand our passion.

Not that you have to have *lived* every story you tell. What I'm saying is that you should bring a long-standing, or at least overwhelming, *desire* to have lived it. Starting a book on the heels of a breakfast conversation is like getting married after a conversation in the checkout line at Costco.

It happens. It never ends well, even in the most romantic of fiction.

The desire to live vicariously in our stories needs to be matched by our passion for the landscape upon which the story will unfold. That's what makes it work. In Nelson Demille's *Night Fall*, for example, he brought back his iconic ex-military hero to investigate the hypothetical cover-up of an exploded airliner (this was based on a real case, TWA Flight 800, which exploded over the coast of Long Island on July 17, 1996, claiming 230 souls and igniting conspiracy theories about a cover-up). There was only one reason to do that: Demille had a passion for it. Perhaps he was furious about what he thought was the truth.

What floats your boat? How would you live your life differently if you could start over? What would you do, who would you be, where would you go, what would you embrace? These are the questions a writer should ask before taking any "*what if?*" idea seriously. Consider hatching an idea from your passion, and then develop a concept that allows you to stage it and explore it.

This crystallized for me one morning while reading about a new J.J. Abrams television show, *Alcatraz*, in which criminals who seemingly disappeared from an island fifty years ago show up in present-day San Francisco and start killing people. They've traveled through time. They might be ghosts. But the dead bodies they leave in their wake are real, and they must be found and stopped.

Now *that* interests me, both on a "what if?" level and a time-tested passion level. I wish to hell I'd thought of it. Time travel is one of the most intriguing premises I can think of ... and yet, I've never written a time travel story.

Hmmm. I should look at that. Because the passion for it is there. All sorts of thematic, dramatic possibilities await within this realm. All I need now is a killer "what if?" proposition that keeps me awake at night. (A side note: *Alcatraz* tanked, cancelled after one season, despite the strength of the idea and the craft of the people who made it. As William Goldman said, "Nobody knows anything." That said, we should pursue that which interests us to the point of obsession and leave our passing fancies on the shelf.)

The books I've published were all, to some extent, grounded in something I have an obsessive, passionate interest in. Something I *know*.

Don't jump too fast at your *"what ifs?"*

They are like items on a menu ... the picture is appealing, and you know it'll taste good. But will it nourish? Will it fill you, does it check something off your bucket list, will it give you focus and joy and challenge? Is the idea worth a year of your life? Do you want to be *remembered* for this story?

These are the questions you need to ask, relative to the initiating idea, before you ask, "What if?"

Write from a place of passion and obsession and innate, time-tested curiosity, a place where issues collide with the conceptual, set in an arena that fuels the drama as much as any characters you can place within it.

Write the story you *should* be writing. If a story is worthy, you should be feeling the story physics tugging at you even before you write a word.

8

THE FLIP SIDE OF CONCEPT
WHEREIN WE LEARN THAT CONCEPT HAS TWO FACES THAT DEMAND ATTENTION.

Concept is one of the Six Core Competencies of successful storytelling. It has two faces, two aspects to consider. One addresses the *what* of the story, and the other addresses the *how*. One is the *creative* realm, in which the story's bones begin to form, and the other is the author's *narrative strategy*, which is the conceptual approach to how the author will *tell* the story.

Both are make-or-break propositions.

THE CREATIVE REALM OF CONCEPT

At its most obvious, *concept* refers to the inherent proposition and invitation of the story on a narrative level. It suggests that if you create a set of characters, concoct a compelling situation to put them in, and mash the two together, literary hijinks will ensue.

Without the *mash*, something is lacking. It's either all plot with characters that are too thin or archetypical or comic bookish, or all character, which could be judged as ... boring.

A great concept is the stuff of thrills, chills, drama, tension, laughter, wonder, turn-ons, emotions, and life lessons that turn good books into great books. Characters *aren't* those things, but they are the windows *into* those things, the vehicles of *vicarious experience.* At its core, it is *concept* that gives great characters a stage upon which to show their stuff, which is the seed from which *theme* emerges.

Notice the interconnectivity in play among the Six Core Competencies and the physics that drive them.

When we think of concept, we often instinctually use a "what if?" proposition (and if you don't, you should, because the goal of concept is to ask *a dramatic question*). Concept points us toward the hook, the Big Question, the compelling conceit of the fiction that is the source of dramatic tension, theme, character arc, and the prospect of engaging a reader's emotions.

But that creative view may not be enough to fully seize the conceptual potential at hand.

There is another realm of execution at this level—another opportunity—that is by definition totally conceptual in nature and execution. If you don't address it and optimize it by making the best possible choices in this realm, it will leave the station without you and define and restrict your story in doing so.

The optimization of concept from a narrative perspective—*how* you are going to tell a story—is the path toward displaying the most powerful story physics possible.

THE MECHANICAL VIEW OF CONCEPT

The *mechanical* take on concept deals with how the story *should best be* told ... a *strategic* approach in a narrative sense. The difference between a story told in first-person present tense and one told in third-person omniscient past tense is one of narrative strategy (a key realm of story physics), which is a conceptual decision in and of itself.

When you choose to write in first person, for example, you've just put a narrative strategy—a conceptual one—into the mix.

This mechanical side of concept is comprised of the choices an author makes about voice, tense, time sequencing, narrative asides, and other little tricks and structures that reside outside of the simply *linear.*

Oftentimes, the simply linear is ideal. But not always. When it isn't, you need a narrative strategy, rendered through concept, that does the job better.

The Help (which is deconstructed in Chapter 23) is told in first person: sometimes in present tense, sometimes in past tense, and sometimes with a mix of the two. Tricky stuff. This is a narrative strategy one should opt for with caution. But the conceptual aspect of this decision went even further: The author decided to use not one, but *three* character narrators.

It was a choice, a decision—a concept—made at some early point in the story development process. This decision, determining the best voice for this narrative, was a product of the author's *search for story*. She could have chosen differently, but Stockett didn't give in to the obvious alternative of singular third-person omniscient narration, because there was a better choice on the table, one that wasn't obvious at all, especially with *three* heroes doing the narrating.

It worked. Oh man, did it ever work.

Alice Sebold could, for example, have written *The Lovely Bones* as a detective story with the same dramatic spine, same hook (young girl is murdered), same conceptual underpinnings (dead girl talks to us from heaven), and same characters and drama. If she had done that, it would have been a conceptual choice that would have defined the entire future of the story. But she didn't. She opted for a first-person narrative that didn't fit cleanly into the mystery genre. Ten million copies later, I conclude that she chose well.

Readers and viewers take these strategic mechanical choices for granted. But if we, as writers, take them for granted as we stare at the blank page, it could be fatal.

Or it can make your career.

Which is why this realm of mechanical conceptualization is so important. Mechanical concepts and strategies *become* creative by means of their ultimate effectiveness.

Remember *Pulp Fiction*? How it jumped around in time? Nothing linear there. That's a *concept*, one residing in the mechanical realm of author decision making.

How about *The Bridges of Madison County*? This had a totally mechanical conceptual choice, in that the story unfolded in two spheres of time, with narrative bridging (no pun intended) to optimize the story physics of pace, tension, and emotion. The daughter's point of view separated this story from the crowd of nostalgic love stories out there.

Structure, while guided by principles, is very much a conceptual decision, because *what goes where* defines your story. The sequence is an issue of story physics, because it determines the level of tension and empathy in play at any given moment. The principles give us a target context, but the content is ours to choose.

Did you see the film *500 Days of Summer*? Did you notice that the screenplay was nominated for an Oscar? Each scene was labeled with graphic subtitles as one of those 500 days, unfolding in what appeared to be a random order. It doesn't begin on Day 1. Day 365, for example, occurs well before, say, Day 21. But it wasn't remotely random from the author's perspective. The story showed us what needed to be revealed in precisely the proper, optimized order according to the contextually driven principles of story structure (which is physics driven), weaving backstory, false climaxes, abandoned hopes, and rekindled passion together into a linear and artful love story that was as much about *how it arrived* at its conclusion as about the conclusion itself.

This, too, is a concept. A tricky one, since a story still needs to unfold in a thematically and dramatically linear fashion *no matter what* mechanical or strategic choice the author makes.

In my 2004 novel, *Bait and Switch*, I combined a first-person narrative alternating with third-person point-of-view chapters showing what was going on behind the curtain of the hero's awareness (once again sending a legion of old-school writing teachers into a catatonic frenzy). According to the folks at *Publishers Weekly*, who named it one of the "Best Books of 2004" after a starred review, apparently it worked. Enough to see it republished in 2013.

A risky choice? Not really. I first beheld and marveled at that technique in Nelson Demille's *The Lion's Game* (2002), and it blew my mind. A whole new world of conceptual possibility opened up simply by seeing it done, and done well. Generations of old-school English Comp teachers are rolling over in their graves, but so be it; it's an exciting new day for writers.

The enlightened writer understands that these two conceptual landscapes—creative and mechanical—are on the table at all times. When seized early, even before a first draft, the storytelling is empowered and/or tested against your vision for it. If you land upon it during the drafting process, this is equally valid, because once that landing occurs, so does the strategic vision for the story.

You can start a successful story without one, but you can't finish a successful story without a vision for it.

So along with asking ourselves *"What would my hero do in this situation?"* and *"What will make the dramatic tension in this scene go vertical?"* (these among a long list of other conceptual questions …) we should also be asking ourselves what *mechanical* options—point of view, time sequencing, dialogue style, even how things looks on the page—best suit the story and our vision for it.

This is where risk, creativity, and courage collide in a brilliant explosion of exhilarating potential.

This is the essence of optimization.

Awareness is a beautiful thing.

A story is also like a child.

Children tend to wander off to explore dangerous and wasted side trips and bad choices—some of which, I'll grant you, yield valuable lessons. It's our job to shepherd our scenes toward the sweet spot of dramatic optimization and relevance.

When *that* happens, know that *both* realms of conceptual decision making are in play … and that you have total control over the options presented by both.

STORY PHYSICS AS NARRATIVE BENCHMARKS

WHEREIN WE REALIZE THAT CHICKEN SALAD AND CHICKEN SH*T ARE BOTH PRODUCTS OF THE SAME ANIMAL.

It is one thing to search for a story and quite another to search for *the best possible story*. Knowing the difference is the stuff writing careers are made of.

Ask anyone who writes fiction how many issues an author needs to think about, how much stuff there is to know and execute, and you may get an answer that amounts to dozens, even hundreds, of elements. That's pretty accurate, actually. Few who have tried it are tempted to oversimplify.

Rather than simplify, let's organize. Let's put what we need to know into two big honkin' boxes. One box is full of dynamite, the other full of tools.

DYNAMITE—THE *FORCES* OF STORYTELLING

Like anyone designing and building an engine (and our stories are nothing if not dramatic *engines*) we need to know what *powers* and *fuels* our stories.

These are the Six Realms of Story Physics:

1. Compelling premise
2. Dramatic tension
3. Pace
4. Hero empathy
5. Vicarious experience
6. Narrative strategy

These realms will make your story explode from the pages. Or reach up to seduce. Or whisper, right before it screams.

Or not. The lack of these, or the mishandling of them, is like pouring gasoline on a book of matches. No spark, no fire.

Execution counts, the concept empowers ... but these are the things readers will *notice*.

Use these elements to fuel your story beats, with the goal of making them sizzle, and your story will be better for it. They will be present on their own, but it's better when we notice and manage the fuel at hand.

Now let's look at the tools that run on story physics. Think of them as power tools. They are the means by which story physics actually make it into your story. Each tool is linked to the essence of the story *physics* it uses.

TOOLBOX: THE SIX CORE COMPETENCIES OF SUCCESSFUL STORYTELLING

1. **CONCEPT:** The dramatic core of *compelling premise*.
2. **CHARACTER:** Crafted with an eye on *empathy* and "rootability."
3. **THEME:** A contextual and subtextual tool that relies on *all six of the story physics*.
4. **STRUCTURE:** A tool for crafting *dramatic tension, pace,* and character arc, from which *empathy* arises.
5. **SCENE EXECUTION:** A tool that puts each story beat into a physics-optimizing form; this is where physics appear on the page.
6. **WRITING VOICE:** A tool to achieve a *differentiated delivery*.

All of these demand your immediate attention *as soon as* you have an idea. Because your story won't work until you've covered each base.

Graphic by Bryan Wiggins, wigginscreative.com

You still have to know dozens, even hundreds of things to write a story well. But now they're in twelve buckets: Six realms of story physics … and Six Core Competencies that define the tools of application. At a glance they tend to overlap, and to the glancing observer they may sound like the same things, but to a professional, they're as different as muscle strength and a barbell.

That being said, each of them is a matter of degree and nuance. As writers, we wear an entire rack of hats: designer, dreamer, engineer, planner, assembler, quality controller, riveter, tester, taster, caterer, and deliverer, not to mention marketer, promoter, and bookkeeper. These are multiple core competencies that we must, without exception, master at a professional level. What separates the laborer and the artist is, in fact, a command of nuance and the sense of how to best use the forces at hand.

And that's how you write the *best* possible story. Not by numbers, not by somebody's paradigm or series of steps, but by honoring the physics and principles that underpin them, and then wielding them like Michelangelo rocked a paintbrush. Admit it, his work was nothing but physics and tools ... color and strokes, rendering an idea he had in his head. It was the integration of it, the heart behind it, and the patience to lie on his back for years on a platform held together by leather thongs ... that's how you write the best possible story.

I can't deliver the genius. But I can show you the physics and the tools.

THE GOOD/BETTER/BEST
OF THE CORE COMPETENCIES

So how do we manage these issues of degree and nuance? While structure tells us when and what, is there a way to determine *how much*? The answer arrives in the form of one's personal tastes and judgment regarding the physics of it all. Just how hot is hot ... how tense is tense ... and how smooth is smooth? We get to decide.

When we make that decision for each story element, each selection of raw materials and tools of execution, we are better equipped to optimize the mix. This is how we create something magical ... without the slightest bit of *magic* involved. We don't settle for good. We assimilate what we've learned and what we know to chase down *better*, in the pursuit of *best*.

Concept

DEFINED: The *Big Evolved Idea* of your story. The basic "what if?" proposition. The dramatic landscape, the window into plot, the source of conflict, the compelling question, the enticing situation, the promise of the story, the stage upon which the character finds something to do.

> **GOOD:** The reader is inherently drawn to the proposition and is attracted to the answer of the dramatic question posed.

> **BETTER:** The reader can inherently experience the hero's journey in pursuit of that answer. He can live the hero's journey vicariously. The story promises an exciting, rewarding ride.

BEST: The reader not only experiences the hero's journey, but also empathetically *feels* what's at stake. He relates to the consequences of the resolution of the story.

EXAMPLE: *The Hunger Games.* The concept alone is a home run. It compels, it promises a ride, and it asks us to feel for and root for the hero, beginning at the conceptual level. The entire notion of kids killing kids for the entertainment and vengeance of a self-declared superior culture is appalling, and as such, captivating. Novels like Jonathan Franzen's *Freedom* rely more on character than concept. Yes, it has one, but it offers nothing particularly compelling at the conceptual level—normal people with normal jobs seeking normal relationships—other than the promise that Franzen can write the heck out of a paragraph. The concept is real life rendered eloquent, with insight.

LESSON: The deeper you are within any given genre, the more critical *concept* becomes. Concept is the stage upon which character is allowed to unfold. And the story physics of dramatic tension and vicarious ride are the forces that will make it work.

You are searching for a concept that delivers the level of power, via story physics, that will allow your story to succeed. Too many writers settle here, failing to get beyond their own fascination with an idea to assess how the market might be drawn to it. A novel about your cousin picking berries one summer is a tough sell. It's not inherently compelling. Franzen could perhaps pull it off, but the rest of us are better served by searching for a concept that demands attention.

Character

DEFINED: The protagonist of the story, presented with layers of backstory, inner psychology, outer dimensions, and a journey that will allow him or her to become heroic as he or she evolves over the course of the story to become the primary catalyst of the story's resolution (which is what heroes do).

GOOD: An interesting protagonist we can root for.

BETTER: A layered protagonist we can *relate* to as we root for her or him.

BEST: A protagonist who feels what we feel, fears what we fear, and steps into the hero's role as we would hope *we* would. In other words, a vicarious juxtaposition between hero and reader on an emotional level. A hero who *gets it done*.

EXAMPLE: Holden Caufield in *The Catcher in the Rye*. He's *us*, at our most basic level of humanity. And yet, he's better than us, because he can describe moments and contexts and dynamics in a way that we can't, but in a way that we immediately relate to.

THE LESSON: The character will work best when we give her or him something interesting to *do* (dramatic tension and hero empathy) and something to *be*, rather than simply writing *about* a character in a static slice-of-life manner.

Theme

DEFINED: The relevance and transparency of the human experience through the dynamics of the story, both in terms of character and conflict. What it all means. An *issue* that informs and becomes catalytic within the story. What the story asks readers to think about, get angry about, question, or feel.

GOOD: A story that shows life as it really *is*, for better or worse. One that allows us to recognize the dynamics of being alive in whatever time the story takes place within, while illuminating universal truths germane to the time and setting. A story about being poor, for example. We can all relate to that, even if we're not.

BETTER: A story that shows the virtues of heroism as they play out on a thematically rich and realistic stage. In showing heroism, it also reflects on the darkness which must be conquered or overcome.

BEST: A story that pushes buttons and doesn't flinch, one that demands the reader see both sides and all the options that attach to the hero's choices, and teaches us truth and reality in the process. A story from which issues arise that are explored and put to the test through the challenges presented to the characters and the consequences of the decisions and actions.

EXAMPLE: John Irving's *The Cider House Rules*, which explores both sides of a polarizing issue through the points of view of the characters on both sides of the question, and on a level that defies politics and religion and doesn't flinch from consequences. A story that at once forces readers to decide and reflect.

And, of course, there's Kathryn Stockett's *The Help*, which is a clinic on theme. The book sells us nothing but allows the reading experience relative to the characters and their journeys to prompt our own personal response.

Structure

DEFINED: The expositional unfolding of the story in a sequence that deepens stakes and presents twists while delivering the reading experience. This paradigm presents target placement (in terms of linear percentage of story) for specific story points, each separating the four parts of story, each of which has its own contextual missions. This mission-driven structural approach differentiates the narrative goals among those four parts of the story, as well as the contextual purpose of the scenes within them.

> **GOOD:** A solid four-part sequential presentation of the story: setup, response (to the First Plot Point), a proactive attack on the problem, and resolution.

> **BETTER:** A sequence that allows the reader to get lost in the story in a vicarious way, which deepens the effectiveness and compelling nature of the four parts that comprise it as well as the nature of the dramatic tension within each.

> **BEST:** A story that surprises, intrigues, captures, and then rewards the reader on both an emotional and intellectual level. The reader simply cannot put it down because the story is un-

veiled, beat by beat, in a way that entices, teases, and ultimately rewards.

EXAMPLE: Dan Brown's *The Da Vinci Code*. Love it or hate it, the story blends all Six Core Competencies into a compelling story that readers—some eighty million of them—literally could not put down. Its structure, which is in complete compliance with the optimal four-part paradigm, is its strength.

The Hunger Games is another clinic in story structure, completely in alignment with the paradigm. It is no coincidence that these novels are two of the most successful franchises in book-selling history precisely *because* of the way their structures optimize story physics. To be clear, it isn't just the strength of the concepts that reside at the core of these two books and success stories like them … it's the pacing and deft touch with which they unfold before the reader's eyes.

Scene Execution

DEFINED: Blocks of narrative exposition that move the story forward in an optimal way, with equal weight given to characterization and dramatic tension. Each scene should have a specific narrative mission, developed in context to its place in the story sequence and the context of the narrative arc.

> **GOOD:** Scenes that are logical in order, that blend into subsequent scenes to create a smooth, sequential story spine.

> **BETTER:** Scenes that play like one-act dramas, each with a setup, confrontation, and resolution, yet yield seamlessly into the next. Scenes that deliver one primary, salient point of plot exposition while contributing to characterization, building layer upon dependent layer of exposition and sequential narrative.

> **BEST:** Scenes that cut quickly to the point (mission) of the scene, that present, frame, and resolve a story beat while setting up a subsequent deepening of stakes, urgency, options, and character arc, including nuances and subtleties such as foreshadowing and subtext. Part One scenes, however, have more latitude for a

leisurely setup, particularly in scenes that first introduce main characters and the dramatic premise.

EXAMPLE: Anything by Michael Connelly, Nelson Demille, or Jodi Picoult, or pretty much anything that spends a day on a bestseller list.

Writing Voice
DEFINED: The flavor, style, and flow of the writing itself (prose), from the reader's point of view.

> **GOOD:** Sentences that are clear and direct and that use adjectives and description sparsely yet effectively. *Clean* writing, void of distractions and overeffort. Prose that is not conscious of itself for the sole purpose of stylistic effect. Words, sentences, and paragraphs that readers don't really notice, one way or the other, as they get lost in the story. Writing that is professional, yet taken for granted precisely for that reason.

> **BETTER:** Prose that illuminates the subtext of the moment and of the characters involved. First-person prose is often better suited to inner characterization than third person in this regard.

> **BEST:** Prose that goes down easy yet often rewards, with a hint of humor and spice, with nuance and subtlety where required, and with the power of a blunt instrument when called for. Prose with personality that works in a less-is-more sense, without showing too much effort. This can result in a style that, like a singer's voice, is easily recognized as that of the author, in a defining, branded way, and thus contributes toward the experience of the read.

EXAMPLE: John Updike was the modern master of voice. Read Colin Harrison, too, who sets the bar higher than anyone still breathing. Dennis Lehane, who writes mostly mysteries, has a voice worthy of a grad-school lit class. The list is long and distinguished, yet, unlike guys like Hemingway and Faulkner and Hammett, defies emulation.

GO DEEPER. HARDER.
Be in command of every moment of your story.

How do you do *that*? By *beginning* with the mission and subtext of every scene you write. By knowing what the story needs in any given moment and searching for it, and then optimizing it with the best feasible creative choice you can conjure, after creatively vetting options that arise.

In other words, instead of relying on the rewriting process, on the assumption that you'll need to pound your story into shape as you write it, you can create your story in context to a fundamental knowledge of the forces that make a scene and ultimately a story *work*, both in terms of physics and the structural paradigm that optimizes it. This leads to clarity on the difference between good, better, and best, and allows you to land on *best* more often than not.

When we don't settle for *good* or even *better*—when we shoot for, recognize, and build our stories around creative choices that optimize story physics—we are then using the search process *qualitatively*, rather than the quantitative approach of simply filling in pages of a raw first draft.

Here's an example.

You come to a place in your story where you need to write a scene in which your hero notices the woman that will, later in the story, seduce him and then frame him for murder. That becomes the mission of the scene. And, with a mission in mind, you have infinite choices on how to get there.

> **GOOD:** Our guy arrives at his car in a parking lot, sees the woman, and notices that she's smiling at him in a way that shows she wants to make a connection. He notices her license plate number and calls in a favor to get her name and address.

> **BETTER:** The smile is laced with promise and mystery, and as he gets in his car he notices she's left a note on his windshield, which reveals she already knows his name and promises that he'll hear from her soon.

> **BEST:** She stages an accident in that parking lot, backing into him in a way that seems random but later, upon reflection,

was clearly a strategy to stage an introduction, one he won't soon forget.

Sequential, concept-driven, structure-governed, and organic story building can work without an endgame in mind (you're still *searching* for your story), provided you have the time, willpower, and continuing love for the story to see it through. You'll have to go back to square one and revise it in context to the discovered ending, once it comes to you. However, when a story is composed of *optimized* elements of story physics from the idea stage and onward through conceptualization, the big picture arc, the creation of a beat sheet, and *then* a first draft … *that* process will get you much closer to the highest vision of your story every time.

The process of searching for your story, then, is critical.

Every bit as critical as the writing of a draft itself. Because that search is inevitable and inescapable, even if you are only writing a draft to get it done, versus planning an outline beforehand. Both are simply different ways to search for a story.

With story physics as your litmus test, your choices will be better informed and already in context to the whole.

THE STORIES WITHIN YOUR STORY
WHEREIN WE PROVE THAT THIS IS A LOT HARDER THAN IT LOOKS.

Usually, when you let it slip that you're a writer, the response is, "Cool ... what do you write?" as if you'd just said the most fascinating and unexpected thing possible. Everybody's a closeted writer, it seems, but hardly anyone admits to it. And when you announce you write "novels" or "screenplays," one of two things is likely to happen.

Most often you'll get a polite nod, perhaps a flash of confusion, and then a conflicted expression that says, *Okay then, we're done with that ... enough about you.*

Once in a rare while you'll score the dreaded conversational follow-up, which for most of us is worse: "Have you published anything?" Now there's a dance and a half for you. The answer is no more comfortable if you can say, "Yes," than it is when you humbly say, "Not yet." Trust me on this.

It's possible, though, that you may encounter someone who, out of genuine curiosity, asks you to tell them your story, asks you what it's about. Good luck with that. You have about a thirty-second window—equivalent to a short elevator pitch, literally—before their eyes glaze over and you find yourself speaking to a blank, albeit polite, stare.

You lost them at, "Well, it's about ..."

And if your answer is, "Well, it's kind of complicated..." then it's *you* who is lost.

If this cocktail or tailgate banter is with an agent or an editor, then buck up, this is your shot. But chances are it's from a James Patterson fan, or more likely from someone who's just being polite. Nonetheless, this is your moment in the spotlight, so make it count. In this nonprofessional setting, your answer could be just about anything, focusing on any one of the four elements of the Six Core Competencies (that's all you'll have time for ... trust me on that, too).

It's about a guy who ... (*your hero/protagonist*).

It's about what would happen if ... (*your concept*).

At it's heart it's a story about ... (*insert your passion or agenda here, because that's your theme*).

It's the story of growing up with an alcoholic mother who ends up in prison ... (*a brief structural overview, possibly inspired by something that actually happened*).

You can make any one of these into a compelling elevator pitch. If your listener is in the business, your best response will contain a strategic blending of all of these ... which becomes, in fact, a statement of your story's *premise*.

Eventually, by the time you have a draft that is worthy of pitching, you absolutely will need to be able to tell the story (in an elevator or elsewhere) in a condensed version, via a *premise*.

But what if you haven't finished it yet? What if you're pitching your story at a workshop, one with important people in the audience? *Which* story will you tell? Which core competency (concept, character, theme, and structure) will you open with, and which will you add next?

You need to know what your story is about from all four contexts as early in the development and execution phases as possible. Knowing this, in fact, is the finish line of your search for story, and jacked-up *story physics* are the jet fuel you use to make sure it all flies.

All of those approaches shown above (for the elevator placeholder answer) are *stories*. They are microstories, existing within the larger context of your macrostory. They are stories that concurrently unfold in combination with the other elements, with edges and transitions known only to you, the author.

Here's a scary little truth about pitching your story: You never know which of the elements a reader/listener might react to first, or strongest. Many agents listen for character. Some hope to hear an original concept. Some are watching your eyes, trying to sniff out a whiff of fear. All of them, though, are listening for something commercial, something they can hit out of the ballpark for you.

Okay, let's be real here ... hit out of the ballpark for *them*.

This has always been true, but what may be new to you is an appreciation for the mind-set of visualizing our stories as a melting pot for several conjoined story lines at once, each of them contributing to the other.

Consider your favorite novels and movies.

You'll discover that there are *many* stories being told, if not at once, then in an interdependent and intertwined way.

A foreground story.

A background story.

A character-driven story.

A plot-driven story, one that depends on dramatic tension.

A subplot story.

A subtextual story.

An arena story.

An emerging story.

A departing story.

A backstory.

A thematic story.

A surprising story.

A touching story.

A gripping story.

A story of empathy.

A story of emotion and meaning.

A story of something that really happened.

An insider's story.

An ironic story.

A poignant story.

A story that ... just *works*.

My intention is not that this list be merely viewed as story descriptions or adjectives. What I'm saying here is that these microstories, like different people occupying the same room, all exist and *unfold* as discreet story lines *within* the pages of *your* manuscript.

Need an example? In *The Da Vinci Code,* the foreground story is Langdon's journey as an interpreter of symbols and clues in pursuit of a killer. His journey, juxtaposed against his own belief systems, becomes a character-driven story as well.

The background story, which emerges gradually, is the underlying cause of this skulduggery, in the form of an ancient sect of Catholic monks hell-bent on hiding the truth behind their religion.

The subplot story involves the nature of the woman called in to help him, which ultimately links to a subtextual story about what really happened two thousand years ago.

The emerging story is the existence of a centuries-old sect of assassins working at the behest of the Church to hide certain truths which pose a challenge to the belief system the Catholic Church has been protecting and wielding for over two thousand years, and what may or may not be true. Which is part of the subtextual story.

The thematic story is the relevance of this hypothesis to our very real modern lives, which haven't been privy to the backstory this novel suggests.

The gripping story (dramatic tension) is Langdon's survival in pursuit of the truth. Will they kill him before he finds that truth? Notice how this differs from the foreground story—the murder mystery—and how it overwhelms that story in the final act.

The story is also gripping in its use of old Leo Da Vinci and his art as a cryptic time capsule of meaning, using the real thing to whet our appetites for more. This is part backstory, part historical story, part speculative story.

A story of emotion and meaning ... because chances are this novel (and the movie) pissed you off or shocked you into doubt, or perhaps confirmed your inner cynic. Which is why you talked about it, and why it exploded in popularity.

Brown's novel was a story of *empathy* because to some extent you cared about poor Langdon, not only because he was in the crosshairs of an assassin, but because he is metaphorically chasing down the truth of a religion that has perhaps troubled you to some extent. Or not. For some readers, Langdon was simply *them*.

All this in one little story that sold over eighty million hardcover copies and just as many paperbacks, fueled two movies, and propelled the author's backlist into immortality.

Do we think Brown *pantsed* all this stuff? Did he stumble upon it as he wrote a draft? Make it up as he went along? And if he did, do you think he got it all down in just a couple of drafts? That he's really that good? Nelson Demille blurbed the book with a multimillion dollar endorsement: "This is pure genius." But was this the genius of Einstein's variety (ninety-nine percent perspiration, one percent inspiration) or simply the outcome for a writer who combined a killer concept and story landscape with a convoy full of story physics?

Maybe this list of microstories allows you to appreciate the architectural complexity and competency of this novel a little more, and hopefully it gives you the inspiration and confidence to go there yourself.

The truth is more likely this: Dan Brown considered all these stories as parts of a whole, then fleshed them out individually and sequentially. He did some of this legwork beforehand, and other parts emerged through the drafts themselves. Drafting was probably part of the process, but because it didn't take half a lifetime to create, I can assure you he was writing *toward* and *in context to* something (i.e., a vision for the macrostory) in each instance, rather than stumbling upon these story lines through the good grace of luck or a whispering, cloud-dwelling muse.

Can *we* do that? *Should* we do that?

The answer to *that* is: Absolutely, we should. If you want to break in, if you want to write a story that leaves a mark, then the answer is a resounding *Yes, indeed.*

If you intend to make it all up as you go along, you must realize that your process is nothing other than, nothing more than, a search for these microstories. And that only after you've discovered them, vetted them, played with them, and tried them out can you hope to optimize a draft that marries them seamlessly.

Have you ever tried to play with an idea—expand it, test its potential, create foreshadowing and then consequences for it—*within* a current working draft? If so, you know how difficult that can be. That's why writers who "pants" their stories sometimes require years to finish one. The good news is that you really can evolve an idea in your head, even through conversation and with the use of hierarchical "what if?" sequences and beat sheets, and you can do it to an almost full extent before you write a word.

Notice how *each* of the various stories in *The Da Vinci Code*, and in virtually every other sophisticated novel that works, has a beginning, middle, and an ending of its own. Notice how the driving force that moves the characters through the four-part story architecture (setup ... response ... attack ... resolution) is *dramatic tension*, which can be defined as something that needs to be done or accomplished, with something opposing it, in context to stakes and consequences for either outcome.

In other words ... something needs to *happen*. Dan Brown's story, from a writer's point of view, wasn't about religion, it was about a hero with a problem and a goal, unfolding in context to stakes and the presence of opposition.

That's what a *story* is for each of these flavors (microspines) of storytelling.

The abyss is wide and deep, and it's calling your name.

As authors with professional aspirations, it's easy to focus on only one or two of these microstories in context to our Big Idea (whichever of the four elements it initially emerges from) and let the others take care of themselves. This trap is all the more deadly, even if these elements do, to some extent, tend to manifest on their own. But as story architects, we benefit from a view of the nuances of *all* the stories that are unfolding in our novels and screenplays, because only with this proactive knowledge can we manipulate and optimize them.

Some authors might bristle at the notion that they are being asked to manipulate the reader. But isn't that what's actually happening in a story that works?

We almost always begin with at least some *story notion* in our heads.

We then attempt, or should attempt, to evolve that idea into a Big Idea. And then, into a bona fide concept. And from there, we should allow it to grow into a rich and fertile *premise*. At this point, we face a critical crossroads.

Do you begin writing a draft ... or do you continue a predraft search for the rest of the microstories (plural intended) that are required to exist arm in arm, dancing to the same music, within the whole of your narrative?

If the writing of drafts is your chosen path toward the discovery of all of these concurrent stories (and there's nothing wrong with that; it's just harder and takes longer, like designing and building a bridge on-site, without an architect's blueprint), then you need to know that you'll have to go back and smooth the edges between the microstories. Because it's virtually impossible to *optimize* this dance until you know the entire arc of *all* the stories.

And you thought this was going to be easy.

THE SEDUCTIVE WHISPER OF SUBTEXT
WHEREIN WE REALIZE WE MIGHT BE TRYING TOO HARD.

All stories have subtext. No exceptions. Life itself is riddled with it. And the stories we write, even when set in other times and worlds and dimensions, are ultimately about life.

The real issue for writers—the real opportunity—becomes this: Will the subtext of your story contribute to the main story's effectiveness, or will it just hide there between the lines without significance? Perhaps worse, will only an English lit professor with commercial sensibilities be able to notice it?

It is an underappreciated truth that in a world full of genre-based fiction and character-driven mainstream stories, subtext is perhaps the most differentiating and inherently powerful nuance of storytelling. If you're looking for an edge, an advanced tip, a secret the bestselling authors don't want you to know, this is it. Master subtext and you're immediately playing in a league of your own.

A writer who doesn't address the issue of subtext with the intention of harnessing its power in her story is like a musician who ignores harmony. There is so much inherent potential above, below, and between the layers of the main melody line. Without the use of differentiating, compelling subtext in your stories, you are singing a cappella. And when was the last time you heard *that* on the Top 100 list?

In fiction, subtext is the offspring of setting, characterization, backstory, and dramatic exposition. It's like stuff growing in your yard. You can seed it and care for it, or you can let it spring up randomly on its own. Either way, it defines the street appeal of your home, either adding to or compromising what you're going for.

That said, subtext is always available as a layer to make your story richer, deeper, and more compelling. The evolved professional writer uses this to his advantage.

Subtext is the universe within which your story unfolds.

It's what defines everything, yet without needing to be referenced.

Imagine a story set at the bottom of the sea. The rules of that submerged universe deliver subtext to the story. If humans are involved, you don't need to explain the need for submarines and air tanks.

Imagine a story populated entirely by criminals. The dynamics between your characters are defined by that subtext, as are the expectations of the reader.

Subtext is the unspoken influence in your story. Social values, political power, nature, and the technological, scientific, and human constraints of time and setting ... these define the possible and impossible, the likely and the unlikely, as well as the mind-sets of the characters.

You already know that you must set your story somewhere. Your story must unfold in a world of your creation, either real or surreal, in a place, a time frame, a culture or society, or even within a family or a workplace dynamic of some kind.

But a story is more than its setting. Subtext often equates to and facilitates *theme*. It's fair to say that setting becomes theme when proactively applied as subtext. When you make choices about setting, physical and cultural, you are choosing your subtext. Because these choices apply certain pressures—forces—that define and influence what happens within the settings and themes you've chosen.

To optimize subtext, to use it as the means toward your intended theme, the writer elects to make the story *dependent* on the setting in a contextual way. The social and physical contexts of time, place, or community become dramatic pressures, actual factors in how the story unfolds.

Remember the movie *Witness* with Harrison Ford? The subtext is religious, as the witness to the crime at the center of the plot is Amish. The Amish belief system applies significant social pressure to the choices of those who adopt it and defines how the outside world views them. And thus that subtext was key to the story. Without that particular subtext, *Witness* is just another mystery, one without eight Academy Award nominations and two wins.

In both the book and film versions of *The Help*, subtext—the racial biases, norms, and inequities of the story's time and place—is the most significant thing about the entire story. Imagine this story unfolding today, anywhere. It might work, but it would be a completely different dramatic paradigm.

When Kathryn Stockett set out to write this novel, she knew her story was *about* this thematic issue, and everything that happens character-wise and plot-wise connects to and is informed by it. It's entirely possible the term *subtext* never entered her mind

And yet she didn't leave it at that. Her story wasn't solely *about* prejudice and social norms. It was about a compelling *plot*, too. One without the other would not have ended up in the same level of stratosphere that *The Help* has achieved.

Remember John Grisham's first novel, *A Time to Kill*? Pure subtext. Without that 1950s southern setting, it would all be old news. When a novel uses subtext to define the times, it seizes an inherent opportunity beyond the compelling nature of its plot.

When you look closely at iconic bestsellers and critically acclaimed movies, you'll see that subtext is the essence in common. Watch, read, and learn.

Examples are everywhere.

In romances, the subtext is often the social barriers that separate lovers. The era of the story and the social norms of the culture define what can happen and what can't. This is the subtext, if not the theme itself.

In mysteries, the subtext is often police corruption, sexual deviation, corporate or political greed and self-service, or a landscape of human darkness springing from jealously, sociopathology, opportunism, fear, or hatred.

In science fiction, the subtext might be the impending death of a planet, a postapocalyptic setting in which survival is defined by the environment, or the presence of nonhuman intelligence. Technology versus humanity.

Every story has subtext.

And once again, we have a choice—we can manage it, or allow it to manage our stories for us. But know this: Without throwing a lasso around it and following up with a harness, it'll run wild and perhaps run away. By capturing and taming subtext, you can lead it somewhere it might not otherwise have gone.

THE OPTIMIZATION OF SUBTEXT

As story developers, we are always making decisions in the realm of setting, character arc, and dramatic tension, so it is easy to overlook or take for granted the role of subtext in how our stories play out.

Subtext is conceptual (*concept* being one of the Six Core Competencies), in that your choice of setting or underlying story forces create the compelling X-factor of the story. If you have a love story set in rural Iowa farmland … you better be Jonathan Franzen or you're bucking the odds.

A love story set in a nunnery … now that's a hook that can make you famous.

THE GREAT AND SILENT STORY KILLER
WHEREIN THE WELL-INTENDED WRITER SHOOTS HIMSELF IN THE FOOT.

It's good to have passion for your story. Good to be passionate about a theme at the heart of your story. Good to write with passion. But passion is an intoxicant. A promise without a plan. And it's addictive. It is cheering rather than playing the game.

It's good to have, but it's worthless as a story-planning asset.

In fact, your passion for a story, the very thing you might believe is your biggest asset going into the writing, might instead be silently, insidiously overwhelming it to the point of smothering the story entirely. It's like a lover who drowns you in affection yet gives you nothing that you need.

A politician can rant for years about how a proposed tax cut can help the middle class. But can he shut himself into a room in the back of IRS headquarters and rewrite the tax code that will make it happen?

Some of us want to save the world with our novels. Some reign it in a little and merely want to save a few souls or at least unburden our own. We are serious about this. Our novels are *important* and necessary, stories that must be told. They matter.

If you asked Kathryn Stockett what her novel *The Help* (see Chapter 23) was about, you might get two answers. The first is a thematic target and rationale, the other a window into the story that reflects a narrative plan:

"*The Help* is the story of black maids in 1962 Jackson, Mississippi, and their oppression and injustice at the hands of their prejudiced white employers. The story will show the strength and humanity of these women and how they helped change the course of racial history in this country."

Yeah ... but where's the *story*? That's just the *subtext*.

"*The Help* is a story of a young writer who's looking to break into publishing and senses a story in the experiences of the black maids of 1962 Jackson, Mississippi. She struggles to enlist their help in writing a book that sheds light on these secret injustices and in doing so discovers both darkness and humanity that exceeds her vision and finds her own position in the community threatened."

Now *that's* a story. Theme will *emerge* from this story organically. A writer needs both answers, always.

Because great craft and an understanding of the mechanisms, architectures, and chemistries involved—a compelling, dramatic premise ... tension and conflict ... antagonism that causes the conflict ... optimal pacing ... heroic empathy ... a vicarious reading experience ... stellar craft in execution—that's the real work behind the thematic promise.

These should be the things the writer talks about *first* and becomes most passionate about once the work is underway. Inherent to this understanding is the certainty that the thematic promises—exciting and important as they are—aren't even in the ballpark until these players are in the shower.

Thematic power is the product of dramatic effectiveness. If your passion is on the wrong end of that sentence, then your story needs a bodyguard, because its life may be in danger.

What is your story *about*?

That last word is a loaded gun pointed at the heart of your manuscript. Your answer exposes you, strips you naked in the light of your story's commercial and mechanical viability. It tells you what you know, and by its absence, also exposes what you don't know.

To make your story compelling in execution, you must have a plot.

Passion without plot will drag your manuscript to the bottom of the Priority Mail bin on its way back to you.

A great story is about a problem, not an ideology. The ideology is subtext. It's *about* a person, your hero, who has something to win or lose in squaring off with his problem and his issues. An external antagonist (bad guy) who stands in his way. A journey to take as the battle builds, ebbs and flows, and allows the hero to grow into his heroic role and begin to act in a manner that solves the problem.

Your hero doesn't need to be a soldier in the problem, but the problem needs to contextually bear on whatever conflict-driven path you put him on.

Read any published story, and you'll find these dynamics present. Read any unpublished story, and they might not be.

Too many writers don't even consider this when approaching a story about pain and injustice and healing and finding love again. All of those targets are themes, and when they work, they are the product—the outcome—of a story well told.

A story with a plot.

This mistake is everywhere.

I read a lot of unpublished work in my role as a story coach. And this problem tops the list: stories that focus on the wrong things. These stories focus on theme over conflict. The authors are writing passionately about *issues*. World peace. Finding love. Finding one's true self in a cold, cruel world. Resolving family stuff. Forgiveness.

I read outlines intended to convey the idea and concept of the story, and I have to ask, "Nice theme, but where's the story? Where's the concept?" A theme is *not* a concept—it's subtext—even if it may lead to a concept at some point. The flip side of this is also true: A theme is never really a concept; it's an intention, a goal for an outcome.

Paragraphs then ensue describing the politics of the day or the backstory of the hero and the dysfunctional family. The author describes how the character feels, and, in a misguided attempt to resolve the story, about how the problem (if there is one) is resolved when the hero one day wakes up and *realizes* something.

As if the juice of the story resides there. It doesn't. It resides in the power of the conflict you bring to it, and in the hero's *actions* to make things right.

Still no story. The writer is practically weeping onto the page. Her pet issue, once illuminated, will be her cathartic salvation, and she puts all of her pain and rage and passion into it. She writes *about* it, often because it's *her own* story.

There's still no story, I tell her. No hero's problem. No external antagonist. No overriding goal to reach, just a litany of internal issues holding her back, told episodically. Nobody and nothing to root for.

She sometimes doesn't see what I mean, until I tell her this:

A story is about a character, a hero ... not a theme. Theme only emerges from the vicarious emotional participation on the part of a reader who empathizes with (and roots for) a hero who faces a problem, a challenge, or a need that launches him down a path of reaction to a new quest. The hero, under pressure from the antagonist and a ticking clock, then proactively manages the new quest toward a desired end.

Variations on this model abound. There's no need to reinvent it.

That's a story. Hero, problem, antagonist, respond, change, attack, regroup, grow, do something heroic, solve the problem.

The word *theme* isn't in there. It doesn't mean anything ... until it does.

A story is about characters *doing* things.

That's it in a nutshell. The sequence and sum of what they *do* is the story. It's not what they see or feel but what they do in response to pressure and stakes and need.

What the story "means" is *subtext*, not the narrative point guard. Subtext is good because it informs what actually does happen, but it's not the driving force. Character decision and action *are* the driving forces. Themes—the messages and focuses you are so passionate about—are *outcomes* of your narrative efforts, like fruit from a planting.

Bad dirt, no water, no sun, no care or craft ... no fruit. And here you are, having promised everyone a lovely fruit salad.

Once you realize that the power of your intended thematic outcome is in your hands, you must comprehend the limits and the upside of what this means.

This isn't true only for stories with bombs and criminals and murders. This applies to *any* story. Because they all require conflict, they all require a plot that arises from it. These two requisite elements—character action and related conflict—define the path toward strong thematic resonance.

Plot is the stage upon which your characters reveal themselves.

Characters are the catalytic moving parts of the plot.

Emotions are the currency of everyone's involvement in the plot.

Stakes are the consequences of the *actions* of the characters in context to that involvement.

A good story coach won't care much about your theme, or the issues. These elements are either there or they aren't, depending on how well the story physics pan out.

We're looking for *story*, in all its phases, contexts, forms, and functions. A doctor doesn't care about your upcoming promotion ... she just cares that you'll be upright and breathing when the day arrives.

THE RELATIONSHIP BETWEEN STRUCTURE AND STORY PHYSICS
WHEREIN THE PARADIGM BEGINS TO LOOK LIKE HOME.

Not everyone understands the difference between a principle and a rule. The truth is, there are no "rules" in art ... but we can lay no claim to art until the principles that underpin effectiveness have been put into play. These principles are known as *craft*.

That's not a paradox as much as it is a major lightbulb going off. An Epiphany. If you haven't heard that glorious little *click* yet, keep reading, I'm pointing you toward the on switch.

Storytelling is a process of executing options.
It's about creative *choices*. To ensure that we don't shoot ourselves in the foot, we have *principles* that guide us in our choices. Principles exist to keep us safe because they help us manage the physics of storytelling and *empower* our stories while allowing us the latitude to interpret and assemble them as we wish.

When someone tells you your story structure is weak, it usually means one of the following: The pacing is sluggish ... there's not enough tension ... there's no discernible character arc ... the story is too one-dimensional ... it's not complex or layered enough to sustain interest. What they're not saying, but what they mean, is that it's dull as dirt. They actually liked your concept when it was pitched to them, or they wouldn't have read your manuscript. From there, though, your story is like a pretty person with a boring personality ... personality is what counts in the writing game.

The truth is, you'll probably hear a critique about your pacing, tension, character arc, and the like *before* you hear anything about your structure. But pay attention to it all, because one is the cause and the other is effect. Compromised structure leads to weakness elsewhere.

Structure is the means toward pace, tension, arc, depth, and compelling interest. It is the road map, the paradigm, that presents them in an optimal way. To mess with structure—to make it up as you please—is to put the story's outcome at risk. Structure is an example of cause and effect, a driven, universal phenomenon. (Ever heard of karma? There's karma in writing stories, too ... your sins will come back to you, and your gifts to it will reap rewards.) The more you understand about cause and effect in your fiction, the better your stories will be.

Structure sets you free to be great.

Step off a cliff and you will fall. Do it with the right gear, something that mitigates the very physics you seek to defy, and you have a shot at living to leap another day. In fact, with the right equipment cliff jumping is considered a sport. But that doesn't soothe the organic writer's natural aversion to having a suggested place to put things in their stories. Some ask why they can't simply write a story any dang way they please?

You can ... provided the story *aligns* with the basic *principles* of fiction. It's not an exact science but an approximate one, a model that needs to balance as a whole as much or more than it requires precision at every target milestone. You can write it any dang way you please if you don't care about getting it published or anyone liking it.

The trouble is, as basic as the principles are, too many writers don't consider them when facing the very choices and moments in a story that will define its ultimate effectiveness.

They just sit down and write. Splash it onto the page. Something comes to them in the flow, and they put it in. And then they move on. It's like setting out on a drive to Florida and suddenly deciding you'd like a pizza from a street vendor in New York. This is fine if it's just you and the family ... but if you're a professional driving a bus full of paying passengers, it's not so good. Not so professional.

Why can't we invent our own structures?

That's a good question, one commonly asked. It's a loaded question, too, a seductive notion if you're looking for an answer that licenses you to ignore the principles of story structure and just do your own thing. Sometimes published writers will allude to this in interviews about their work, implying or even stating outright that this is what they do, that they don't use a model or an architectural principle when creating their stories.

But that's wrong. Even if they said it. Even if they *believe* it.

If the story works, the principles they decry or claim to ignore are already in play, even if they don't want to own up to it. Even if they don't *realize* it. Even if a person believes the earth is flat, their belief doesn't change what *is*. If, in the creation of their drafts, these nonstructure-loving writers sense something isn't right, or are told so, the revision almost always sends them back, however blindly, into the comfy confines of the classic structural paradigm.

The issue in that case is the vernacular of our trade.

Some storytelling terms are close enough to be interchangeable (concept versus theme, for example), but not always accurate in application, especially for those of us looking for insight into craft.

Many writers carelessly use words like *idea*, *concept*, *premise*, and *theme* interchangeably, and yet each of these terms is a separate and important issue of craft. They don't mean the same thing.

The more precisely you want to hone your craft, the more you need to pay attention to this.

If Dan Brown were to say, for example, that his *theme* for *The Da Vinci Code* is a man caught up in a murder mystery going back over two thousand years, that's a mash-up of an old axiom. It's an inaccurate statement of theme, one that echoes throughout the writing world.

The two-thousand-year-old mystery was his *concept*. The veracity of an entire religion into question is his *theme*.

Sometimes these writers actually don't know the difference. They're like athletes who refer to *muscleclature* (look it up, but you won't find it; I've heard that one a lot on ESPN). They don't know how they applied craft to get where they are; instead, they say "I just sit down and write until I get it right. I have no idea how my stories are going to end." Which is total bull, by the way ... they do know how it will end, I guarantee you, in the draft they submit. When it works, they'll have revised that draft to be in context to their newly discovered ending ... thus rendering prior drafts a part of their search for story. It all just sounds so much more mysterious and sexy and brilliant to imply they just suddenly "got it" at the eleventh hour of a final draft, but in terms of understanding what just happened, they didn't really "get it" at all.

When a writer talks about how he planned his story by implying or saying explicitly that he invented his own structure, it could mean two things. The first is misleading because it implies exactly the wrong thing and is therefore dangerous to writers who don't know the difference between structure and strategy. In this first case, the writer meant to say "strategy" instead of "structure." He meant that he looked for scenes or narrative content that fit neatly into the classic four-part story paradigm (which he didn't invent), with the First Plot Point, Midpoint, Second Plot Point, etc., right where they should be (which he may not have understood, but simply had a sense about pace that happened to align with these labels). This is a correct approach, despite the confusion between "structure" and "strategy," and if that's what he meant, then good on him.

But what if he didn't mean that? What if instead he meant he has no clue about four-part structure and feels he needs to—that he *can*—invent whatever structure he wants? Does that mean he's the exception, and we should strive to be one, too? I think not. That's like taking the lead from someone who fell off a bridge and lived to tell about it. It's is a dangerous implication.

Or ... what if he really meant that he needed to *plan* his narrative strategy? What if he was using the word *structure* to merely play casual with the actual writer-specific definition of the word? It's like someone who needs marriage counseling claiming they need structure in their marriage—that could mean anything at all.

I'm thinking this hypothetical writer is saying that he needed to figure out how he was going to write his story and what his plan for it would be. We all need to do that, by the way ... just don't call that need for clarity "structure." Structure is like gravity; you can't mess with it to any degree. It just *is*. It's flexible, yes, to a degree, but only minimally. How you handle and apply it—via trampoline, airplane, nine iron, balloon ride, balance beam, or cliff diving—is all *strategy*.

The physics never change. How you *deal* with them ... that's *strategy*. In storytelling, it's called narrative strategy.

EXAMPLES OF NARRATIVE STRATEGY

Let's look at three massively successful novels, all of which inspired equally successful films: *The Da Vinci Code*, *The Help*, and *The Hunger Games* (these last two are deconstructed and analyzed in Chapters 23 and 24, respectively). These novels and films *prove* the principles of structure, which rely on story physics for their validity. They all had identical structural architectures. They used the same model, *the* model that works and is an expectation in today's publishing world. (If the authors stumbled upon it, so be it, but they didn't *invent* it. Instead, they had to work to *align* their stories with it.) They were all presented as four quartile-proximate parts ... with effective story milestones at very-close-to-optimal locations ... and contextual flows and character arcs that aligned with these principles.

They are textbook examples of the principles of story structure. The paradigm (which they didn't invent) served as the *framework* for their genius concepts and narrative skills.

If you don't like the word *structure*, think of it as a generic *framework*, waiting to keep your story from folding in on itself.

So, what if one of *those* authors had said in an interview that she had to first "plan her structure?"

It could mean two things: She did indeed distribute her narrative across this classic structural grid ... or she meant to say that she "planned her narrative *strategy*."

Now that's something we can learn from.

Because all the authors *did* plan their narrative strategies. Notice that all three stories, while unfolding along the same structural paradigm, had very different *narrative* strategies.

So what's the difference?

Let's allow the stories to answer this question.

In *The Da Vinci Code*, Dan Brown chose to tell the story through multiple points of view, all written in classic third-person omniscient narrative prose. We were with Langdon as he discovered clues, as he ran, as he uncovered a dark truth. We were with the bad French cops as they chased him down. We were with that albino, self-whipping, whack-job assassin as he received his orders and went out looking for his next victim.

This was Dan Brown's narrative *strategy*, not his *structure*. His structure was classic four-part exposition.

In *The Help*, Kathryn Stockett told the story through three points of view, each in the first-person past tense (with a dash of present context) of three different characters. This wasn't structure ... this was narrative *strategy*.

In *The Hunger Games*, Suzanne Collins used a very different strategy than the folks who made a movie out of her story. Both, by the way, used the exact same structure, which was also identical to that of *The Da Vinci Code, The Help, Gone Girl,* and virtually any other bestseller you can name (because it's a universal structure), even if the author can't or won't describe it that way. But Collins's narrative strategy was to tell the story in first-person present through the mind of Katniss, her hero. The novel didn't use a single moment from behind the curtain of her awareness (though this *was* the case in the film).

Pure narrative strategy. In each case, it was executed across the same, identical structural grid.

The one you and I should be using.

Tarantino uses it, even if he mangles timelines to make it look like his story is jumping all over the place (*Pulp Fiction* comes to mind). In terms of context, it doesn't randomly jump around. It flows perfectly, totally in line with the principles as they relate to context.

Most stories are told sequentially in terms of time itself. But story structure isn't about that, it's about context, one that optimizes the physics of dramatic tension and pace.

It's the same with the film *500 Days of Summer*, the strategy of which was to sequence random days from the five hundred days of the title, making it look like a structure. But the structure, the context of how the conflict and the character arcs were presented, was textbook four-part contextual beauty.

Structure is something we use to populate our narrative sequence with concept, characters, theme, and our beautiful, clever words. Structure is already there, like gravity, waiting for us to harness its power.

But narrative strategy ... that's ours to decide upon and even to invent. There really are no rules for this. Just our choices, which we must live or die with.

TAKING STRUCTURE TO THE BANK

When you see story structure as an application of principles of story physics rather than a constriction borne of rules, you're onto something. This shift is perhaps the most critical milestone in a writer's development, because without it one remains alone and without a compass in a sea of creative choices that will drown your story in a heartbeat.

These universal literary forces don't care if you understand them or not. They will always be there to influence your story, to either drag it down or lift it up ... depending on how you apply them.

What do best-selling authors know that you don't?

Sometimes the answer is ... absolutely nothing. The same goes for agents. I participated in a panel discussion at a conference a while back, during which an agent claimed he could tell if a story was going to work and if he wanted to represent an author after reading the first page.

See, even agents are clueless sometimes. (Just don't tell them I told you that.)

This isn't about the freedom to break what you might perceive to be rules. Rather, successful authors inherently, if not consciously, understand the awesome power of applying the principles of literary physics within a story. If you're looking to define the nature of *writing talent*, this could be it. It is the certain knowledge that the principles themselves bestow freedom to our choices, in context to the certainty that to violate them is a sure route to literary suicide.

If that sounds harsh, it won't once you understand what specific principles I'm talking about here. If you don't recognize them as essential, then you don't understand fiction.

And if you want to call them rules ... it doesn't matter. Rules don't care; they'll still kill you if you ignore them.

THE RHETORIC OF RULES VERSUS PRINCIPLES

The real issue isn't labeling which is which; the importance lies in the author's relationship with the physics of storytelling. When, perhaps unknowingly, you write from a desire to break "rules" and do something you believe to be outside of the box, by definition you are thus confused about what commercial creativity even means. It's almost impossible to cite an example of a story that has proven successful without story physics in play.

Go ahead, break some rules. Obliterate them. Just don't abandon the power of story physics in doing so. Better to understand how to harness these story forces to make your story as good as possible within the parameters of your own making. When physics are bent or stretched, they aren't broken rules but examples of creativity and strategy. But the absence of any specific realm of story physics is a broken rule, one that never works.

Sometimes you get lucky and tap into one or more of the elements of story physics intuitively as you unspool your narrative, but more often you succeed when you are conscious of these forces and don't allow yourself to settle ... when you push your story with the intent of optimizing the very forces that will give it wings.

And how do you do *that*?

By understanding the elements, context, and mission of story architecture as it manifests on the page via structure.

Where you start, what comes next, what comes after that, what and where and why to twist and evolve the story, how to end it ... you optimize these details not from the pure genius of your learning curve, savvy, intuitive self, but from a proactive application of the role and inevitable presence of story physics in your vetting and selection of the elements and moments in your story.

Story structure isn't a rule. It is the means toward the freedom to create without risk. It is a set of illuminated principles that make a story work.

14

HOW TO CHALLENGE YOUR HERO
WHEREIN WE REALIZE OUR PROTAGONIST NEEDS SOMETHING TO DO.

The enlightened writer understands that plot and character, at their most effective, are separate yet interdependent essences, both driven by story physics. Plot is the stage upon which character is allowed to unfold, where dramatic tension is launched, escalated through pace, and ultimately resolved. Character is the means by which plot becomes relevant and meaningful, the realm of empathy and vicarious experience.

The search for optimal story physics seeks to create harmony and balance across these two critical story elements, without a myopic focus on either.

Characterization is complex.

If you can grasp the nuance of subtext and *inner dialogue*, if your concept becomes a tension-driven stage upon which this plays, then you'll have the chops to make your characters more vivid and visceral than you thought possible. Characters are almost always more interesting and transparent when they're doing something, rather than thinking about something or waxing eloquent in a vacuum. Or worse, being written *about*.

Just look deeper at your life and relationships and you'll notice all manner of dialogue going on everywhere. People are constantly engaged in conversations with their most deeply hidden, most despised, and most coveted inner *selves*. The "self" that is actually in charge is usually up for debate, and in our fiction, that's the fun of it. It's not a verbal thing, per se: Folks aren't going around muttering quietly to themselves, nor should your characters, unless that's part of their deal.

Often there is a very clear, sometimes palpable gap between one's inner thoughts and his exterior behavior and attitude. That gap is something most people are dealing with right beneath the surface, sometimes 24-7.

The shy person who must contrive an air of confidence and warmth in a crowd.

The insecure person who walks through the world with a cloak of bluster.

The person who conforms to fit in, even when he realizes this isn't who he is.

The person faking it in a marriage. At work. In church.

The self-absorbed person sitting with friends at dinner in a nice restaurant, uttering not a single word, totally checked out or waiting until the conversation circles around to his favorite topic—himself.

The seething person hiding hate, resentment, bitterness, and fear behind a mask of calm.

Moods, both good and bad, are part of an inner dialogue. But sometimes the inner noise isn't obvious.

The extent to which someone—including your hero *and* your villain—*recognizes* the gap between her true thoughts, beliefs, preferences, and comfort zones, and the way she chooses to behave or appear in spite of them … is *inner dialogue*. A constant tug-of-war within the psyche. A devil on one shoulder, an angel on the other. Or at least, the voice of reason, whose hat is borrowed from either of the former.

Inner dialogue is also something readers will relate to, and when they can relate, it jacks the element of *empathy*.

If a character has no idea how conflicted he or she is, well, that's a dialogue of another sort. The person can't see it, though everybody else can. Don't kid yourself, though, most of us (even those who aren't in therapy) usually *know*. The façade, or the vacancy, is a *choice*.

So what to do with this?

Before you square off with this dramatic can of worms, think about it. Go through a roster of people you know, and suddenly you'll realize how transparent the wall behind which this inner dialogue plays can be. The better you know the person, the more aware *you* are of what's going on inside *him*.

He thinks he's fooling everybody ... but not so much.

Scary, isn't it?

Chances are that, because you are human, *you* are among these inner conversationalists. All the better to put this to use in your fiction.

Now imagine you're casting this person—or you—in your story. Consider the possibilities of revealing that inner tension, the inherent contradiction as narrated by an inner dialogue, in a dramatic moment.

Walking into a crowded room. Lying about what you did last night. Asking a girl out for the first time. Feigning joy while considering suicide.

This faux existence is too often the human experience. When depicted artfully in your story, it will evoke empathy from readers on both sides of the hero-villain proposition. In recognizing this, you now have another arrow in your quiver of character-building weapons. Go as deep as you like, picking your moments to maximize revelation, tension, and complexity.

First-person narrative invites this, but you can pull it off in third person, too. Start to look for inner dialogue and character layering in the work of folks like Stephen King, Dennis Lehane, Jonathan Franzen, John Irving, and probably your favorite writer.

Heroes are obvious candidates for inner dialogue. But if you can bring this complexity to your antagonists, as well—who may or may not be human, so write accordingly—you'll have achieved a new level of depth there, too. This depth will set your story apart.

THE MAGIC PILL OF COMPELLING CHARACTERIZATION

Just like a writer's discovery of story architecture (for some, an epiphany), the sudden recognition and understanding of what you're seeing on the inside of your characters, and how that relates to what they *do* on the outside, can change everything about your ability to write compelling characters.

This is huge. Get ready to go to the next level the moment this sinks in.

This is as much about recognizing and verbalizing the *essence* of something that resists description as it is about leaving it to literary instinct or experiential happenstance. The same case can be made for structure and, perhaps, the story physics that drive it.

Let there be characterization.

The nuances of characterization cannot be fully appreciated until one first grasps the fundamentals, which are unto themselves eternally challenging. You can't negotiate the order of that evolution.

In my previous writing book I described several basic facets of characterization technique: backstory, inner conflict versus exterior conflict, character arc, the three dimensions of characterization (infused with much subtlety and nuance), the seven realms of characterization … all within the context of a journey, quest, or need that is thrust upon the hero by the author. The latter, by the way, is the "give your character something to do" part, the stage upon which character shows itself.

That's Character 101, a class from which we should never consider ourselves graduated. But where compelling character excellence is concerned, you must dig deeper. Like concept, it's best to begin crafting character with something compelling in mind.

The most compelling way to suck us into a story and have us immediately understand and root for a character (or hate her, your call), the best way to give your story a shot at *huge* success, is to show us *how the character feels about* and *responds* to the journey you've set before her.

This means character surfaces *in the here and now*, and along the path to come. This is the hero's humanity, for better or worse: her opinions, fears, feelings, judgments, and *inner response to the moment*. Too often writers depend on backstory to show character landscape, but that's only one opportunity. The more effective window into character is having her act out and respond.

And *that* goes far beyond showing us what she says and does.

The writer who commands this advanced technique of characterization isn't just showing us what *happens*. He's allowing us *into the head* of the character *as it happens*, and in a way that allows us to interpret (or misinterpret), emotionally respond to, assess, fear, plan against, flee from, or otherwise form opinions about all that is being processed in a given moment or situation.

This is, at a simplistic level, called *point of view*. This is where the power of hero empathy kicks in.

But it is an *informed* point of view, because we are made aware of how the world in any given moment *feels* and how it is *interpreted* by the character. And in doing so, we immediately empathize.

The key word here is *interpreted*. It's beyond simple characterization. It's mind-melding the hero with the reader from an emotional, analytical, and sociological point of view.

When done well, it's the magic pill of characterization. Empathy, leading to *rooting*, is the most empowering thing a writer can achieve in the relationship between hero and reader.

It is the whole point.

A DEEPER VICARIOUS EXPERIENCE
WHEREIN THE READER GETS A RIDE-ALONG.

It's good to find an edge. But sometimes an edge is hard to find.

It's rare to extract a gold nugget from the vast wealth of storytelling tips, techniques, principles, and strategies that are already on your radar; yet when you know what it is, you see it everywhere. Once recognized and understood, you begin to see how it elevates a story into print, onto bestseller lists, and into theaters.

Any genre. Any writer. Any story.

The nice thing about the little kernel of literary gold I'm about to reveal is that it makes virtually any story better, even stories in which setting, in a more obvious context, isn't critical. Sometimes this little tactic is precisely what makes such a story a winner.

All the writer has to do is recognize its power and choose to build the story around it. To optimize this ingredient.

It's called *vicarious experience*, one of the major underlying story forces that impart power, weight, and impact to novels and screenplays. We've described it, seen it in examples, and easily related to it. Now let's go deeper, in context to our present focus: how to search for the *best* possible story out there.

Vicarious experience is delivered either through setting or though social, cultural, or relational dynamics. By definition, it means transporting the reader to a place, time, or situation that:

a. they can't or probably won't ever experience in real life.

b. is inherently exciting, curious, dangerous, titillating, or rewarding.

c. is forbidden and/or impossible.

d. is inherently compelling for some other reason; for instance, it's a true-life event.

Referencing the letters above, this translates to: a) afterlife stories, historical stories, supernatural stories; b) arena stories (The Vatican, a corrupt law firm, a crack den, a major league baseball office, heaven or hell), adventure stories (Clive Cussler), mob stories (*The Godfather*), stories about storms and mountains and sinking ships, dark love stories, prison stories; c) ghost stories, meth lab stories, corrupt cop stories, speculative fiction; and d) issue-driven stories (*The Help*), true stories, war stories, historical event stories, and so on.

Vicarious experience is so common that it is often taken for granted.

Every story unfolds upon a dramatic stage. You must recognize the opportunity to make that stage—both in support of your story and as an independent source of focus and fascination—more compelling. This is the forgotten stepchild of both story planning and story "pantsing," when in fact it can empower either process.

A love story set in rural Idaho? This relies almost entirely on the character dynamic, because nobody out there is really wondering about the experience of hanging out in Twin Falls. But a love story set in, say ... the White House ... a nunnery ... a pro sports team ... the space shuttle ... another planet ... the afterlife ... a big-time Hollywood talent agency or studio ... you get the idea. Same love story, better setting. It's vicariously rewarding just to be there. The setting itself has inherent appeal and reward for the reader. It becomes *subtext* for all that happens there. The subtext of Idaho ... french fries. The subtext of a federal prison ... watch your back.

It is the nature of being in such a setting that delivers vicarious experience. We can't go back to 1962 Jackson, Mississippi, (nor would we choose to), but we can go there in *The Help*, which empowers its thematic intentions with the vivid subtext of its setting.

When you add your story to a setting that delivers vicarious experience—when you set your story within this time, place, or context that is, when regarded alone, inherently *interesting*—you are rewarded with a whole in excess of its parts.

Some stories are almost entirely about the vicarious experience. Remember *Top Gun*? It's a pretty pedestrian story. Like I said earlier, I tend to get slammed for even bringing it up, but it's a model for both good and bad. And yet, it puts us in the cockpit of a jet fighter, resulting in a billion dollar box office.

You've seen this executed over and over, but perhaps haven't recognized what it has contributed to the reader (or viewing) experience.

Never again. That's why we, as writers, need to keep our writer goggles on when reading or watching a film, even if it's "for pleasure." Writers never get a day off; we're always researching life, sometimes through the lenses of others.

Let me show you how this exists right now.

One of the hot new novels these days (at this writing) is *The Darlings* by Cristina Alger. It's a coming-of-age story set during the 2008 financial collapse and focuses on a family of billionaires living in the Upper East Side in Manhattan. The reviews almost entirely focused on this contextual setting—how it takes us into this forbidden realm—made all the juicier by the fact that the author is the daughter of a real-life hedge fund Big Cheese.

Pure vicarious experience. If the same story were set on a cattle farm in Kansas, it wouldn't fly, wouldn't get the buzz. In fact, notice that in many major media reviews of novels, the "takes us into a world ..." focus is common.

A while back, Anne Rice's book, *The Wolf Gift*, occupied the #6 position on *The New York Times* bestseller list. It was about—wait for it—werewolves. It's fantasy, but like all of Rice's novels, it's *vicarious* in that it allows us to live inside a world in which such creatures not only exist, but love.

The Harry Potter series, the Twilight saga, and The Hunger Games trilogy all rely on a strong vicarious experience. We get to go to Hogwarts, make love to the living and gorgeous dead, or live in a postapocalyptic world in which moral sensibilities have melted down and the kid next door wants to rip your throat out. All of these stories have characters and plots and subplots—the authors could have set them virtually anywhere and in any time—but they are rendered special and defined by the vicarious experiences they deliver.

When Stephenie Meyer decided to write about vampires (and largely reinvent the mythology), she was opting to deliver a vicarious experience. When a writer is creating a story partly for her own vicarious experience, it usually translates well on the page.

The same goes for James Cameron when he made *Titanic*. The vicarious experience of being on that ship as it went down was the central appeal of the whole thing, assisted by some killer digital visual effects.

I lived this firsthand with my 2004 novel *Bait and Switch*. Virtually every review (including the starred one from *Publishers Weekly*) mentioned "the world into which" I took the reader, that of Silicon Valley and high-tech billionaires and their trophy wives—a place where none of us can go, many of us wonder about, and intrigue, danger, and private jets await.

THE GOAL IS GOOSEBUMPS

Vicarious experience, as a goal and as a brute force of story physics, can be more than simply time and place. It can be delivered through social and character dynamics as well. It's like that old fortune cookie gag, where you add the words "in bed" to the end of any message. Just add "What would it be like...?" to the beginning of your setting or situation, and you're already delving into vicarious experience.

What would it be like to be married to a serial killer?

To discover your child has supernatural abilities?

To suddenly possess supernatural abilities?

To live in a world in which aliens have taken over?

To live in a world in which an alien is elected President?

To be told your spouse is having an affair?

To win the lottery?

To suddenly be able to read minds?

To be locked in your own body without the ability to move or communicate?

To go to heaven? To go to hell?

To talk to God directly ... and get responses via e-mail or text?

The answers to each of these is pure *vicarious experience.* These and an infinite list of others are contextual, conceptual, thematic, and even character-centric landscapes that could unfold in any place, at any time, and within any social system. These are things readers will never experience ... until you give them that experience in your pages.

So there it is, a secret writing weapon just waiting for you.

Take a look at your story and ask yourself what kind of vicarious experience you are delivering to your reader. All stories take us out of our own lives and into another existence, but does your setting—either time, place, contextual, or relational—contribute to the reading experience in an exciting, compelling, or even frightening way? One that is vicarious? One that readers will be drawn to—drawn into—by virtue of this alone?

When you understand the power and consequences of your choices, you begin to comprehend more than ever that the upside of your story is yours to craft, because the outcome is almost entirely rooted in vicarious experience.

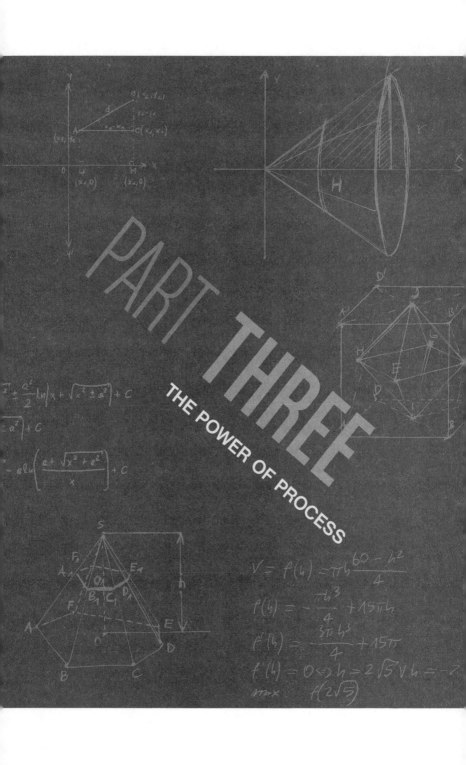

PART THREE

THE POWER OF PROCESS

16

THE HIGHEST GOAL OF YOUR WRITING PROCESS

WHEREIN WE FINALLY AGREE THAT THERE IS MORE THAN ONE WAY TO SKIN A MANUSCRIPT.

Stories have a natural flow. The underlying forces of a story are best served when the writer recognizes where and how within that flow to *apply* those forces and how to connect them as the narrative unfolds. One's process defines where, how, and how soon the idea for a story will dissolve seamlessly into a concept that sets the stage for the layered sequential narrative of an effective story. And in doing so, she defines when and how story physics will be applied.

Since I started writing about story architecture and story physics, I sometimes feel like I've been in a street fight. Pantsers vs. Planners. Jets vs. Sharks. Right vs. Left. Good vs. Evil. You would not believe the vitriolic venom sent my way when I've suggested that there exists an underlying, matrix-like set of structural principles and aesthetic sensibilities that, like gods looking down from Olympus through their enchanted reading glasses, determine the fate of our stories.

But no gray exists in the truth about what makes a story work, and there are only some shades of gray (fifty perhaps?) regarding the process of getting there. Many roads will take you to Rome, but only one city bears that name, at least in Italy. We're talking about physics and tools, which can be used to build just about anything. But you can't write *anything* you want and call it a story. Not if you intend to throw your story out there in the hopes of finding an audience.

I think I stumbled upon it. Like the previously quoted truisms on writing about *something happening*, this, too, warrants a place on your writing wall, written in blood:

Write your story however you need to write it, process-wise. But don't turn a blind eye to what's true about the bones of the story itself, however you get there. What the story demands from you in order for it to work is nonnegotiable.

The highest goal of any writing process is to find and execute the best possible story. If your process is part of the problem—for writers who can't seem to get it right, or get it published, it usually is—then the process should be taken apart and changed.

This means that, at the end of the day, *planners* and *pantsers* are two names given to writers with the same pursuit. It's the same game, with different paths and styles. But there is only one finish line.

Like many epiphanies, the problem is simplified when clarified. And the polarization vanishes like smoke blown away in a relieved sigh of recognition.

You can build a castle with a blueprint and a forklift, or you can build it one handful of sand at a time. The latter may be more romantic, it may be the only way you can wrap your head around it, but that doesn't change the above epiphany.

I believe that the more you understand those principles and criteria, the more you'll be prone to plan, or at least to engage *the search for story* in real time, rather than continue to write drafts and put blind trust in a muse that you hope will show you the path. Or at least how your story will end.

Either way, though, the truth and the destination are clear. Only the path remains shrouded in an intoxicating mist.

THE TRANSFORMATIVE POWER OF MISSION-DRIVEN STORYTELLING

WHEREIN THE MOST POWERFUL WRITING TIP EVER STEPS FORWARD TO CHANGE EVERYTHING ... IN A GOOD WAY.

As a prolific and often loud provider of writing tips, I am sometimes asked what my very favorite piece of advice or most treasured morsel of writing wisdom might be. I don't hesitate in answering. The most valuable writing advice I can impart is focused on the principles of mission-driven storytelling.

Let me break that down:

- Mission-driven ... in that there are four distinct, sequential, context-defined parts to a story, and each of these parts is roughly the same length. Everything that appears within those parts should be crafted and executed in context to the mission at hand, each of which is unique.
- Mission-driven ... in that each individual scene has a goal it strives to execute, a single piece of narrative contribution to story exposition, rendered within the parameters of the characters and settings the author has established. If the scene has too many missions to deliver upon, then dramatic tension is

compromised. If it skips on exposition altogether and simply characterizes or perhaps offers up a little essay on something—a very common gaffe in unpublished manuscripts—then pacing is compromised.

Notice, too, that dramatic tension and pacing are two of the most powerful elements of story physics. This is another way to realize that all this stuff is connected—mission-driven storytelling strives to optimize story physics.

It boils down to this: For each and every scene in your story, ask *"What's the primary, singular, expositional mission of this scene?"* If you have trouble answering, or you have more than one answer, then odds are the scene is in trouble. When this happens consistently in a story, the whole thing may already be wearing a toe tag. When you ask this question—and properly answer it—*before* you write the scene, it's like filing a flight plan for it, and your odds of success go up exponentially.

The Mission-Driven Context applies to any and all processes.

Organic drafters who write without a clear story plan are at risk on both counts. Successful drafters have already mastered this contextual, mission-driven ethic, which enables them to focus on the right exposition in the right way, at the right time in their stories. It might take a few drafts to get it right, but they know this is what needs to happen for things to work.

Planners address mission-driven writing predraft. In fact, the mission for their scenes is the highest order of vision for what ends up on the page. They write *toward* the mission and craft scenes to deliver the best, most entertaining and artful way to have the scene say what it needs to say, and no more.

Mission-driven writing is a context that applies on multiple levels. It brings macrocontext (the whole story) to the flow of the narrative, keeping the spine of the story crisp and relevant and avoiding unnecessary side trips. It allows each scene to be optimally effective through an understanding of the specific expositional information it must convey, and how it connects to subsequent scenes. It also allows the writer to layer in subtext, including theme, character arc, and subplot, without allowing those goals to overwhelm the central purpose of the scene itself.

Before you can pay something off, you need to set it up.

Before you ask someone to invest, you must make a promise.

Before there is a story, there is conflict.

Before anyone cares, there must be stakes.

Getting all of that in motion in your story is the mission of your first twenty to twenty-five percent, or Part One, of the story's length. And if you do it right, you'll *need* all of those pages.

The whole *Part One Setup leading to the First Plot Point* enchilada can be confusing, and for some, sounds like something a mad rogue screenwriter is trying to jam down your novelist throat. As someone who is all three—a screenwriter, a novelist, and completely mad—I assure you that this is equally valid thinking for both page and screen.

Essential stuff.

A story unfolds in four basic parts.

Some say it's three (the film industry, for example), but because the middle part in the model, which is twice as long as the parts on either side of it, breaks down into two separate missions, four is actually more accurate.

The key word here is *mission*.

Each of the four parts has a *different* one in a contextual sense. This means that the scenes within each part should align contextually with that mission and thus bear a different context than scenes from the other parts. That's critical to understand—it's the difference between a writer who knows what she's doing and one who is faking it or imitating what she's read and mislabeling it as *knowing how to write*.

The order of the missions of the four parts is, by virtue of the nature of storytelling, ordained. You mess with that order at your own peril. Your story won't work until it lines up with this contextual sequence.

The first part is called "the setup."

It contains a *hook*, one or more *inciting incidents*, an introduction of the hero, foreshadowing, the planting of narrative seeds (including subplot), and the establishment of context, arena, setting, time, and voice.

The mission of this opening quartile is to *invest the reader in the story* through empathy for the hero, which depends on the establishment of stakes and a clearly defined dramatic question at the heart of the story.

Like … who did it? What will happen? How will it turn out? What will I experience if I (the reader) stick with this story? It promises to answer another question: Why will I care?

The last thing that happens in the Part One setup is called "the First Plot Point." Its appearance is a milestone in the story because it signals the end of Part One and the beginning of Part Two.

Don't mess with that, either. Rather, learn what this all means, and discover the creative freedom that comes with knowing you are within the realm of what *works*.

Once you get this down, you'll see a First Plot Point at work in every published story. No exceptions. It'll be like a curtain parting for you, inviting you to come backstage and hang out with the writer.

Why this can be confusing.

It's confusing because the *terms* can be confusing. *Inciting incident* versus *hook*. *Inciting incident* versus *First Plot Point*. *Narrative exposition* versus *character development*. *Dramatic tension* versus *plot*. Back in the days when the first storytellers were spinning tales over a fire and the carcass of a yak, the word *rhetoric* was pronounced *blah blah blah*. Which is what the unenlightened writer still hears.

Don't be *that* guy.

To add to the confusion … a hook *can* be an inciting incident, but it can *never* be the First Plot Point, which, at the twentieth to twenty-fifth percentile, is *way* too late for a hook. An inciting incident *can* be the First Plot Point, but inciting incidents (scenes that change things and inject major story elements) can also appear in the *middle* of the

Part One setup pages (in which case it still isn't a First Plot Point), or even at the beginning of it. In which case, it becomes a hook.

So let's clear this up.

By any other description or nametag, when something really compelling happens in the first scene of your story, or the first ten pages, if it isn't in the first scene, that's a *hook*. Big or little. Yeah, it may indeed *be* an inciting incident (something happens that connects to the forthcoming story line) ... but it doesn't have to be.

Your hook could be unconnected to plot and entirely connected to characterization, like the revelation on page 1 that the narrator of this story is a ghost. That's a *hook*.

When it's not connected to plot, it's not an inciting *incident*.

If the event, however, is huge, like someone murdering someone on page 1, or leaving them, or hiring them, or painting them with stars and stripes, then it is an inciting incident *and* a hook.

If that happens on, say, page 45, that's not a hook at all, but it is an inciting incident. But it's still not the First Plot Point ... unless it is.

Having fun yet? And you thought all these supposedly rigid paradigms and principles and structural guidelines would restrict you.

The fact is, you're lost without them, because your story will fail without them. The moment you realize that they actually set you free ... you become *empowered*.

The key to understanding the First Plot Point.

Lots of stuff can and should happen in your Part One setup. But not all of it *connects to the hero* in a meaningful and relevant way ... yet. The core story, the specific conflict, doesn't kick in with full disclosure and meaning until the First Plot Point at the end of Part One, which introduces the forthcoming journey, quest, or mission you are giving your hero.

Read that again. It's the key to everything.

Your story *must* impart to your hero a journey, need, quest, mission, problem to solve, or goal to attain. That's precisely what your story *is*: a vicarious sharing, an unveiling, of that *journey, need, quest, mission, problem to solve, or goal to attain.*

That said, the key to wrapping your head around this is under-standing that this *hero's journey, need, quest, mission, problem to solve, or goal to attain* is, by intention and design, launched, fully rendered, put in motion, and unquestionably underway ... at the First Plot Point. At the end of your Part One setup. Not before.

Here's a really nifty way to get this clear in your head.

The First Plot Point is the moment the hero becomes *involved*, sub-jected to, in quest of or otherwise impacted by, the hook and incit-ing incident(s) that you've put into the flow prior to it. To the whole of your Part One. It's when your hero assumes the starring role in the story and suddenly finds himself in deep water. It is here that he *earns* his stardom.

At the First Plot Point the hero (and/or the reader) is suddenly *aware* of what all the stuff that happened in the Part One setup *means*. And because of the stakes you have put in place *prior* to this moment, it's also the point at which we (the readers) become truly *invested* in the story.

Prior to that, it's all just ingredients set out on a counter and/or simmering in a pot, emitting an enticing scent, drawing us in ... but it's not yet a meal to be consumed until you serve it on a platter for the reader at the First Plot Point. Dinner is served, the story has finally kicked in and is fully underway. This happens when you connect it all to the hero's forthcoming *journey, need, quest, mission, problem to solve, or goal to attain.*

Serve the potatoes before the gravy is warm, and your dinner will suck.

In *The Da Vinci Code*, a body is discovered in a museum. Hook? Yes. Inciting incident? Yes. But ... it doesn't yet connect to the hero's core *journey, need, quest, mission, problem to solve, or goal to attain* that the story puts before him. *It just sets it up.* It doesn't *mean* any-thing yet, at least in context to the story to come. It's just stuff that comes into play later. This context alone—despite happening early—means that it's not yet the First Plot Point.

The reader learns that the police are out to pin this on the hero, who has been innocently called in to help investigate. This adds tension. We can smell what's cooking, and its name is story physics.

But is it the First Plot Point?

Nope. Not yet. It's just a cool inciting incident. Because it doesn't *yet* connect to the hero (even though we see it coming), and it doesn't ignite, or otherwise launch or define, the hero's *journey, need, quest, mission, problem to solve, or goal to attain.*

Begin noticing this in the stories you read.

And the movies you see. In fact, you can see the First Plot Point in most movie trailers, preceded by a quick synopsis of the Part One setup:

> "Meet the Joneses, your average American family ... two and a
> half kids, a dog, a mortgage ... until the bottom falls out when
> the wife is kidnapped by her ex-husband and the new hubby
> has to defy the FBI, CIA, and the Mob to get her back."

The hero might actually begin a journey in Part One, but when that happens you can bet this journey won't be the *precise* core story line to come. You can bet it will *change and evolve*. It will take on deeper meaning and stakes. It's all just part of the setup.

Until it isn't. Until—based as much on location and timing and mission—a story beat arrives that changes everything. It imparts meaning and direction and thrust and stakes by revealing the real hero's *journey, need, quest, mission, problem to solve, or goal to attain* within the world this story creates.

This is where most uninitiated writers screw up. They have quite isolated their core story, or they get to it too soon, or too late. When that happens, story physics have been maimed, and its time to go back to the principles of four-part story architecture to nurse them back to optimal health.

MISSION-CRITICAL SCENE WRITING
WHEREIN WE EXAMINE WHERE AND HOW WE MAKE OR BREAK OUR STORIES, EVEN WHEN EVERYTHING ELSE WORKS.

Two words have emerged from the computer programming world into the lexicon of writing fiction. (It's actually *three*, if you count the word *architecture*, which the pioneering computer geeks actually borrowed from the building trade to describe programming in a *design* context.) Those two high-tech words are *paradigm* and *optimize*.

Ironically, it is *architecture* that programmers—and writers—seek to *optimize*. As for *paradigm*—the framework of assumptions and expectations that put a fence around a task or element—everything depends on *which* paradigm you work from.

Like diets and cures, all paradigms are not created equal.

Republicans and Democrats ... different political paradigms. Fiction and nonfiction ... different at every level. Planning and pantsing ... not as different as you'd think (both are a search for story), but regarded as different *process* paradigms.

To *optimize* is to make something the very best it can be, given its use, context, and mission. The latter caveat is critical to one's understanding of the goal of optimization. Sometimes a whisper is the optimal corrective tool, and sometimes it's a two-by-four. That's why *context* is critical to this understanding.

There is a fourth term the geeks have also snatched and applied to enterprise-level software: *mission-critical*. As in, the whole thing goes up in flames if *this* doesn't work.

So it is with my very favorite writing tip. If you don't completely know where a story is going, there is no way you can *optimize* your scenes. You can write them or string them together, but until you clarify their destination they are just your best in-the-moment guesses. Writers who claim they can optimize their stories one scene at a time in linear order within an early draft are one of three things: patient, geniuses, or unpublished. Trust me, if such a process results in a published and successful book or script—and it really does happen— there was a honkin' rewrite in there somewhere. My position is that, through an understanding of these principles (which will, over time, lead you toward story planning, at least as a part of your process) you can cut down on the number of drafts required (reducing to one or two, in fact), and the time that expires between starting and finishing.

Mission-driven, mission-critical scene construction and execution is the make-or-break skill set of storytelling. You can plan like a mad genius, but if you can't *execute* scenes at a professional level, then all that planning collapses in a heaving mass of unfulfilled *intention*.

Planning is the creation of an architecturally sound blueprint. Successful planning is when the mission-critical story beats—Hook, First Plot Point, First Pinch Point, Midpoint, Second Pinch Point, Second Plot Point, and the Climax scenes—have been optimized based on stellar story physics. Scene writing is all hammers and nails and drywall, assembled with the touch of a master craftsman. Without a seamless blueprint, it's like putting a granite and cherry kitchen into a tent.

This is why scene writing is one of the essential Six Core Competencies.

Scene writing is always risky without a contextual *mission* that melds into a master plan. Without a mission, too often the result is scenes that don't forward exposition or hit the pause button on the story with a side trip or overwrought backstory. To complicate matters, there are different species (categories) of scenes with differing contextual missions and therefore discreet forms.

Opening scenes read differently than expositional scenes ... which are different than milestone scenes ... which are again different from scenes with unique and vital roles in a story (like flashbacks, behind-the-curtain cutaways, first-person reflections, etc.). To a great extent these differences are defined by an understanding of the four different contextual realms of a story (which go a long way toward defining the context of the scenes within them; see Chapter 22), and what happens just before and after a given scene.

A scene that is *just* characterization, with nothing added to the exposition, is not good. Not optimized. When you add a piece of narrative exposition to that characterization, the scene has a *mission*. When you add a second or third mission to a single scene, you risk compromising power and clarity. James Patterson has mastered this, and it has become the accepted model of effective scene writing today: One mission per scene.

Think of each scene as a frame in a PowerPoint presentation. That single bullet of information is the mission. What you might *say* about that frame in live presentation ... that's what you insert in your beat sheet or outline, or, if you can keep it all straight in your head, in the actual execution of a scene.

Ask yourself: What does this scene need to accomplish? Why is it here? How does it propel the story forward? What about it is interesting or emotionally resonant? What is the conflict in this scene? The subtext?

Sometimes a key *moment* within a story calls for a microcosmic drama that stands alone as a chunk of dramatic power. Big moments certainly call for big scenes, and often for preliminary setup scenes. Other times, scenes can be in and out, quick and clear. You get to make that call, but in either case, your scenes work best—they are *optimized*—when conceived and then executed from a mission-driven perspective.

Once you know the mission for each scene, the next step is to conceive a creative *treatment* (approach) for the scene, using the power of story physics to drive it home. This treatment should make the scene as effective—scary, dramatic, multifaceted, mysterious, impactful, sexy, or whatever it needs to be—to best fulfill its mission. This, too, is the *art* of writing ... an intuitive feel for the type of creative treatment that is indeed optimal.

The more you understand the Big Picture of your story and the principles that prop it up, the quicker and closer you'll come to that intuitive creative solution.

PRINCIPLES FOR EFFECTIVE SCENE WRITING

Enter your scene at the *last possible moment*. This can only happen if you do, in fact, *understand* the mission of the scene and have defined the single kernel of essential exposition it delivers to the reader.

Is the setup of the scene necessary? Are there extraneous chit-chatty character greetings or side conversations? Is there gratuitous characterization or unnecessary backstory? Are descriptions of places and people required to get the point (the mission) across? Are you giving the reader enough credit to see and *get* the moment, without slamming them over the head with the obvious or mundane?

The deeper you go into a story, the less this type of minutia should be present. Even then, don't describe things that don't need describing; that is, details the reader can intuitively understand. Don't describe how a coffeemaker looks, even when coffee is being served in a scene. Believe me, it happens in those unpublished manuscripts you don't get to see.

Get to the point. Get to *it*. Less is more.

If your story leans to the more literate and character-driven variety, these rules *still* apply, but with a different veneer. If your words don't reveal and connect to a mission, to a *purpose*, then chances are they should be economized or reconsidered.

Make your scenes microcosms of dramatic theory. They should apply story physics directly to the mission at hand. If there is a major reveal, lead into it, then deliver the blow (the key revelation at the heart of the scene's mission) at the last moment of the scene. This is called a cut and thrust, and it propels the reader into the scene that follows so she can learn more about what just happened.

Many scenes have a setup (done with prior context), a confrontation, and a resolution. Sometimes the elements can be implied and not shown; that's your choice. A great scene asks and, to some extent, answers a dramatic question. Just know that *overwriting* a scene is a deal killer, a pace sucker. Give the reader credit for the ability to make leaps. Explain only what requires explaining.

And, going back to Writing 101—*show*, don't tell. When you can. This is a flexible principle that needs to be applied artfully. But don't show *everything* ... because everything doesn't need to be on the page. The subtext of a vicarious journey (one of the realms of story physics) is allowing readers to visualize settings and circumstances through their own frames of reference.

19

YOUR STORY IN NINE BAD SENTENCES

WHEREIN WE SEE HOW WELL YOU REALLY KNOW YOUR STORY.

This is an exercise. Don't panic ... breathe. I'm not advocating bad sentences. I'm not suggesting you throw your kids into the deep end as a means of teaching them how to swim. This is a grammatical timeout to help us *make a point* and learn something about our stories. This is a *tool*, like a singer belting out the scales, something nobody pays to hear.

Any story—the whole story—can be reduced to nine sentences.

It can actually be reduced to one, but nine can tell the whole story with structural resolution, albeit at a ten thousand-foot level. Go ahead, try this on your story at any stage, or apply it to your favorite novels. It'll test your knowledge of story architecture while pointing you toward it—which is the whole point of the exercise.

This is something you can use when developing a story or when finishing one. It's an acid test, of sorts. If you struggle with it, then your story is possibly in trouble.

The goal isn't to finish, but to *optimize*. To make your story the very best it can be within the context and confines of your driving concept.

These nine sentences aren't the first step in story development, by the way. Or at least they shouldn't be. The first step is the identification of an idea. The goal then becomes to expand the idea into a concept, and then to lay it out over these specific nine sentences, each of which is assigned a mission.

When you do that, you've just structured your entire novel.

The number nine isn't arbitrary here. Solid stories have five major milestones, and they unfold in four parts. Do the math: That's nine specific turns and essences and differentiated contexts and/or subtexts that need to be identified and broken down into individual scene treatments.

The real value of this exercise comes when these nine sentences expand into more sentences, with each sentence ultimately describing a scene in your story. At that point, congratulations are in order—you've just written an entire outline.

Here are the nine sentences you are going for:

1. Hook
2. Part One Exposition (setup)
3. First Plot Point
4. Part Two Exposition (response, journey begins)
5. Midpoint
6. Part Three Exposition (hero becomes proactive)
7. Second Plot Point
8. Part Four Exposition (hero becomes catalyst for…)
9. Ending/Resolution

The Hunger Games in Nine Sentences

Pay attention to the labels that identify the four parts and the five milestones.

This is important because these sentences need to be in a specific order and target specific content … and they all need to be covered. Here we go:

1. The HOOK is when, after meeting Katniss and her family in the first chapter, we see her sister Prim selected as a Tribute in the District 12 Reaping ceremony, and then Katniss (our hero) steps up to volunteer to take her place in the Games.

2. The SETUP continues (Part One of the story, or about the first twenty percent of the total length) with scenes that simultaneously show us the life Katniss had been living, including her skills in the forest, and the process of saying goodbye and then traveling to the Capitol city, where she and the other District 12 Tribute, Peeta, prepare and train under the guidance of assigned mentors and caretakers.

3. The story changes (kicks into a higher gear) at the FIRST PLOT POINT when Katniss, after being unsure about a strategy that pairs her romantically with Peeta, appears to accept this strategic union, thus uniting them as partners in the Games and spinning the subtextual story arc of their relationship, which becomes the source of hope.

4. In the PART TWO scenes (our hero's response to this newly defined quest/journey), we see Katniss finish her final preparations with a flourish and then enter the Games and survive a near-miss attack before fleeing into the woods, eluding others and searching for shelter and water, and discovering that Peeta has joined a pack that is targeting her.

5. The MIDPOINT transforms Katniss from a wandering potential victim into a warrior, as she attacks the Tributes waiting to kill her with a hive of killer wasps and begins an alliance with the lovable and clever Tribute Rue.

6. In the PART THREE scenes, Katniss, now partnered with Rue and recovering from wasp stings that made her hallucinate about Peeta actually helping her escape, tends to her injuries while hatching a plan to attack the food and supplies of the dominant surviving pack of Tributes (which includes Peeta), a plan that succeeds but causes Rue's death.

7. The SECOND PLOT POINT reunites a badly injured Peeta with Katniss, where their reconciled relationship returns to what is now a seemingly genuine romantic affection that is also their best shot at survival, and as such, sets up the ending sequence.

8. The PART FOUR scenes show Katniss and Peeta taking shelter so Peeta can safely heal, while Katniss leaves him behind

to go to a Gamekeeper-arranged gifting, where she is nearly killed before being saved by Rue's District co-Tribute (acting in gratitude for her kindness to Rue), and then, when it is announced that the rules will change to permit two surviving Tributes from the same district to win the games, they must escape the release of killer mutts that chase them onto the Cornucopia itself for a final showdown.

9. At the END of the story, Katniss and Peeta, after surviving the mutts and a final confrontation with the lone and most sinister surviving Tribute, are pronounced winners of the 74th Annual Hunger Games and taken back to the city for recovery and celebration, which takes a dark turn when their mentor warns them that the President is not happy that their near death pact/bluff has humiliated the Capitol and tarnished the Games, and that they are not yet out of danger (thus setting up the sequels).

Okay, those are admittedly some big, ugly, Faulkneresque sentences, contrived to cover ground (especially when working backwards from a completed story). But they began as short sentences or bullet points in a beat sheet, and they worked as placeholders until the writer better understood what would happen at a particular point.

This is a tool that can unblock you.

It can become the primary spine of your story development, something much easier and faster to revise than a draft. It works because it forces you to consider the major moving parts of your story and opens the door to the creation of specific scenes within the parts that you've identified. It is also an exercise in story physics, which become, in effect, the endgame of the key scenes in the sequence.

My advice: Use these nine sentences as a means of fleshing out your story before you write. If you can't create that way (thousands tell me they can't, so you might be one of them), then use this exercise to keep your organic scene sequence on track with the optimal generic architecture of the story.

Can you reduce your story to nine sentences that cover the four parts (setup, response, attack, resolution), divided by the five major story milestones (Hook, First Plot Point, Midpoint, Second Plot Point, Ending)?

Try it. You'll be amazed, if not with what you have, then with the clarity of what you *don't* yet have (or perhaps have in the wrong place), which is just as valuable.

Once you've written your nine sentences, stir in character arc and context, thematic subtext, and specific scenes that flesh out these sentences, and you're in business.

Ask Suzanne Collins, and she'll certainly agree … business is good for *The Hunger Games*.

THE BEAT SHEET

WHEREIN THE STORYTELLING BLUEPRINT BECOMES A GUIDE INSTEAD OF AN OBSTACLE COURSE.

The "beat" in the title of this chapter is meant quite literally, at least from a musicality perspective (versus, say, a pugilistic one). I'm talking about *story* beats—moments, or expository steps forward, best rendered as individual scenes—that are first represented as bullets, sentence fragments, or lines of description, written upon just about anything. (As in, a line of yellow sticky notes. Or index cards thumb-tacked to your wall. Or sheets of printer paper, scotch taped floor to ceiling.)

Those pieces of paper contain your story, one beat at a time. It's called a "beat sheet," and infinite variations and media upon which to write them are available to you. Simply writing numbers *1* through *60* in Microsoft Word, each followed by a story beat, is my favorite.

Each story beat begins as either a one-word mission or a bulleted phrase.

Which then becomes a sentence.

Which then becomes a paragraph.

Which then becomes a scene, crafted to optimize the story beat.

Each and every one of those iterations drives toward the mission for the scene itself, either generically ("boy meets girl") or specifically ("boy hits girl's car in stadium parking lot").

Your beat sheet is the skeleton of your story plan. You can write a draft directly from it, or you can keep expanding it until it becomes a rich story outline, or at the extreme, the draft itself.

THE INITIAL GENERIC ITEMS ON YOUR BEAT SHEET

Whether you start with that empty list of numbers *1* through *60* or a sequence of sixty blank sticky notes or 3" × 5" index cards, you should insert generic missions in five places.

For scene 1, write "Hook."

For scenes 12 to 15 (pick one, it doesn't matter at this point), write "First Plot Point."

For scene 30, write "Midpoint."

For scenes 42 to 46 (again, it doesn't matter which one you pick for now), write "Second Plot Point."

For scene 60 write "Ending."

Now you have a framework to develop scenes toward, and in context to. At some point—the sooner the better—you will add specific scene content and treatment to those same five beats, and suddenly you're in full story-planning gear. With those scenes in place you'll find yourself naturally imagining the scenes between them—the connective tissue.

You can group the beat sheet cards (or numbers) into the four parts, which would be roughly fifteen beats each. The nice thing about this process is that you can cut or add or shift or start over ... which is far preferable to doing so within an actual draft.

After you fill in all sixty scenes—by then it could be forty-one or eighty-eight in total, because *you* ultimately determine the number; just make sure the percentages across the four parts come close to the optimal lengths—will it be *final*? No. Will it be structurally sound? Yes, if you don't quit before you're done.

Everything from that point forward—the actual writing and revising of the manuscript—is pure, blissful upside, rather than a random search for your story.

That's what the beat sheet is for.

And here's what the beat sheet looks like. For a printable version, go to writersdigest.com/story-physics-beat-sheet.

THE BEAT SHEET—A FLEXIBLE TEMPLATE FOR YOUR STORY

The first section allows you to create a targeted direction and narrative flow for your story. Fill these in, and you'll find specific scene ideas popping into your head.

That's next.

Each blank line in the template represents a scene. Fill them in as your story takes form with either a) a singular narrative mission for the scene (example: hero meets love interest for first time), and/or b) the narrative content of the scene (example: Bob and Shirley run into each other at the reunion).

Conceptual hook/appeal: _____

_____

_____

_____

Theme(s): _____

_____

_____

_____

Through-line: _____

_____

_____

_____

PART ONE—SETUP:

1.1 _____

1.2 _____

1.3 _____

1.4 _____

1.5 _____

1.6 _____

1.7 _____

1.8 _____

1.9 _____

1.10 _____

1.11 _____

1.12 _____

1.13 _____

1.14 _____

1.15 (First Plot Point) _____

YOUR STORY ON STEROIDS
WHEREIN WE SHOOT FOR THE OPTIMIZATION OF STORY PHYSICS ACROSS ALL ELEMENTS.

Some writers equate writing with *power* to writing with *eloquence*. In other words, writing with descriptive genius, lots of cool adjectives, and the occasional adverb. But that's not writing with power, it's like writing with gobs of slathered-on purple prose. Too often, this is the work of a newbie. It can come off as trying too hard. How often do we see a published book dripping with purple? Not so much.

To fully understand what *writing with power* really means, one has to know the difference and then *recognize it* when it crosses your path. We should understand that power has as much to do with sentences as good looks have to do with integrity and I.Q. (Have you seen a picture of Einstein or Kim Kardashian lately?)

It's good to have both, but eloquence alone won't get you published. Earlier I mentioned an agent who claimed he could tell if he wanted to represent a book after reading only the first page. Odds are he was easily seduced by eloquence. Odds are, too, that by the time he reached page fifty, he'd often changed his mind. Of course, that doesn't sound as edgy in a panel discussion (that's the trouble with venues like that—there are far too many generalizations, polarizations, and one-offs to cast any of them in stone).

Let me show you an example of a powerful *moment*.

In the trailer for the film *We Bought a Zoo*, there's a line spoken by Matt Damon to his struggling teenage son that, in my opinion, qualifies as powerful:

"All you need is twenty seconds of insane courage, and I promise you something great will come of it."

Man, do I wish my dad had said something like that to me. And man, do I wish I'd thought of it and used it in my own work first.

There's only one adjective in there. My jaw dropped into my popcorn when I heard this line (great lines often make it into the trailer). We should strive to write lines like that. This line is powerful because of what it *means*, and the truth and the simple eloquence of it forces you to notice.

Simple eloquence trumps souped-up purple eloquence every time.

Power is not about adjectives. Power is all about impact ... subtext, relevance, illumination, irony, clarity, truth, heart, soul ... the poignant moment, stripped of pretense.

Here's another example.

Go to Amazon.com to read the first page of a novel called *Manhattan Nocturne*, by Colin Harrison, originally published in 1997 to astounding critical acclaim and republished in 2008. Study that first paragraph, the one that begins with: "I sell mayhem, scandal, murder and doom."

I believe the term *OMG!* applies. I've read this aloud at many workshops, and the universal response is the silent mouthing of the word *wow*. Only two of the sentences contain a total of four adjectives. And yet, this is as descriptive and compelling as it gets. That author, by the way, was once dubbed "the poet laureate of American thriller writers," and it wasn't solely because of his prose. It was because of his ability to write with *power,* which fueled his solid story lines.

Writing with power is nothing other than taking all the essences of story physics to a higher level.

Power depends on timing, cadence, and relevance.

You have to understand what a scene is *going for*—indeed, what the thematic essence of the *entire* story is—in order to optimize your ability to write it *powerfully*. Once again, being *mission driven* is the key. Don't try to make every sentence quotable. If you *season* your writing with powerful *moments*, with only the occasional swing for the prosaic fence, you'll imbue the whole thing with a powerful essence.

It's hard to really *learn* this. It's a sensibility, a nuance, a deft *touch*. Over time you can *discover* it from deep within yourself, and discovery always begins by *noticing* it when you see it. To write powerfully, you need to summon your inner poet, copywriter, philosopher, favorite uncle, JFK's speechwriter, and Abraham Lincoln, all fused and staged with an exquisite sense of timing.

Don't force it, just look for it, recognize it, and understand it. And then look for *just the right moment* to go for it in your own work.

What have you written lately?

If you expect to sell your first novel or screenplay—as in, the first story you've ever *written*—then you've just anointed yourself *special*. It hardly ever happens. A career as a fiction writer is a long-haul proposition. Getting published isn't the benchmark ... staying *at it* is. "On to the next" is the mantra of the successful writer.

That said, here's a career-making question: Is your muse driving the bus, or waiting on a bench?

I had dinner recently with my beautiful stepdaughter. She was an English Lit major, and she's a passionate consumer of novels. She's someone in close touch with energies and enlightenments that would send many of us into hiding, or to a shrink's office.

She has "the gift."

I've talked to her for the last fifteen years about writing a novel. Her life has led her to a point where, one could argue, the time has arrived.

I asked her a question with interesting implications: What was she waiting for? Was she expecting, and therefore waiting on, one of the Muses to suddenly tell her it was the right time, and thus bestow a story idea upon her? Was she waiting for a cosmic shoulder tap that whispers the arrival of a Big Idea?

Before she could answer, I suggested that she may indeed be waiting on her Muse or a sign from the cosmos. And then I also suggested that she flip this whole proposition on its naive ear to see what might happen. What if, I postulated, the muse was *waiting on her*? Waiting for her to click into story-search mode, eager to climb on board if only she'd declare the intention and cast a net.

She said this was an interesting idea. She'd think about it.

I'm hoping you'll do the same.

What have you written lately? If the answer is, "Not much," then what are you waiting for?

The craft is already here. It's yours for the taking.

So is the Muse, and so is the Big Idea.

The latter, however, is still out there, possibly hiding in plain sight. Possibly closer than you can imagine. But it must survive some vetting before you invest in it.

What if? Marry those two words with something that fascinates you, frightens you, challenges you, or calls to you ... and summon the Muse out of hiding. Send some story physics her way ... and who knows what might happen?

She won't say the words for you ... but she's listening closely.

Tick tock.

PART FOUR

STORY PHYSICS IN
THE REAL WRITING WORLD

THE SIX CORE COMPETENCIES OF SUCCESSFUL STORYTELLING: A 101 REVIEW

WHEREIN WE PLAY CATCH-UP, ESPECIALLY IF THIS MODEL IS NEW TO YOU.

You've seen these words many times thus far in this book: *the Six Core Competencies*. They refer to what I like to think of as a *tool chest*—facets of knowledge and skill, separate but interdependent within the whole of the storytelling process—comprised of four story development *elements* and two *execution skills*. Each has a subordinated list of criteria and alternative forms and benchmarks for determining how well they will work within a story. Together they are the antithesis of *make-it-up-as-you-go-and just-throw-it-into-the-wind-and-see-what-happens* storytelling.

The four *elements* of the Six Core Competencies are actually *aspects and qualities* that are essential for a story's effectiveness. If you skip one or if one is weak, you may have just rendered your story unpublishable. These elements are:

- concept
- character

- theme
- structure

The remaining two of the Six Core Competencies are specific *tasks and skills* of execution, the actions through which you implement the previous four elements:

- scene execution
- voice and style

Some writers are surprised to find they need to *do* only two things—versus six things they need to *know*—in order to write a book: Write scenes, and create them using sentences. Everything you do while looking at a screen with your fingers on a keyboard falls under the category of one of those two things.

An anesthesiologist has to *do* only one thing well: Put the patient under without killing him. But she has to *know* about five hundred things to do it successfully. It is the same with a writer: There are four arenas you need to know about ... and only two skill sets you need to master in context to that knowledge.

Oversimplification? Hardly. Within those six buckets are literally hundreds of things you need to be aware of and be able to implement. Organizing them, however, allows you to inventory your knowledge, rather than just spilling words onto a page randomly, instinctively, imitatively, or from some misguided belief system.

CORE COMPETENCIES VS. STORY PHYSICS

Let me be clear here—the Six Core Competencies are *not* the same elements as the six essences of story *physics*, which are the focus of this book. To think they are the same is like thinking an airplane is the same thing as gravity or that surfing is the same thing as the ocean tides. Or that a stick of dynamite is the same thing as an explosion.

The Six Core Competencies are made up of tools or activities that require tools, while story physics are essences, forces, catalysts for an outcome. They are the *objects* of the tools. Story physics make the tools useful, and make them work in the first place.

The fact that both models are measured and described with *six* separate component realms is coincidental, though potentially confusing. They refer to completely different things. Yet—like airplanes and gravity—they are connected at the hip, in that the six basic essences of story physics—compelling premise, dramatic tension, pacing, hero empathy, vicarious experience, and narrative strategy—are the *underlying forces* that make the Six Core Competencies necessary and effective. The more powerful the forces, the better the tools work.

Viewed in context to the whole of the story development and execution process, when the integration of the Six Core Competencies and story physics is understood, they become a complete—and completely empowering—survey of what a writer needs to understand and execute within a story. The writer now has six things she needs to *put into* a story ... and six reasons (forces) why she should. Story physics are six variables you can manipulate by applying the Six Core Competencies. Even if someone uses different terminology to describe them—which is the case more often than not—all twelve *will* be present in an effectively told story.

This is what's known in the academic world as a *model*. It's a window into clarity. If you're looking to truly understand what needs to be done—what ground you need to cover—to write an effective story, then both of these six-part models will serve you. Otherwise, you better hope that what spills out of your head when you sit down and write will cover all those bases naturally.

This "phenomenon" occurs all the time in the real world, even for best-selling authors who, in their interviews, seduce the uninitiated into believing that writing without utilizing the tools and forces of storytelling is a tried and true practice that will work for everyone. Good luck with that. For every writer who succeeds by simply stumbling upon proper balance and structure, or through instinct or a learning curve (the pain of many failures), there are crowds of writers who were rejected because of flaws that feed on this very approach.

It's theoretically possible to successfully complete an appendectomy or an amputation without really knowing what you're doing, and we hear about it when it happens. But the odds are better that in such situations somebody's going to die instead. Medical school is a better avenue to take to doing appendectomies and such, because the procedures are exceedingly complex. The same is the case for writing an effective novel or screenplay. The Six Core Competencies and story physics models are the medical school of storytelling.

The objective of this chapter is to introduce the Six Core Competencies to you—perhaps *again*, if you've read *Story Engineering* and/or my website—independent of the context within which they have been referred to in this book. It's sort of like studying the nature and chemistry of spices before discussing them in context to cooking a killer meal. Or, switching analogies here, it's good to know the building blocks, the ingredients—units of weight-bearing structure and force-applying aesthetic potential—before we set out to erect a building.

THE ORIGIN OF THIS MODEL

The core competencies were the subject of my first writing book, *Story Engineering: Mastering the Six Core Competencies of Successful Writing* (2011, Writer's Digest Books). They represent a vast collection of the things writers need to know, boiled down into six categories, or buckets of information. Six wasn't the target, but it just turned out that way after studying this stuff for more than thirty years. I concluded that just about anything out there in the writing void can be placed inside one of these buckets, and each bucket is unique enough to warrant its own category.

A concept is not a theme. A concept is not structure. Structure is not conceptual, until the writer makes it so. Character is not theme until it marries concept. A scene is separate from and subordinated to the macroconcept. Words are just drops of water in a large lake of story. Each of these is worthy and necessary, but each is separate and requires integration with the others.

It's like the skills required of a quarterback: throwing strength, footwork in the pocket, field vision, speed, ability to take a hit ... each is a separate talent. They are all requisite core competencies.

And yet, all of these—speed, toughness, field vision—can be possessed by an eighth grader. A player can be positioned at quarterback at any level: grade school, high school, small college, D-1, and professional. The difference between good and great at any level is the underlying *physics* of each of those core competencies. Strength, speed, sensibility, decision-making, creativity, courage, and something indefinably special ... these are the football *physics* that define the future of the player.

So it is with our stories. We must master the core competencies to play at the professional level, and the better our understanding of the story physics that make each of those core competencies work, the sooner we'll see our books in the window of a bookstore.

THE ANTE-IN TO THE PROFESSIONAL LEVEL

In order to achieve effective story development, *all* the Six Core Competencies need to be effectively rendered within a story. This means an author is best served by understanding each of them as both stand-alone elements and skills, as well as pieces of an integrated whole.

We do this by understanding and applying the strongest forces of story physics to our stories, in just the right places, in just the right way, with just the right touch. All of which splats a cream pie into the face of anyone who claims that either of these models results in formulaic storytelling. The number of potential outcomes that result from infinite degrees of application within each element of the models is ... infinite.

You need to nail *all six competencies* to get into the publishing game and deliver a story that readers will feel and remember. And even then, success isn't guaranteed, because agents, editors, and readers decide the definition of "nail." We are left to simply do the best we can, and our efforts are always empowered through awareness and knowledge.

Which is to say, nailing them may not be enough.

Not every skilled athlete makes it in his sport. In that world, being *gifted* has a lot to do with it. While many major league athletes do everything well, most do one or two things *very* well, better than their almost-made-it peers. Ask your club golf or tennis pro about this ... on paper he has the same level of excellence as the touring pros relative to form, consistency, and power. And yet, he's giving lessons for forty bucks an hour instead of being interviewed by John McEnroe. The reason behind this corresponds to getting published: You need something *special*, something extraordinary (as well as a bit of good fortune), to break in and have a book rise to the level of a bestseller. And, lucky for us, it doesn't require a genetic gift. It does require, however, the application of literary physics in a way similar to an athlete's genetic gifts of power and speed. We can get there if we obtain knowledge and awareness, and evolve a nuanced touch and sensibility.

Here's how the core competencies relate to story physics.

- When one *concept* (a core competency) works better than another—when it is simply more appealing and compelling—it's because of *story physics*: The concept is stronger because it possesses more dramatic tension and effective pace, and provides a vicarious experience for the reader.
- When one *character* (a core competency) springs from the pages more vividly than another, it's because of *story physics*: The character has greater hero empathy and more "rootability."
- When a story's *theme* (a core competency) hits home with people, when it pushes their buttons, it's because of *story physics*: A compelling premise gives visibility into something we care about, with resultant hero empathy and an intense vicarious experience.
- When a story's *structure* (a key core competency, the one most writers struggle with) works, it's because of *story physics*: Dramatic tension and pace are spooled out in a way that optimizes reader attention and retention and allows for the building of other essences of physics along the way, such as hero empathy and vicarious experience. (If you've ever started reading a book and felt the urge to put it down, it's probably because

the story structure isn't strong ... it could technically be right, but competitively isn't at the level it should be.)

- When the *scenes* in a story (a core competency) work well, it's because of *story physics*: Dramatic tension and pace, as well as vicarious experience, are all present.
- When a writer's *voice* and style (a core competency) add value to a story, it's because of *story physics*: The voice differentiates effective execution. At minimum, the style doesn't detract from the reading experience, and, at best, it's a pleasure to read. (We don't see published examples of styles that detract from the reading experience because these stories don't get published.)

Notice that all the core competencies are dependent on one or more of the essences of story physics and that they can all be rendered as a matter of degree. In *The Hunger Games*, for example, the competition concocted by the Capitol city could have been a bake-off. But that's not nearly as gripping (compelling premise, dramatic tension, hero empathy, vicarious experience) as the death match we see in the novels. Not by a long shot. We get to choose our level of story physics through the application of the core competencies. And Suzanne Collins chose well (see Chapter 24 for an analysis of the story physics in her novel).

Memorize this if you really want to master it: The core competencies are the *what*, the underlying story physics that make them work are the *why*, and the writer's skill at execution and integration is the *how*. In an effective story, there is always a dance, or give and take, between the core competencies and the underlying story physics.

Maybe you're like a lot of writers out there, still searching for the *how* or for a better grip on the *what* and the *why*. Maybe you feel that too much of the teaching related to telling stories comes off like a big white cloud, a body of thought that morphs and moves and separates and then gathers itself again, constantly defying any sort of box a well-intended teacher might want to stuff it into. You'll hear sage advice, and all of it will be true and valid: *You have to make the reader root for your hero ... you must include emotional stakes and resonance ... you need to have a theme and subtext ... the denouement needs to be contextually aligned with the narrative exposition ... the character arc needs to spark a sense of empathy ... and so on.*

Say what? All of these cloudy concepts are usually missing both a *how* and a *why* component. Story physics, on the other hand, *is* the *how* and the *why*. It is the match you put to your fuse. It is the fuel you pour onto the pile you intend to ignite. When you focus too much on the pile, without regard to the fuel, you'll end up with a pile of dry wood.

But how the hell do you go about *doing* any of it? It's like telling an artist how to paint without talking about the brush. Where do you start, and what do you start with? And after you do finally start, what comes next? How do you know *what* to write? In what order do you write it in? How do you even approach conjuring those esoteric literary clouds?

The Six Core Competencies model endeavors to answer these questions, and in doing so provides a set of standards and criteria for achieving the aforementioned vaporous aesthetics.

It does this through criteria-driven, content-specific modeling of a successful story. Yes, regardless of form or content, all successful stories—novels and screenplays—share certain elements, internal dynamics, and standards. It's not a formula, per se, but an accepted structure.

I'll say it again: Omit any of the Six Core Competencies, and your story will suffer for it. Take a swing at one and miss (through mediocre ideas or poor execution) and your manuscript will reek of "newbie-ism." Most writers begin their journeys with a sense of these issues of craftsmanship, but lack a box to put them in, or, if you prefer, a fence to put around them. They just set off down the storytelling trail and wing it, armed only with the motivation that comes with believing they can write a story every bit as good as the one they just finished reading, or (if it's a movie) watching.

It really is harder than it looks.

You've heard a lot of people in your life say, "I'd like to write a novel someday." Or a screenplay, perhaps. Or some variation thereof. And if you're already a writer yourself (definition of a writer: someone who actually writes) you may have thought at the time, *Good luck with that, it's a lot harder than it looks.*

And while I willingly say that I created the Six Core Competencies model to make the utterly complex clearer and more accessible, please don't think that I'm saying it's remotely easy. No, my view is quite the opposite. The bar is higher than you know. But once you get inside the Six Core Competencies model, you'll see that it carves a road map through the creative jungle toward writing a publishable manuscript, a process that's about as clear and left-brained as a highly right-brained endeavor can be. And it's a journey rendered safer and more efficient—and more fun—through an understanding of the story physics that make it all work.

Never forget that solid writing, like any professional skill or craft, looks easy when in the hands of a true pro. Much like software code lurking behind the most simple and beautiful web page, successful writers have an entire infrastructure in place, invisible to the untrained eye, that empowers the program to run.

THE SIX CORE COMPETENCIES, DEFINED AND SUMMARIZED

The core competencies first appear in Chapter 8, after many references and contextual nods. Here they are, listed and defined for you:

1. **CONCEPT:** The idea that evolves into a platform for a story. Best expressed as a "what if?" question, which becomes a series of *dramatic questions* that define the story's inherent compelling nature. A story without a concept leads to a story without dramatic tension and a resultant focus on character, which leads to a character who has nothing interesting to do or achieve. Concept leads to premise, which leads to plot, which is a good thing in professional commercial fiction. (See Chapter 23 for a deeper exploration of concept, both generically and as demonstrated in *The Help*.)

2. **CHARACTER:** At minimum, a protagonist who is usually the story's hero. The character's journey becomes the stage

upon which inner layers and emerging arc are displayed. A story without a hero is a story without a heart, a story that is too journalistic.

3. **THEME:** Yes, it's like putting smoke into a bottle, but it can be done. Theme is the emerging meaning of the story as it relates to real life outside the story—issues, problems, the human condition, and specific elements such as love, loss, old age, government, societal decay, or corruption. Theme is most powerful when it becomes visible via the *outcome*— the residual takeaway for the reader—relative to whatever issues are involved.

4. **STRUCTURE:** What comes first, what comes next, and so forth ... and why. Structure breaks down into a four-part sequence. Each part has a mission and unique context and is separated by a story beat (a moment of transition and illumination) with its own unique mission and context. This is where the vast majority of rejected manuscripts can find their Achilles' heel, because structure exists to optimize the underlying story physics, especially dramatic tension and pace. Writers mess with this structure at their own peril. It appears in pretty much every successful novel or film.

5. **SCENE CONSTRUCTION:** You can know the game, but if you can't play it well, you can't win. Scene construction is where principles and theory meet reality through the creation of units of dramatic exposition that drive a story forward. Many defining principles and parameters apply, and again, writers who choose to challenge them do so at their own peril.

6. **WRITING VOICE:** The coat of paint, or if you prefer, the suit of clothes that delivers it all to the reader. If your story is a house, structure is the foundation and weight-bearing walls, character is the architectural style, and concept is the exact floor plan ... and voice is the paint and tile and carpeting and adorning accoutrements (gargoyles on the gutters, for example) that give the place a personality.

A CLOSER LOOK AT STORY STRUCTURE

Story structure is the Big Enchilada of the Six Core Competencies. Most writers bring some semblance of learning curve and intuitive sense to the other five, but structure is both terrifying and liberating. It becomes a guideline, a contextual road map, that shows you what to write (contextually, in terms of the missions of the scenes) and where to put it.

For many, mastering structure seems, well, impossible. But here's the career-changing epiphany that challenges you to either do this properly, from this model, or remain a vagabond wandering across the vast landscape of story possibilities: Structure is everywhere. When you realize this, you'll see it in virtually every book you've ever read and movie you've even seen. (This includes, with a stretch, the classics. But I submit to you that you're not writing a classic but a book that seeks an audience in *this* day and age, which, like it or not, responds to this set of principles, not the ones that Shakespeare and Cervantes and even St. Paul had to deal with.) Not because it's a rule—rules suck—but because, like gravity, it's the paradigm within which the underlying story physics work best.

Like an airplane wing, there are many designs. But they all, despite their size, have basically the same shape, because of the physics involved.

Same with our stories.

On the following pages are the basics of story structure in graphic form. Stare at it for ... the rest of your career. This is it, the Holy Grail of injecting powerful story physics into your story. Even if an agent or editor doesn't subscribe to this, they're likely to reject a story that doesn't align with it.

Compromised story physics will be the reason they reject you. And structure will likely be the culprit.

Depart from these proportions and target beats at your own peril, but it'll be like skydiving with a bedroom sheet if you do.

And if you doubt it, I encourage you to test it.

Deconstruct any book or movie against this model. You'll experience a curtain parting ... the long-lost truth that nobody has told you in all those workshops ... at least not in as simplified a form. They actually have told you, but without a complete contextual Big Picture grasp of it, those truths float free, unconnected to a bigger whole.

What follows is perhaps the most empowering part of this book. It's where you'll see the power of story physics at work in two recent bestsellers: *The Help* and *The Hunger Games*.

These chapters present a significant opportunity for learning, as points of story architecture and story physics are reviewed both generically and in context to these stories. The more angles we take as we look at these things, the clearer your understanding will be.

If you haven't read the books, I encourage you to do so. Or, if you want to get up to speed quickly, as a review in preparation for these deconstructions, I recommend you watch the DVDs, as they'll suffice for purposes of this analysis (and I do point out where and how the films differ from the books). In fact, you may want to actually see the DVDs again after reading this ... because once you see story architecture and story physics at work, you can't *un-see* them. You'll find yourself analyzing every book and movie you enjoy from now on, just like any professional who is also a *consumer* in her field.

1. SETUP

PART ONE: Set up the plot by creating stakes (what the hero has to lose), backstory (including inner demons), and character empathy, while perhaps foreshadowing the forthcoming conflict. Part One ends when the hero is made aware of something new in his life through decision, action, or offstage news. The arrival of the First Plot Point (FPP) at the end of Part One is the first full view of the story's primary antagonistic force. **THE FIVE GOALS OF SETUP:** 1) Killer hook, 2) Introduce hero, 3) Establish stakes, 4) Foreshadow coming events, 5) Prep for FPP launch.

FPP DEFINITION: The moment when something enters the story in a manner that affects and alters the hero's status, plans, and beliefs, forcing him to take action in response, and thus defining the contextual nature of the hero's experience from that point forward, now with tangible stakes and obvious opposition in place. **FPP MISSION:** Define Conflict. FPP, Midpoint (MP), and Second Plot Point (SPP) are three major story tent poles—all else sags from or rises to each of these points.

FIRST PLOT POINT

INCITING INCIDENT

Something huge, dramatic, and game-changing. Differs from FPP, because FPP bestows "meaning" on the hero, reader, or both. The inciting incident simply presents the one-way door the hero passes through to the future.

HOOK

Tension and conflict presented in the first few pages simply to "hook" the reader. The reader does not know what it means yet.

TENSION

Story Length

ORPHAN: The hero is unsure of what will happen to him next. We empathize with him and care about him. The story—the quest you give the hero—adopts him going forward.

2. RESPONSE

PART TWO: The hero's response to the introduction of the new situation (the conflict) presented by the FPP. Part Two is about a reaction, through action, decision, or indecision, to the antagonistic force, and the launch of a new quest to fulfill a newly defined need. Determine why the reader will empathize with the hero's response to this force.

MP DEFINITION: New information that enters squarely in the middle of the story that changes the *contextual* experience and understanding of the reader, the hero, or both.

MIDPOINT

An example or a reminder of the nature and implications of the antagonistic force that is not filtered by the hero's experience. The reader sees for herself in a direct form.

PINCH POINT 1

WANDERER: The hero is a wanderer, staggering through a forest of options and risks, not sure where to go or what to do next. He is no longer an orphan.

3. ATTACK

PART THREE: The hero begins to try to fix things. He becomes proactive, courageous, and ingenious in the quest to attain his goal, which continues to evolve and becomes stronger and more adaptive to the sudden heroics. The hero attacks both the objects before him *and* his inner demons. He understands that he needs to change if he is to succeed. The Midpoint provides him with the new information and/or awareness that serves as the catalyst to inspire his attack.

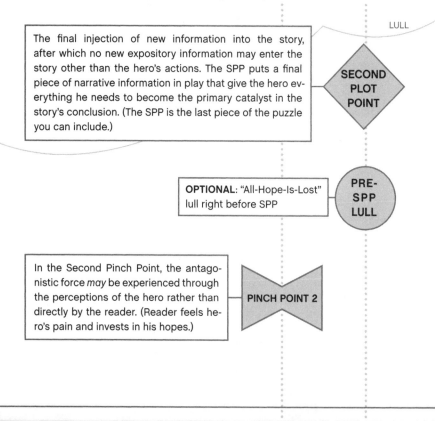

LULL

The final injection of new information into the story, after which no new expository information may enter the story other than the hero's actions. The SPP puts a final piece of narrative information in play that give the hero everything he needs to become the primary catalyst in the story's conclusion. (The SPP is the last piece of the puzzle you can include.)

SECOND PLOT POINT

OPTIONAL: "All-Hope-Is-Lost" lull right before SPP

PRE-SPP LULL

In the Second Pinch Point, the antagonistic force *may* be experienced through the perceptions of the hero rather than directly by the reader. (Reader feels hero's pain and invests in his hopes.)

PINCH POINT 2

CHARACTER DEVELOPMENT

WARRIOR: The hero has stopped reacting and started pursuing. He escalates his courage and creativity to respond to the antagonistic forces instead of running from them.

4. RESOLUTION

CLIMAX

PART FOUR: (10-12 scenes) Shows how the hero summons the courage and growth to come forward with a solution to the problem, to reach the goal, to overcome the inner obstacles in order to conquer the story's antagonistic force and achieve his goal. **RULE:** No new information can enter the story after the Second Plot Point. **GUIDELINES:** The hero needs to be the primary catalyst in the resolution of the story. We should see evidence of how he's grown throughout. The writer's goal by the end of the story is to have the reader cry, cheer, and applaud.

BEAT SHEET STORY PLANNING

1. For each scene, create a single-bullet list that defines the scene's mission (why it's there, how it serves to further the story's exposition) and content.
2. Expand each bullet into a descriptive sentence.
3. Expand each sentence into a summary paragraph.
4. Write the novel from the summary paragraphs.

DENOUEMENT

Story Length: 40–70 Scenes

MARTYR: The hero does not have to die (although he might) but he does have to do whatever is necessary, to be *willing* to die, to achieve his goal. That is what makes him a martyr.

Graphic by Bryan Wiggins, wigginscreative.com

23

STORY PHYSICS AT WORK IN *THE HELP*

WHEREIN WE COME TO UNDERSTAND WHY THIS BOOK WENT VIRAL.

Kathryn Stockett's mega-bestseller, *The Help*, is a clinic in story physics. The author's process, whether it required ten drafts or a single outline, doesn't matter as much as the presence of story physics. The story works on all levels—dramatic tension, pace, hero empathy (there are three heroes here, and we root for each of them equally), vicarious ride, and the stellar execution that allows these forces to shine.

The plot points are right where they're supposed to be, doing what they're supposed to do, and the contextual missions of the four story *parts* unfold in fully aligned, textbook glory.

The Help was Stockett's *first* novel, which adds to the utter shock and awe of its performance, both commercially and critically. It brags the usual litany of home-run credentials: It was a #1 *New York Times* bestseller for more than a year and topped all the other bestseller lists as well, including spending some time at #1 on the *New York Times* paperback list. Reviewers praised the book for its power, "pitch-perfect" delivery (a phrase used over and over, speaking to the core competency of "writing voice"), and humor and heart (hero empathy). Reviews rarely mention the plot, but the enlightened writer understands that plot is the stage upon which to showcase the things reviewers do rave about: the power and emotional resonance—the way a book *explores* an arena or thematic issue—of the reading outcome.

And of course there's that inevitable major movie deal, with amazing reviews, Oscar nominations, and career-making box office receipts ... all made possible *because* of story physics.

Can we deduce, through the book and film's success, that Stockett is a literary genius? I say *yes*. Her execution is spot-on. Does the success have anything to do with her choice of subject matter? Absolutely. A compelling premise that opens the gates for the other forces to come forth is the first of the story physics discussed in this book. Was it a lucky break? Only if you don't consider perseverance an element of skill and effort, because this book, like many home runs, was rejected multiple times before it stuck.

In fact, forty-five literary agents rejected it—an all too common and depressing detail in the behind-the-scenes stories of many bestsellers and classics. All of those short-sighted agents were professionals looking for the next Big Thing. (The lesson: Don't believe agents when they say your book *isn't* the next Big Thing ... but *do* use it as an opportunity to reexamine your story and make it better.) As I said before, William Goldman, the sage Oscar-winning screenwriter and novelist, said of the movie business, "Nobody knows anything," and it's equally true of the publishing business.

The Help defies genre categorization, and in many ways qualifies as The Great American Novel. It probably won't end up with that title, since it illuminates one of the darkest periods in American modern history and culture. That said, it's a historical novel that's about humanity more than it is about history.

I coach many writers who seek to write a book like this, that at its heart is about an *issue*. As I've explored elsewhere in this book, the mistake they make is *writing about the issue* rather than crafting a story from which the issue *emerges*, clarified, empowered, and even polarized toward the author's intent. That's precisely what Stockett did in *The Help*.

Not one critic praised the *structure* of the book, though many held the story up as iconic and important. The structure is *perfect*, and, for us, is something worth noticing. Nobody notices when this happens because they're too busy swooning over the other five core competencies, which are empowered by structure.

That's a loaded sentence that I encourage you to read again. It nails the relationship between structure and the rest of the elements that will make a story successful. Nothing works without structure.

It's like a perfectly designed vehicle. Most people don't notice the engineering; they just appreciate *the ride*.

THE FIRST LESSON OF *THE HELP*

The story has three point-of-view narrators—right there, it's already outside of the box, causing a generation of academic creative writing teachers to roll over in their graves—and any one of them could be nominated as the protagonist. Notice how this "out-of-box" thinking is not remotely in violation of basic story physics or the principles of the Six Core Competencies, yet it flies in the face of the few old "rules" that suggest this is a mistake. Story physics never hold you back or inhibit your creativity, and they don't care about your high school teacher's rules.

The more you read, the more you realize the centerpiece hero of this story is *Skeeter*, a rich and not remotely spoiled young woman embarking on her career in 1962 Jackson, Mississippi. (This is much like the author, who confesses the story was inspired by her own childhood spent living with women of color who worked as domestic help for her parents).

Skeeter desperately wants to be a *writer*, which echoes more details of the author's own life. There's a key lesson for us here: Stockett's inspiring *idea* didn't end up as the focus of the novel, but in fictionalizing it, she evolved it into a *concept*, and then a *premise*. *The Help* isn't a lecture on racism, and it never gets preachy. It's a drama that showcases the consequences of behaviors on both sides of a theme.

In fact (and this is a lesson in *concepting*, one of the Six Core Competencies), Skeeter's chosen profession as a writer is the driving catalyst of the entire story. Without it, *The Help* is nothing but a series of character profiles told from a historical context.

Without Skeeter's career choice, there is no story.

At first, like so many of us, Skeeter just wants to *write*. She's not sure what or even why, and she'll take any job that requires a typewriter. Which she soon does, writing household tips for a local daily newspaper for what amounts to little more than cigarette money (remember, this was 1962, when the belief systems of the day—which also reside at the heart and soul of this story—ruled without question or surgeon general warnings).

Skeeter gets in touch with a Big Time Book Editor in New York, who barely gives her the time of day (*that* much hasn't changed since 1962, by the way). But she does manage to offer some life-changing career advice, and Skeeter listens.

One wonders if Stockett herself lived this little epiphany in her own writing journey. It could be that the book began *there*, rather than through some lifelong burning desire to write about the civil rights movement. Or not. The two may have collided in an inspired moment of story planning fate.

That's often what happens, too. Only Ms. Stockett knows. Collisions between creative sparks and burning themes can be a very good thing.

That grouchy editor's advice was this: *Write something worth writing.* Something that hits people right where they live. Something that challenges. That upsets a farmer's market full of apple carts. That lacks respect for the status quo. That makes the establishment uncomfortable. That rights wrongs and exposes truth.

That pisses people off … because it's so *right*.

DECONSTRUCTING *THE HELP*

My opinion: After all the workshops … all the how-to books … all the blogs … after all the resources available to help us, I think the most illuminating, clarifying, and empowering thing writers can do to improve their craft is to read or see—and then *analyze*—stories in all genres. Break them down into their component parts and milestones with a view toward seeing what makes them tick, and behold the power of story architecture at work. Again, once you know it, once you see it, you can't un-see it. It'll be there in every story you read or view going forward.

Med students have cadavers, we have bestsellers and great films.

We have *The Help*, a story that is still very much alive and kicking.

Dead or alive, you can learn much in the transitory space—also known as a slippery slope—between theory and reality.

The Help is a study in place, setting, and character.

None of which, by the way, compete with or compromise the unfolding dramatic tension across a textbook-perfect four-part story arc—*structure*—punctuated by specific, easily identified narrative milestones. Many scenes, while remaining mission driven, seem to drop us into a moment in time in which character dynamics are exposed, seemingly without much forward-moving plot exposition.

But don't be fooled or lulled into complacency. Subtext is raging on every page.

The Help is nothing if not filled with subtext.

A reader of thrillers might get impatient with this aspect of *The Help*, but it is there by design. Why? Because the weight of our relationships with these characters, driven by our vicarious witnessing of their dynamics and inner responses, is the key to the entire novel.

What *happens* in the story is given weight by what the characters are feeling, which connects hero empathy to vicarious experience. And while those feelings are worth writing about, the story ultimately focuses on what they *do*.

The author fully understood this subtlety. The story could have easily become lost in a sea of characterized vignettes—for a while I thought that was where it was going—but I always had a sense that the story was leading somewhere, and heading toward risks and stakes worth dying for.

For me, this is the essence of character-driven storytelling that still delivers a story that is, purely in a dramatic sense, rich with tension and subtext. We keep reading to find out what happens, and yet we wouldn't *care* about what happens if Stockett hadn't balanced such a rich tableau of character, culture, and setting so perfectly.

A WINDOW INTO THEME

To put it another way, *The Help* blends craft and art in a way that is rare. And like Dan Brown's *The Da Vinci Code*, the core competency that propelled it into the hearts and minds of critics and readers alike is its *theme*. The theme is what makes this story *important* and rewarding on many levels. The book shows us how vital *importance* is to the success of the story.

THE HELP: STRUCTURE FROM 10,000 FEET

As you've probably noticed, I'm a big fan of *context*. It informs and empowers each moment of a story on several levels. Context is more than structural—it applies with equal power to all Six Core Competencies—though the topic of structure is where we'll begin our deconstruction of *The Help*.

Everything hangs on structure.

Ms. Stockett may or may not have had any idea that her story aligned with anything at all in terms of structural *principles*. Or she may be a raving story engineer, like me.

It doesn't matter. The story *works*. And these principles, planned, painfully extracted, intuitively graced, or otherwise, are the reason it works. As we study the linear structure of the book, which is textbook perfect, notice the contexts put into place by the various parts and milestones.[1]

The Hook

The mission of a *hook* is to grab the reader early—very early—by establishing dramatic tension or posing a question (a can of worms) that compels further interest and promises a rewarding ride. Sometimes it's huge, sometimes it's more subtle.

---

[1] All page numbers here refer to the paperback edition.

In *The Help*, the hook is directly theme-related and therefore somewhat subtle. Either way, it announces that this story will push your buttons, that it is *important*.

As hooks go, pushing someone's buttons relative to worldview and personal belief systems almost always throws open the door to a killer story. John Irving did it in *The Cider House Rules*, Dan Brown did it in *The Da Vinci Code*, and Kathryn Stockett does it in *The Help*. Take note: All three were iconic bestsellers.

In *The Help*, the hook occurs at the end of the first chapter, which is a great place for a hook to appear in any story. In case you missed it, it happens again at the end of the second chapter, thereby bookending the first hook.

It's on page 13, in the final sentence. The entire chapter has set up the emotional resonance of this moment, and we meet a compelling narrator who we already care about and a villain who we already dislike. The hook makes clear to the reader that the pivotal issue of this story involves a bigoted young white woman in 1962 Jackson, Mississippi, who announces that she intends to build a "colored bathroom" for her maid, and that it is no longer acceptable that the maid use the "white bathroom," which is the *only* bathroom in the house.

And there it is. We're hooked on a macro level because of the size of that universal can of worms. We're also hooked on a character level because we learn this through the narrative point of view of a woman who has already shown us her humanity.

The *mission* of the first scene/chapter is to *set up* this hook. Story physics are already in play, and in a big way.

The First Plot Point

In looking at any First Plot Point, it's critical to remember that the moment has already been set up in the previous chapters, or about twenty to twenty-five percent of the story's length. It almost always changes the plot (in many cases it *begins* the plot), but more importantly, it defines the forthcoming landscape of *dramatic tension* while defining stakes (*hero empathy*) and a direction for the hero's resultant/responding quest, need, or journey.

In *The Help* we have been introduced to three almost equal protagonists by the time we get to the First Plot Point. When it arrives, it changes the story for all three.

The First Plot Point in *The Help* occurs on page 104 (at almost exactly the twentieth percentile of the story), at the end of Chapter Six, as narrated by Miss Skeeter. By now the worldview and pre-First-Plot-Point life of each character has been established (stakes), as have the issues and potential responses that will drive the story post First Plot Point. The reader, in terms of story physics, already feels deep empathy for these characters. Only now, when something changes, when an opportunity is recognized or seized, or when the hero steps through a portal of no return, does the story make a shift from showing the characters to showing *what they must do*. This is the primary mission of the First Plot Point moment.

In *The Help*, the First Plot Point is when Miss Skeeter realizes that she *must* and will write her book about the lives of the maids in Jackson, Mississippi. Until that moment, it has been nothing other than a vague notion, a scary idea, and a seemingly impossible dream. As long as it remained in that space, it wasn't dangerous. The moment it became real, it became *The Story*.

Nothing is the same for any of these characters once this fuse is lit. The story really *begins* here. Everything prior to this moment has been a setup for it, and for what happens after it.

The Midpoint

The mission of the Midpoint is to pull back the curtain of awareness for the hero, the reader, or both, by inserting new information that has already been in play as an influencing dynamic of the story, but is now exposed on one of those levels. Or it can be something new, if that's what it takes to create a new context, though in this case foreshadowing would be helpful. If the hero is privy to this new awareness, it alters her experience going forward.

In *The Help*, the Midpoint occurs on page 248 (at the forty-eighth percentile). Once again, context is critical to understanding how and why this new information changes and empowers the story.

Until now the other maids (besides Aibileen and Minny) have resisted contributing to Skeeter's book. At the Midpoint, new stakes on the table: Medgar Evans has been murdered by local racial bigots, and Miss Hilly (who is among the bigots in an oh-so-proper but nonetheless spiritually lethal way) is closing in on Minny's secret (her employment with Miss Celia).

On page 248, the most resistant and vocal of the other maids, Yule May, quietly tells Aibileen that she wants to contribute to Skeeter's book, which means they'll *all* want in, for reasons that are bigger than their fears. It is now worth the risk.

Miss Skeeter's book is now alive and dangerous ... and inevitable.

The Second Plot Point

The Second Plot Point occurs on page 398 (the seventy-seventh percentile), when the Big Secret is let out of the bag. If you've read the book, you know what it was: the nature of the pie Minny baked for Hilly, the pie that was as metaphoric as it was catalytic to the story.

That moment changes everything. It jacks the stakes. It accelerates pace and tension. The end of the fuse is right around the corner. The consequences take on new fear and danger. The inevitable resolution forces the characters to take action and face those consequences like never before.

And because we've been moved to care for them so deeply, the destiny of these characters is something we, the readers, find ourselves deeply invested in.

Which is why this story works so well.

The Conclusion

Structurally speaking, the end of a book is a milestone that is defined by all that has conspired to bring it about. And thus it stands apart from generic criteria or standards other than the need to convey some level of closure, meaning, and emotion.

The ending of *The Help* was inevitably going to be a sticky wicket, as Ms. Stockett couldn't realistically show these women single-handedly solving global issues while absolving prejudice in the South through their actions. No, the ending always had to be personal, and perhaps the first of many quiet dominoes toppling in an important cultural shift. This ending is a quiet yet satisfying resolution to what has been so brilliantly put in place before it.

If Skeeter hadn't seen and felt the fear and resistance of the maids, and thus the weight of the stakes, we wouldn't have cared about her decision—indeed, her *need*—to write this book for the right reasons. If the First Plot Point had come too early, it would have compromised this essence, and had it come too late the story would have been marking time unnecessarily.

The First Plot Point occurs at the twentieth to twenty-fifth percentile for a *reason*. We see it work in full glory in this book. If it had happened earlier, the degree of empathy and character depth, driven by the aforementioned stakes, would have been compromised. If it had come later, the dramatic tension would have thinned, and it would have taken too long for something to *happen* in the story outside of each character's private life.

The Midpoint is a tool that facilitates dramatic tension. We needed to experience the resistance of the maids and Skeeter's quest to figure out the logistics of her exposé. And we needed to move forward once it was determined that the book would actually be written. Inserting this shift in the *middle* of a story ensures a balanced flow of dramatic tension.

The story needed something external, in addition to the thematic element, to facilitate a big ending. It would benefit from something other than the release of Skeeter's book and the humiliation of the white women of Jackson. More was required to escalate things at this point. Readers needed the visceral satisfaction of seeing Miss Hilly get nailed. To swallow her own medicine. That justice was facilitated by the Second Plot Point, which, had it come later, would have compromised the anticipation, and had it come too soon, would have lingered in a false sense of lost pacing.

The timing of these milestones isn't arbitrary. They are proven. They are *physics*. *The Help* allows us to see how and why they work.

And now that we do, let's go back and look at the four contextual, sequential parts of this story.

THE OPENING ACT

The most critical thing writers need to understand about Part One— *any* Part One, including yours—is that its highest calling is to introduce and *set up* the story elements in such a way that when the First Plot Point arrives, it is reinforced by stakes, emotional empathy, the shadow of an emerging antagonistic force, and foreshadowing of other elements that await down the road.

Timing and exposition in Part One are everything. Get too eager and you'll be serving up the main dish before the silverware arrives.

Certainly, though, some seriously dramatic stuff *can* happen in Part One. Character introduction and backstory drop us into the lives of three narrators, and the action here is character defining rather than story defining.

The mission of these Part One scenes is clear: Make us *feel* like we're there (vicarious experience), so that we see dynamics that the characters cannot (hero empathy). The characters *feel* them—and you can certainly make that feeling visceral—but for them it isn't a *story* yet, it's just their lives. This is brilliant narrative strategy, as the reader is on edge before the characters are.

This story is out to *change* the characters' lives. But we need to ease into it strategically. Knowing *what* has to change (racism as a social norm) and the reason *why* (the emerging social phenomenon of racial equality) is where the dramatic juice comes from. It's what will push readers' buttons, and Stockett milks them for all they're worth.

A *story* best unfolds when the First Plot Point changes everything. Before then, the story was just *coming*.

The novel's Part One spans six chapters with forty-three total *scenes*. Each scene is separated by white space (skipped lines), and represents a change of setting, time, or focus. For example, the author will break away from a scene to show us a quick flashback from a character's childhood or home life, then back into a new scene that picks up sequentially where it left off before the flashback. Many of these scenes are less than a page, while primary exposition scenes go as long as twenty pages.

This demonstrates *mission-driven scene writing* at its finest, which I believe is one of the most powerful principles in storytelling.

You'll first notice this mission-driven technique early in the first chapter, at the bottom of page 2, when the narrator (Aibileen) cuts away from talking about the child she's caring for to tell us about her own child (a scene which, by the way, reverts back to *past* tense, which is why this is so hard to make work ... (try this sometime ... the next thing you know, you'll need a scene in *future* tense and that'll cause all the clocks in all the bookstores on the planet to run backwards). Both scenes have a characterization goal of showing this woman's heart and her passion for the children in her care, which is important because it makes us like and root for her going forward. They also have an expositional mission of setting up the contextual factors that will come into play once this story really launches.

Could the author have lumped them together? Perhaps. But that probably wouldn't have been as effective (if nothing but for the mixing of tenses) or clear. Mission-driven scenes go straight at one thing and (usually) one thing only, using the narrative build toward the delivery of that mission as context. That said, characterization is the goal of every scene as well, even in the presence of an expositional mission.

The First Plot Point arrives (page 104) when Miss Skeeter realizes that she *will* write the book that will change the lives of all the players in this story. The core dramatic story is now in play. Prior to that point it is just a dangerous *idea*, one that nobody seems to like. It is when a character turns a notion she is pondering and exploring into *a plan and a commitment* that a setup evolves into a story.

Read Part One of the book again. Notice how everything—all six chapters, all forty-three scenes—are contributing toward that First Plot Point moment: revealing backstory ... giving it stakes ... infusing it with tension and fear and anticipation. Those 104 pages invest the reader in this moment as much as they set up, in a mechanical sense, the participation of the players.

The average reader experiences this but probably doesn't realize what's going on at a structural level. The writer, however, *should* strive to notice, because this is precisely what should happen in any effective story.

Notice also that the author delivers clean narrative POV symmetry in the first six chapters of Part One. She has three narrators who all must be introduced and given their turns at the microphone.

Two chapters are devoted to each of them, because all three points of view are critical to the setup. Each character has her own subplot and subtext unique unto themselves.

The story would not be as effective had we not come to know, love, and empathize with each of them, had we not felt their oppression and need, recognized the social pressures in play, sensed the palpable fear of defying those pressures, and then anticipated that something was going to upset this apple cart.

That pretty much summarizes all of what this Part One—and *any* Part One—sets out to accomplish, and in this case, the novel does so with stellar effectiveness. It truly is an exercise in story physics, planting seeds for dramatic tension and empathy, tightening the strings for forthcoming pace, and presenting a premise that gives it all a compelling framework.

By the time Miss Skeeter confesses that the idea for her book is not going away, when she realizes that it is bigger than she is (which, again, is the First Plot Point), we *know* this is the path the story will take. Inherent to that path is the conflict, dramatic tension, character arc, and thematic power that reside at the heart of any good story, and it makes this one a home run on every level.

If this isn't clear, I recommend that you read the setup again and look for these mission-critical narrative outcomes. It's all *setup*, manipulating the reader's emotional investment in the characters and their feelings about the thematic issues at hand.

Let's review how the chapters contribute toward this mission.

In Chapter One we meet Aibileen. We see her heart as she truly loves the child in her care and out-mothers the mother. We meet her employer and feel the chill of the empty and shallow place in her soul. We are immersed in the culture that defines the dynamics of these relationships.

We also meet the story's narrative hero, Miss Skeeter, through Aibileen's eyes. The primary plot device—telling the collective story of the maids in Jackson—is foreshadowed at that moment. But dramatic tension is already at work: Aibileen isn't too keen on being the voice that exposes the racism of the day. She has a job, a family to care for, and a little white girl that *needs* her.

Aibileen is brought to life, and her life *matters*. At the end of the chapter we learn that her employer is building a "colored bathroom" in the garage for her use, after which she will no longer be allowed to use the "family" facilities.

Chances are you felt your face flushing with outrage as you read that.

We are hooked. The thematic gauntlet has been thrown down. And a character we already root for is squarely in the crosshairs of a coming showdown.

All of this is established in thirteen pages.

Chapter Two, still told from Aibileen's POV, shows us more of her life while introducing us to her friend Minny (also a maid, and soon to be another narrator in this story), and to the villain, Miss Hilly, who arrogantly represents the voice and ignorance of the culture's racial prejudice.

Chapter Three switches to Minny, who has a different set of problems and stakes. Miss Hilly is falsely accusing her of stealing silverware, and the backstory tells us all we need to know about the nature of the villain in this story and the stakes they create for the heroes. Notice two antagonistic forces are at work here: racial prejudice in general, and Miss Hilly as the embodiment of it. The story wouldn't work as well without Miss Hilly, or if Stockett had written "about" the theme in a general way. This is a mistake that newer writers with big thematic intentions often make. They don't humanize the antagonism by giving us *someone*, rather than some*thing*, to root against.

In Chapter Four we go deeper into Minny's world and point of view, including Aibileen's revelation that the white lady, Miss Skeeter, wants to write about how they're being treated by their white employers. At this point participating in such an exposé would be unthinkable, thus creating and foreshadowing part of the story's conflict and resistance going forward.

Chapter Five introduces Miss Skeeter, the primary catalyst of the story and thus, by definition, its primary hero. We look at her life as a well-off white girl cared for by a loving and well-loved black maid, Constantine, who years earlier had mysteriously disappeared.

In Chapter Five and again in Chapter Six we learn about Miss Hilly's intention to set Miss Skeeter up with her husband's stuffy cousin, as it's high time a nice girl settle down to make a home for a proper Southern gentleman. Meanwhile Skeeter has a different vision for her life: She wants to be a writer. This is a primary motivator for everything that happens. When personal motivation collides with conscience and outrage, stuff happens.

THE AUTHOR'S NARRATIVE STRATEGY

The goals and missions of a scene in an effective Part One can seem distant from the story itself. They are outcomes, rather than narrative techniques, and require a narrative strategy in order to be effective.

Stockett pops us in and out of moments and flashbacks just long enough to get a taste for the social dynamics at hand, and moreover, to feel the subtext of prejudice, danger, and injustice. And she does it without compromising the forward-moving pace, which is a nice trick. Some scenes play like little stories, complete with microstakes and outcomes, while others just offer a day-in-the-life view that allows us to understand what those characters are feeling and why in the current spine of the story.

Most important, this stuff can all be *planned* ahead of time. It can be planned in terms of a sequence of beat-sheeted missions that need to be accomplished so the story can drive forward, and it can be planned in terms of how to populate those mission-driven scenes with characters, action, dialogue, and stakes in the form of a microstory.

But it doesn't *have* to be planned. It can be pounded on and edited until the right combination of anecdotes, flashbacks, and real-time moments achieve just the right pacing and level of exposition. I'm not sure which approach Ms. Stockett used here, but it doesn't matter. However you get there, the result will be the same.

These first six chapters also effectively set up several subplots that become influencing factors to the primary plotline. Aibileen's relationship to little Mae Mobley, the daughter of her clueless employer, creates stakes for rocking the racial boats in this town. Minny's new employer is up to something odd and is hiding a secret that will become the primary McGuffin later in the story. And Miss Skeeter juggles an awkward budding romance while pursuing a writing career, which includes a book deal from Random House *if*, and only if, she can send them something worth reading.

It is that last part, in context to Skeeter's goals, that creates the spine of this story. A book exposing the lives and employment dynamics of the black maids of 1962 Jackson, Mississippi, would be a social time bomb, and if Skeeter can get the maids to help her at the risk of their jobs and even their personal safety, she will have that time bomb on her hands.

When you read Part One, notice how little airtime Skeeter's book receives, even though it will later surface as the primary plot device. It's barely there at all, and when it is, it's used as foreshadowing. And yet the book is the subtext all along: It is always there, waiting to emerge as the story's driving force and most critical mechanical element.

When you notice this—that it's not there until page 104—you'll then appreciate what you are witnessing on the page: scenes fully dedicated to setting up the First Plot Point moment and rendering it powerful and richly layered.

Nothing *happens*, and nothing is *resolved*. Rather, elements are *launched*, factors and dynamics are put into play.

It's all just *setup*.

THE TIMING OF THE FIRST PLOT POINT

When you realize the sheer narrative bulk necessary to build these contextual elements with emotional resonance, it becomes clear why the First Plot Point *can't* come any earlier than it does. Shortcutting the optimal insertion point would compromise the weight of the story physics that make it work.

If Skeeter had launched her book with the maids as, say, the hook (at about page 25 or so), the underlying stakes and personal demons attached to the decision wouldn't have stood a chance at making an impact. And their impact is *everything* in this story.

Test this in other stories you are reading, and in the movies you see. You'll find this paradigm to be consistent and almost universally inflexible. After seeing it called out and explained in *The Help*, I'm hoping you'll understand why.

Prior to the First Plot Point, the story was all characterization. But Miss Skeeter's project changes everything, at least in a story sensibility, because now there is *conflict* ... dramatic tension. It creates danger and anxiety. It creates a journey for everyone involved in the project. It establishes a clear line in the sand: On one side are Miss Skeeter and the maids, and on the other side are the villains, led by the going-straight-to-hell-someday Miss Hilly.

Rent the DVD tonight, and you'll see it happen. Somewhere between eighteen and twenty-six minutes or so, the story will *shift*. Change. Twist. Turn into something that has only been hinted at (foreshadowed) or promised prior to that moment. The instant Miss Skeeter realizes she will—she must—write her book about the maids of Jackson, everything about this story changes.

The acknowledgment of the moral compass that drives her decision to write the book suddenly informs all her relationships: with her mother, her social group, the maids, her career plans, the prospect of a new romance, and even the memory of her beloved childhood family maid, Constantine (which becomes a subplot in this story and links tightly to the theme).

These relationships are all different now, because all of these people in her life have a stance on this issue. And in Miss Skeeter's mind, that stance *defines* them.

The maids, especially Aibileen and Minny, experience a shift in their world view. They evolve from feeling fear (of rebellion) and safety (because they're still employed) to courage and purpose. They suddenly have a ray of hope, never overstated in terms of changing the world, but on a higher level worth dying for, because it will expose the truth.

This opens the thematic can of worms that this story represents. What is worth risking your job, safety, and even your life to expose, champion, and speak for? And does your answer to that question define you?

An immediate and multilayered dramatic arc materializes the moment Miss Skeeter launches, in her own head, the intention to write that book.

The stakes become relevant the moment the First Plot Point surfaces.

Little Mae Mobley will grow up without love if Aibileen goes away, and she will go away if exposed as part of Miss Skeeter's project. Minny will continue to hide and face inevitable wrath from Miss Hilly if she's exposed before she can shove her leveraged revenge in the woman's face.

And man, do we ever root for *that*.

CONTEXT AND SUBTEXT

In story architecture, the contextual mission of Part Two is to show the character *responding* to the newly launched, or at least newly twisted, path established at the First Plot Point. Why? Because—and this is story physics again—the reader is thinking, *I wonder what I would do in this situation.* Which, of course, is vicarious experience.

This circles us back to another point: If you don't deliver that situation at the First Plot Point, the reader will have little to empathize with or experience vicariously. One of the first things that should happen in a story planning process is a notion about what will happen at the First Plot Point. When those two things are on the table—the concept and a First Plot Point twist—almost everything that follows, both in terms of planning and execution, happens in *context* to them.

But I digress.

Regardless of when it enters the story planning and execution process, context supplies the subtext for the entire story. It's like ambiance in a restaurant or interior design in a hotel. What's interesting, though, is that with storytelling there is no order of creation in the dance between context and concept. When one materializes, the other soon follows.

The same is true with theme: It can enter a story anytime in the development process. Theme can lead to concept and thus context (because theme is inherently contextual), and vice versa. Katherine Stockett had a life experience—the treatment of "colored" employees in her well-to-do Southern home—that moved her into the realm of theme, and from that thematic context a *concept* (both creative and mechanical) was hatched. She knew enough not to write an on-the-nose story about racial conditions in the South, but rather, to write a story in which this thematic issue is explored through the point of view and context of characters who are living within it.

Huge stuff. Critical writer awareness. It's a make-or-break-level skill set.

THE CONCEPT IN *THE HELP*

It's Miss Skeeter's book. Call it a McGuffin, a plot device, or a metaphor. The moment Stockett dreamed up Skeeter's book idea, she had her concept: What if a socially connected white woman secretly worked with the black maids in a 1962 racially prejudiced Southern town to write a book about their experiences, good and bad, as employees and often second-class citizens in the eyes of their employers?

Everything else—the strong characters, the heavy themes—lacks relevant story physics until that concept is applied. Without that dramatic concept, or at least another concept equally as catalytic (it is critically important to recognize that a great concept's power as a catalyst for the other three story elements of character, theme, and structure is its primary mission), this story goes nowhere. Because it has nowhere to go.

This concept *creates* the journey because it creates *conflict* in the story. It identifies a need, a quest, a problem to solve, or darkness to avoid, all with stakes hanging in the balance, and in the presence of an antagonistic force.

Otherwise this book is just a bunch of short vignettes about maids working in the homes of clueless and often heartless employers—another day in the neighborhood—and a woman named Miss Skeeter realizing that something is deeply wrong with this picture.

She must *do something* about it before it becomes a *story*. Concept gives her something to do and thus becomes the *purpose* of structure.

Structure is the narrative device that drives the concept forward into exposition, with a beginning (the Part One setup) ... middle (Parts Two and Three, separated by a context-shifting Midpoint) ... and a resolution (Part Four).

They are rendered perfectly in *The Help*. They imbue the story with a means by which the huge themes and strong characters have purpose, a chance to strut their stuff.

But notice that this concept was not the original *idea* for the story. It was an inevitable product of the evolution of her sparked idea. Many writers fail to differentiate between the two, even though in execution they will have evolved their idea *into* a concept by adding dramatic tension.

In the author's note after the story concludes, Kathryn Stockett tells us that her *idea* for this book came when she realized that it never occurred to her to ask her beloved childhood maid what it was like to be black in that time and place, what it was like to live with and work with a white family who, despite fairness and caring, never thought to regard her as an equal, and who lived with different expectations and rules on the other side of town.

She evolved and grew that idea to embrace the other core competencies, as well as latch onto story physics. Her emotions around the idea led to the plight of her family's racially incited life situation. She wanted to explore what it was like for them (vicarious experience and empathy), to right these wrongs by exposing this human injustice. *That* was the stuff of Kathryn Stockett's starting point, her idea. But a story didn't exist ... yet. The idea had become pure theme. She needed more. Three more ingredients, in fact: concept, character, and structure.

Fortunately, this author knew she needed to give her characters something to do. They needed a quest, which would become a conflict-driven framework on which to hang these themes. Something that presented risk, had options, had opposition and stakes hanging in the balance.

Miss Skeeter's *book* was that concept. A plot device that unlocked everything she wanted to say in this novel.

As you read *The Help* (or watch the DVD) through the lens of a writer, be sure to notice how the context of this concept begins on page 1 and influences each and every scene thereafter. How, without the context of this concept, none of this happens.

Notice how the First Plot Point is where the concept of this story really kicks in. Notice, too, that it happens at the ideal target location, where the conceptual thrust of the story (Skeeter's book) ignites the quest (to work together on the book), as well as the stakes (what they're risking by opting in) ... and in doing so creates dramatic context *and* content going forward.

The same fundamentals apply to your story as well. What's your concept, and how does it create a platform for your other story elements—character, theme, and structure—to fully explode into the minds and hearts of your readers?

What *journey* are you launching for your characters? And thus for your readers?

The answer to *that* question is the key to writing a great story.

The Help is nothing if not a book of architectural subtleties.

The major plot points in this story are primarily contextual in nature. In many stories they're loud and self-announcing, but not here. The story simply eases into a turn, naturally and gracefully, and suddenly everything has changed.

When Skeeter admits to herself (and thus to us) that she *will* write a book about the maids of Jackson and the racially influenced realities that define their lives, her emerging notion suddenly graduates to an *intention*, something to take *action* on. Her intention is not just about her and her career, it is about something important to tell the world (hero empathy). The dramatic arc of this story is now in play. Everything prior to this moment has merely been a *setup* for it.

It creates a *goal* for Skeeter and thus for the maids. The pursuit of that goal, for all of them, is the story. Prior to the First Plot Point, it was about a *situation*, which is rarely a story.

Their mission is rendered empathetic—something we can *root* for—by virtue of how Part One (the setup) unfolds, via deep characterizations, thematic resonance, and the presentation of a set of worldviews in dire need of examination and change. The reader cares about the book at this point. If it came any earlier, that caring wouldn't have legs. Any later and the story would have lagged. Because of Part One, *consequences* are in play the moment the First Plot Point lights the fuse for the rest of the story. The story kicks into another gear and never looks back.

We are now thrust into Part Two of the story.

While it feels smooth in the reading, the context of this story is now completely different. A shift in *purpose* has occurred. Everything that happens from this point on relates to, in some way, the elements that were put into play at the First Plot Point—Skeeter's book.

Everything that takes place going forward, either directly or indirectly, is a *response* to this new context.

Part Two consists of ten chapters and fifty-one short, mission-driven scenes. Not all of them directly show a character-specific *response* to the new context; indeed, some Part Two scenes seek to create deeper stakes and consequences. But the primary heroic journey has now been launched, and any deepened stakes are, by definition, in context to the new thrust of the story: the book the women are writing together.

Which, we should remind ourselves, *wasn't* in play in Part One.

Let's look at what happens in Part Two and examine how these events are *responses* to the unfolding birth of Skeeter's book and the roles of the women who conspire with her to write it.

Notice how the exposition in Part Two continues to deepen the dramatic tension, ratchet up the stakes, and unpeel yet more layers of characterization. Nothing is solved, but things only get darker and more urgent. Skeeter needs to nail down Aibileen's involvement in the project. But fear is keeping Aibileen from participating—fear of losing her job, fear of rocking the community boat, fear of something unspeakable. This is all in context to—in *response* to—Skeeter's book.

Meanwhile, the subplot of Skeeter's prospective date with a proper Southern gentleman launches. These scenes, which at a glance don't seem to relate to her book, are in context to Skeeter's *inner journey* (which took a sharp turn at the First Plot Point), because now everything that is normal and expected in her life as a privileged young white woman in Jackson is under the spotlight of her new awareness.

We see Miss Hilly's truly ugly moral compass and the blackness of her soul. It's good to ramp up the villain's repulsion factor in Part Two, as this becomes important, in context to what Skeeter is working toward, to the reader's investment. Not only do we root for Skeeter's book and the women who are writing it, we root for Miss Hilly to go down in flames.

Subplots are everywhere in Part Two.

Minny and Miss Celia are engaged in a power struggle with an underlying dark secret. Minny has an unhappy home life. Miss Skeeter is fetching library books on both sides of the racial issue and delivering them to Aibileen, fueling her passion for the project. All of these subplots are contextually related to the primary dramatic device of the story—the book.

Make sure you notice this: The book the women are writing is the heart and soul of the story. It's the vehicle, the machine by which the thematic level emerges.

Minnie joins the team after much urging, albeit reluctantly. She becomes the voice of fear and cynicism that defines the tone of the times. This is part of the unfolding dramatic tension: Will Skeeter get *enough* maids involved? Will the risks surface in ugly ways? Will Skeeter finish in time? What will become of her, and the maids, if she does?

In Chapter Fifteen a piece of actual history drops into the story: Medgar Evers is shot in cold blood by white racists on his own porch, just around the corner from where our maids live. The community's reaction, the maids' response, and the white women villains' attempt to sweep it under the rug only deepen the reader's investment in the success of Miss Skeeter's book. Story physics are raging here.

The Midpoint comes at the end of Chapter Sixteen.

It's subtle and easy to miss, but impossible to ignore if you are looking for story architecture. It feels like a natural evolution of things ... but it's not. Its placement is intentional, downright architectural.

The author could have brought in the Medgar Evans murder at any time in the story, or not at all. But she uses it in *The Help* as the catalyst for her Midpoint, because it changes the context of everything.

The murder isn't the Midpoint, but it is a setup for it. When the characters are suddenly aware of a new context for their journey *because* of a new event or situation, the Midpoint has occurred.

Remember the mission of the Midpoint: To add something to the story that serves as a parting of the narrative curtain—for either the hero(es), the reader, or both—in such a way that the story transitions from response mode into *attack* mode.

Which is precisely what happens at the Midpoint in *The Help*.

First, the black church gathers to voice their concerns over the Evans murder and what it means for their community. Their lives are in danger in a way they weren't before. Something must be done about it. Steam and momentum are building among the oppressed community.

The unspoken sentiment is that if the maids' participation in Skeeter's book is ever exposed, their lives will be in grave danger. And we know that Miss Hilly is capable of going to that extent.

The stakes just went up. The risk—and the necessity—of Skeeter's book is orders of magnitude more significant and important, as are the story physics of dramatic tension and hero empathy.

The other element of the Midpoint is when one of the most resistant of the maids, Yule May (who worked for Miss Hilly), tells Aibileen that she wants *in*. She wants to be among the maids who are telling their stories to the world. The context now is one of an entire community coming together to correct this situation, using Skeeter's book as a starting point.

And because Yule May's employer is the most heinous racist in town (or least in this book), her stakes carry the highest risk of all.

Until this moment, one of the points of dramatic tension was Skeeter's ability to get enough maids involved to meet the publisher's deadline, which was suddenly moved up because of the impending Martin Luther King march.

But now it's *on*.

Skeeter has her maids. They all have their unified purpose and a shared mission. And the villains have even more ammunition and an implied willingness to do whatever is necessary to silence dissent.

What happens from this point on has a new *context*.

It's now onto Part Three *attack* mode (the generic contextual mission of Part Three scenes), but with the same sense of subtlety that defines the rest of the novel. The requisite Part Two *responding* is done, and the Part Three *proactive forward movement* is underway, in the face of even more risk and more significant stakes than before.

Whether Kathryn Stockett developed and nailed all this via planning or explored and experimented and revised toward it through drafting—though almost certainly it was some combination of the two processes—isn't important. What is important is that this structural, conceptual, and contextual outcome was reached successfully.

In Part Three of *The Help*, each of the fifty-one scenes delivered within its ten chapters share this context of *attack*. The characters know what they must do, and they set out to get 'er done.

Milly is now all in. That Part Two reactionary phase (her fear, hesitance, and cynicism) has been dealt with, and the players are no longer fleeing, doubting, or considering other choices. They're in.

The game has changed. The essential dramatic question, which in Part Two was "will Miss Skeeter get enough of the maids involved?" has become "will the book get finished and published, and what will become of them when it does?"

They're attacking the problem, or if you prefer, the goal. Proactively. In full view of the impending consequences. Showing courage and resourcefulness along the way. Everything they try isn't working yet, but they're *trying*. That's the key to Part Three.

All of these plot elements were lurking in the subtext of Part Two, but here in Part Three they push their way to the forefront. Not by some narrative accident, but through the author's intentions, beginning at page 1.

A SUBTLETY OF PART THREE

Part Three isn't about resolution, so don't be in a hurry to get there. The story *is still building in tension and momentum and stakes*. Things are changing here, but the outcome remains in doubt, or at least in jeopardy.

This is a critical, empowering subtlety, and one that doesn't often happen by accident.

The Part Three shift and elevation of tension implies that the antagonist is *also* evolving, meeting the new vigor of the heroes with even darker, more compelling threats and introducing danger through cleverness and proactive efforts of her own.

That, too, is a critical subtlety. Actually, it's not a subtlety at all, come to think of it, it's the fuel that makes the story work. It's story physics, which in Part Three are not subtle at all.

In the third quartile of *The Help*, beginning after the Midpoint, Minnie and Aibileen align and support each other as voices in Miss Skeeter's book. Each of them, in doing so, comes closer to exposure and the dangers of their rebellion, which for them are bigger and more personal than Skeeter and her career. That collision of choices and consequences unfolds alongside the fate of Miss Skeeter's book, albeit *because* of it.

Subplots evolve in Part Three, but in context to the new urgency of the primary plot. Minnie emerges as the stronger part of the liaison with her employer, Miss Celia (a white woman), thus juxtaposing the balance of power and soul beneath the skin of the culture in which they exist.

Skeeter realizes her new boyfriend is too steeped in the culture she is trying to expose. This puts her family status in danger, as well as her social well-being. Meanwhile, she's getting closer to the prize— a career as a published writer.

Toward the end of Part Three, in a major twist that demonstrates that you can insert all the curveballs you want apart from and in addition to those that become your plot and midpoints, Skeeter learns that the book *will* be published after all. This lights a fuse in each of the character arcs, because the consequences have just stepped up from *if* to *when*.

Of course, no Part Three would be complete without experiencing a last-ditch threat from the villain, and Miss Hilly doesn't disappoint. She succeeds in getting Skeeter fired from her newsletter gig and putting her own maid in jail on trumped-up charges. Her potential for evil and her threat to our beloved heroes (hero empathy again) is clearer than ever. However, this evil is not remotely, accidentally, or coincidentally as relevant to the more personal exposure she is risking through the outing of Minnie's pie story.

You see, the antagonist (Miss Hilly) also has a goal. She has stakes that are critically, passionately important to her, and will suffer consequences if she doesn't win. Stakes and consequences are what drive your villain, and they must be part of the narrative exposition.

For those of you who haven't read the book or seen the movie, Millie's pie story is critical. It's a killer plot device that's both literal and metaphorical. After 397 pages of tension building, it suddenly and deliciously (no pun intended) jacks the stakes to a new, unexpected level for everyone.

The Second Plot Point happens when that little kitty is let out of the bag. Minnie reveals the Big Secret that went down between her and Miss Hilly, which, when presented to the world via her narrative in Skeeter's book, will rock both of their worlds. It becomes the centerpiece of the story's consequences. In fact, it might just get Minnie killed, or at least thrown in jail as a result of yet another of Miss Hilly's lies.

Or it might, in fact, expose Miss Hilly for the pitiful human being she is. Which, after all this brilliant reader manipulation on the author's part, would be wonderful and gratifying. It's something to really root for.

It's worth staying up all night to read, in fact. Which is precisely what happened for millions of readers, mostly because of vicarious experience. We just don't want to leave these characters alone with their problems.

The reader is *there* with Aibileen in Jackson. We *must* know what happens, not because the pie story is inherently consequential—it's a somewhat sophomoric story that doesn't directly impact anything other than reputations and karma—but because we, the readers, want it so desperately.

Make no mistake, the reason we're so invested has as much to do with the architecture of the story and the story physics they deliver as it does with its themes.

FIRST PINCH POINT

Be careful, because the eyes play tricks: This is the *pinch* point, not the *plot* point.

The First Pinch Point—a story beat at the exact middle of Part Two—occurs on page 184 of the trade paperback, which is the thirty-fifth percentile mark in the story. It's when Miss Hilly casually announces over coffee and cards that she's going to publish her "Home Help Sanitation Initiative" in the local newspaper. She intends to institutionalize and legitimize racism in the community by imposing standards and consequences of behavior to the contrary.

This is the villain baring her fangs. Not only is this Pinch Point very nearly perfectly placed (the optimal target placement is at the thirty-sixth to thirty-seventh percent mark, smack in the middle of Part Two), it's a textbook example of its narrative mission.

Everything else stops for a moment so the darkness can have the podium. This elevates dramatic tension, hero empathy, and vicarious experience, story physics all.

There's another pinch point a few pages before the "official" one described above, which is perfectly fine, as it further elevates story physics. Miss Skeeter confesses that after several interviews with Aibileen she only has twelve words of transcription to show for it, all of them "Yes, ma'am." It's a classic Pinch moment, as it calls forth the primary challenge or risk of the hero's journey (Skeeter needs to get at least twelve maids into her book). Skeeter's inability to get the maids to play ball is precisely what she's up against in Part Two.

Another minor pinch occurs as Skeeter mails the first draft of the interviews to the editor in New York, prompting fear-driven nightmares. It reminds us of the obstacles that are threatening her goal.

But when you compare these examples, all of which appear in Part Two, it's easy to see that the most dangerous and meaningful of them is Miss Hilly's racist diatribe. It's the highest level of antagonism in the whole story ... and thus it's not a coincidence that it appears very near the optimal target moment, in the middle of the story's second quartile. It is *the* First Pinch Point, architecturally speaking.

SUBTEXT VIA SUBPLOT

We all know what sub*plot* means. It's the events in a story that aren't directly connected to or dependent upon the main plotline ... yet.

But sub*text* ... that's a 202 term in a 101 world.

This gets sticky, because the distinction between context and subtext is subtle. We know that each of the four parts of a story has a mission (setup, response, attack, resolution)—that's context. But the unspoken dynamics of what the characters are dealing with (racism, danger, social pressure, job security, resentment)—these are all subtext.

Subtext is the state and nature of the world in terms of what is going on in a story and what drives and affects the *characters*. Whereas context is what the *story* is doing at a given moment, subtext is determined by the contextual mission of the quartile in which it appears.

Let's create an example before we relate this to *The Help*, which is rich in both context and subtext. A family of four goes to church. The youngest child goes to daycare, the oldest goes to teen Sunday school, and the parents go to coffee hour and then the service. All three have different contexts, because the purpose of each is unique and specific to the attendees.

But it's *church*, and permeating everything, in all three experiences, is a *belief system*. That's the *subtext* of this example.

In *The Help*, each of the four parts offers the reader a fresh context and a unique subtext for the scenes within it. This is basic story architecture, but at a more advanced level. As such, it's not coincidental that the contextual missions of each of the four parts—setup, response, attack, and resolution—are, in fact, descriptors of the subtext itself.

You could say that context is for the author (your scenes must align with the proper context of the part you are putting them in), and subtext is for the characters (the unspoken social and human forces in play should influence their feelings, decisions, actions, and outcome).

The Four Subtexts of *The Help*

In Part One, (where the context is *setup*) no solution has been presented for the problem of racism or the specific problems in the lives of the characters. None of that is on the table ... yet. The *subtext* of everything is that this is just how things are. And it sucks.

In Part Two, (where the context is *response*), the subtext shifts. Now, because Miss Skeeter's book project is a very real possibility, it becomes the primary source of dramatic energy, tension, and momentum, via the central dramatic questions it poses: Will the book get written? If it does, what consequences will come of it? The characters have hope that wasn't there before ... which is the new subtext in this second quartile.

The scenes in Part Two read very much the same as the scenes in Part One, but *the context and the subtext* are different. Each character has thoughts and considers options in relation to their awareness of the possibility of their participation in Skeeter's book. They are hearing and evaluating everything through fresh eyes and keener sensitivity—indeed, this is hope emerging in their lives—and they are considering the possible risks and rewards of participating.

In Part Three (where the context is a *proactive attack* on the problem) the subtext shifts yet again: The characters must consider real life-and-death consequences, and they must counter them. Each participant is *in* and past the point of no return, and the injustices of their lives—or, if they're on the bigoted side of the fence, the threat and utter outrage of what seems to be happening—take on a new urgency and danger. They must take *action*, and they do.

In Part Four (where the context is *resolution*), after the Second Plot Point revelation of Minnie's Big Secret and the potential consequences of Miss Hilly's reaction to it being made public, an edgy new subtext has emerged: The book has been published and the players have a public face, with consequences ensuing.

PART FOUR: THE RESOLUTION

Great endings are hard to craft. They're rewarding to read because the author has successfully tapped into the story physics of empathy and vicarious experience, and easy to take for granted when they're *really* good. Endings are very noticeable only when they bomb.

My favorite author, Nelson Demille, totally tanked the ending of *Night Fall* (the first novel to oust *The Da Vinci Code* from the #1 bestseller slot during its run) when he concluded the story with a *deus ex machina* (the hand of God, or blind chance, entering the story to create resolution) of preposterous proportions. After hundreds of pages of rooting for the hero as he gathers evidence and positions the antagonists for a hard and gratifying fall, the ending shows a meeting with the press and the FBI for a come-to-Jesus outing of the truth ... in the north tower of the World Trade Center on September 11, 2001.

Even Demille admitted later that he really didn't know how to end this thing. Which shows that, even at his level—believe me when I say these A-list brand-name authors have different standards than the rest of us, and sometimes they're lower—at some point in the process we need to write our stories with a specific ending in mind.

Kathryn Stockett begins setting up the ending of *The Help* at the Second Plot Point, which occurs on page 452, when Miss Skeeter tells her co-authors that Harper & Row has accepted their book for publication. It's *on*. No turning back now. The consequences of their actions are inevitable. She might as well have told the women, "Ladies, a new subtext is in town. Deal with it."

It is the anticipation and unfolding of those consequences that create the contextual mission (resolution) for each of the remaining scenes in the book. Several story lines need to wrap up, and each gets its moment at center stage.

Skeeter leaves town and gets a career. Aibileen gets framed and fired, but it doesn't bother her, because she's liberated. And Minny … well, Minny certainly gets her pound of flesh (again, no pun intended) out of the hide of Miss Hilly, who deserves much worse.

If you're like me, I'm guessing that as you read this book you visualized possible endings. I was expecting to see Skeeter's book explode the entire community into a frenzy of rebellion, violence, and ultimately a change in the culture. Perhaps the book would influence the entire civil rights movement, a Rosa Parks catalyst delivered in hardcover.

But Stockett went nowhere near that type of ending. And in doing so, she teaches us how powerful a more subtle and character-driven ending can be.

To have an ending that impacted society as a whole would have been a departure from the realistic tonality the book maintains from the first page. It would have been too Hollywood, as if Michael Bay had taken a crack at the final draft.

In a story that sought to be a serious thematic inquiry into a dark slice of American history, in retrospect I realize that the lighter touch was the only viable option.

Miss Skeeter's book didn't liberate the country from racism. It didn't even set the characters free from it. Rather, it gave those characters *hope* because racism no longer *defined* them. Through their courageous acts of defiance and outrage, they became something more than their oppressors. All the characters march forward into their lives as better people, as quiet heroes who fought for and won their own freedom of will, clearing the way for others to continue the fight.

This is one of the many lessons we can take from *The Help*.

In a character-driven story, the ending must be character specific and thematically powerful. In a plot-driven story, the ending can get away with being bigger and more Hollywood.

This book challenges us to aim high, to bestow a gift to the world that reflects darkness through a lens of hope. It's a book that invests the reader in the characters in a way that transcends empathy, that indeed becomes *transcendent*.

The book presents so many lessons for writers to learn by studying it, and so many lessons for human beings to learn by reading it.

The only real *rule* for an ending is this: It must remain true to the story and reward the reader with something that resonates. No jumping the shark. No *deus ex machina*. The goal is to implant the ending into the hearts and minds of readers, which is possible only if you've recruited their empathy long before the ending enters the picture.

Beyond that, this is the one place in a story where the writer is alone with her instincts and the nature of the corner into which she's painted herself. The question then becomes, "Is this corner the one you planned on and hoped for? Or are you stuck there, with no options?"

The principles of story architecture—the power of story physics implemented via the Six Core Competencies—guide the writer to this point, but the ending is where story and writer become one, and together they make their fate.

STORY PHYSICS AT WORK IN
THE HUNGER GAMES
WHEREIN WE BECOME BETTER STORYTELLERS BY DECONSTRUCT-ING AN ICONIC BESTSELLER.

I can't think of a better literary lab rat than *The Hunger Games* (specific here to the first book in the trilogy), at least at the commercial level. This story is a glowing example of each of the Six Core Competencies in play, as well as the underlying story physics that energize a story—any story—toward greatness.

Like the Harry Potter stories, Suzanne Collins's The Hunger Games trilogy broke out from a young adult niche to cross over into mainstream juggernaut territory, selling nearly thirty million copies and inspiring a blockbuster film. The film is a very true adaptation of the first book in the series, even though it adds extra scenes from a point of view not delivered in the novel.

You won't hear me claim that this story is *perfect*.

Anytime a genre book reaches these heights, somebody always steps up to slam the writing. I've heard such comments about *The Hunger Games*—I don't agree, by the way; I think it's well written—but that level of analysis isn't the focus of this discussion. This is about story-building craft, and on that count the novel is, if not a perfect story, at least a perfect specimen and learning tool.

It hasn't blown up because it sucks, folks. It's compelling and disturbing, as well as vicariously delicious.

Aesthetics are a matter of taste, and many won't care for the violence and the fantasy elements of the story. But reading outside your own writing niche can be very helpful, especially when a story hits all the notes relative to craft, as *The Hunger Games* certainly does.

Here are a few things to look for as you experience this story.

Notice how *context* and *subtext* play a huge role in the reader/audience experience.

Part One (before the First Plot Point) is especially driven by the subtext of the hero's impending and nearly certain death. She realizes she may die from square one. This informs and colors everything—every scene, every nuance, every line of dialogue—with a certain irony and a creepy flavor of fear, and it's one of the things that emotionally penetrates early in the story. This is the author leveraging the power of story physics early on, through reader *empathy*.

Collins makes it easy to root for her protagonist. Katniss, the young heroine, emerges as a strong yet vulnerable character with a large amount of rootability (another realm of story physics), which is a key reason this story has resonated, particularly with younger audiences.

You may not notice it at first, but at its heart this is a *love story*.

In fact, that particular subtext becomes the backbone of the entire structure, over and above the exterior plot (romance writers, take note). This notion alone might pop a few story development light bulbs for you as we go through the book.

The Hunger Games is no Harry Potter, however, even though both stories take us on a trip to the dark side with elements of fantasy and, in the former case, science fiction (*Hunger* has both). Harry Potter's vicarious juice is enchantment and wonder, while *Hunger Games* presents pure terror and a creepy sense of cultural hopelessness that echoes our own reality-television-loving society a little too closely.

THEMATIC OBJECTIVES

The Hunger Games became a home run due in part to some accidental kismet and pure luck. Other novels, past and present, are just as good and never get a fraction of this attention, and some don't even get published. Writing is not an exact science, and while we all plan for and seek to create a tremendous outcome, we are not anywhere close to having *complete* or even significant control over getting there.

Collins makes some challenging choices in her narrative strategy. She mashes her scenes together like a skillet breakfast at Denny's (don't mistake scenes for chapters; they are very different in this book). This is a function of time-spanning first-person narrative, wherein the narrator flashes back to things and then returns to the present, moving through her journey as a memory told to a long lost friend. You have to pay close attention to the scene strategy, but it's there, and it works.

First-person point of view was the best and only real choice for a story like this.

Notice how (unlike the movie), the book remains true to the hero/narrator's (Katniss) point of view for the entire journey. This limits the author, but it also empowers a deeper dive into what things *mean* and what they *could* mean, and creates a sense of fear, anger, paranoia, and hope that is as much subtextual as it is sometimes right on the nose.

Subtext is critical to the success of this story.

The subtext in *The Hunger Games* infiltrates and informs virtually every scene, thereby elevating dramatic moments into something more than simply eating on a train or sleeping in a tree or schmoozing with a freaky television host as part of the Game's pageantry. Impending darkness, death, distrust, and terror are always right below the surface, always unspoken. This alone imbues the story with one of the key elements of story physics: *reader empathy*. We are scared *for* Katniss from the moment she steps forward as a Tribute.

And thus we *root* for her because of *who* she is (her courage is quickly displayed when she steps forward to save her sister). She deserves our empathy.

Katniss is, in all probability, going to die. Horribly. She knows it, and everybody else knows it. And she's going to kill others before that happens. She will kill children who, like her, don't deserve to die.

This, too, enlists our empathy and engages us from a dark and complex emotional place.

One of the creepiest elements of the subtext is that these actions—the killing she will do and her own impending death—are precisely the point. They are the delicious inevitability and largely hopeless stakes of the Games. They sate the lust and fascination of a society that is just like *us*—which is yet another genius dose of subtext at a thematic level.

But the real killer subtext in this narrative, alongside the more thematic ones, is her unfolding relationship with Peeta. In fact, this is the expositional *spine* of the structure—you may be surprised to hear that, but I'll show you—and it becomes the heart and soul of the story itself.

Titanic was more about a *relationship* than a sinking ship. The ship and the dire situation were pure *subtext*. The outcome of *that* was never in doubt.

Same with *The Hunger Games*. This story is also more about a relationship than an impending disaster. In both cases it is the danger, the proximity of death, and the impact of fear that become the driving empathetic essence (an element of story *physics*), and in Collins's case, the primary source of dramatic tension.

The danger is a *catalyst* for an unfolding relationship. If that budding relationship had taken place outside of the Games, it would have been dull as soap opera dirt. But here in the arena it is deeply compelling at a level only story physics can empower.

I ask you, did *you* ever for a moment consider that Katniss might die? No. It's a trilogy, and the hero never dies in a story like this. So that's not the primary source of tension. Which leaves ... what? The answer: *How* she'll survive, which is completely linked to Peeta, because *he* is positioned as potentially dangerous to Katniss—especially in her own mind—from the moment his name is called as a Tribute.

Maybe subtext isn't something you've noticed as a reader, but it is certainly something you need to understand and command as an author. It is all-powerful in storytelling, and in *The Hunger Games* it is the very thing that sparks *reader empathy*.

And as a result, it showcases a masterpiece of reader manipulation.

THE BEAT SHEET

Collins uses a flowing, organic first-person narrative in this story, which defines her scene strategy. The book, unlike the movie, is 100 percent from Katniss's point of view, which puts a fence around what is shown to the reader. It makes the delineation of scenes—separating one from the next—tough to call, because they flow into each other seamlessly, with vague transitions or none at all. When one of these segments has no real expositional mission but flows into one that does, I consider that a single scene (the first is a "setup" moment for the next). So this scene breakdown is imprecise, though each time and place shift (the criteria for a new scene) is noted.

Also note—and don't be confused by—the fact that Collins's structure of titled "parts" within the novel do *not* align with the dramatic paradigm of the four-part structure, at least in terms of chapter and part *numbers*. Dramatically, however, they are totally in sync with the model. The dramatic contextual parts, the plot points, and the character arc are all right where they should be, despite her chapterization and part labels. Whether she planned this or it came about as a result of her very well-developed sense of story optimization, we can't say. It doesn't matter though, because this is how a professional structures an optimally effective story, no matter how she got there.

One final note before the Beat Sheet: Ask yourself, as you read this, if you think Collins prepared this sequence of scenes, perhaps at the high level of detail presented below, before she wrote a draft. The truth is, we don't know ... but she could have. Which means you can do this, too, prior to writing a draft (it's basically creating the entire arc of the story beforehand). Or, after a draft, you can summarize it this way with a view toward determining what needs to change in the next draft.

Either way, a completed Beat Sheet tells a whole story. And when that story works at this level, the odds of completing a successful draft are significantly improved.

Here we go. ...

PART ONE: THE TRIBUTES

Chapter One Scenes

1. World building … Katniss wakes up on day of reaping. This is a fast start; the concept kicks in immediately. No slow ramp-up here.

2. Katniss in the forest … shows us her hunting and survival skills, as well as the "rules" of her world. We also meet Gale (this establishes stakes and lays groundwork for future books, as Gale has little involvement in the first book).

3. Visiting the market … establishes how her world works, shows relationships and foreshadowing.

4. Back home (after flashback), helping her sister Prim prepare for the reaping ceremony; introduction to her family dynamics … establishes stakes.

5. Arriving at the reaping ceremony and background on what this all means … sets up the big reveal: Her sister, Prim, has been chosen as the first District Twelve Tribute. (Note: This is the first of two hooks … but it is *not* the First Plot Point, which doesn't happen until page 72.)

Chapter Two Scenes

6. A continuation of the moment of Prim's selection (this is an example of using chapterization to create emphasis or a "cut and thrust" into the next scene). Katniss quickly steps up to volunteer thus saving her sister (which wouldn't work emotionally if those first five setup scenes hadn't existed). We meet Haymitch (the only previous Games winner from District Twelve). Peeta is chosen as the other District Twelve Tribute. (All of this is delivered in one scene. You could validly argue these are multiple expositional points that, by definition, become their own scene.)

7. Flashback to her first encounter with Peeta, where he discretely throws her bread … establishes her initial context for the ensuing relationship, and we also meet Peeta's father. (This is criti-

cal setup and foreshadowing, because the story ultimately becomes about Katniss's relationship with Peeta.)

8. Back to the reaping ceremony, where Katniss and Peeta are presented to the crowd. Katniss realizes that to win, she'll have to kill him if someone doesn't do it for or before her. (Important context: The only person having fun here is Effie, her handler for the Games. This is important foreshadowing of the city we'll soon visit.)

Chapter Three Scenes

9. A series of emotional farewells from family (stakes and empathy), Peeta's father (who kindly gives Katniss some cookies for their journey), and finally Gale (prospective love interest; provides conflict in unfolding relationship with Peeta), who encourages her to make a bow in the wild to use as a weapon. Katniss is certain she'll never see any of them again, just as she is sure Peeta must die if she is to win (reader empathy and tension established). You could argue that each of these farewells is a separate scene, though Collins narrates them as a single episodic scene.

10. The train ride to the Capitol city. Collins uses this to give us specific background about the Games. Katniss and Peeta see a video about the Tributes from the other Districts, thus showing us the antagonists who will face them in the forest. Continued dynamics with her handlers, Effie and Haymitch. Continued tension with Peeta, who is enigmatic (we don't know his intentions at this point, because all of this is told from Katniss's first-person point of view).

Chapter Four Scenes

11. Still on the train, we see Peeta caring for Katniss (what's his game?), which causes her confusion and skepticism. She resists getting close. As a metaphor for her quiet declaration of independence (and opposition?) to Peeta, she throws the cookies Peeta's father had given her off the train.

12. Another flashback scene showcasing her skills as a hunter with a bow. We learn the backstory of her family, specifically her father's death and her mother's crippling reaction to it, casting Katniss into the lead role as provider for the family.
13. Back on the train ... Haymitch continues to prep Katniss and Peeta with advice on how to survive the opening minutes in the arena Cornucopia. His advice: Run in the opposite direction.
14. A narrative bridge ... Katniss reflects on all of this information as the train arrives at the Capitol. She realizes and believes that Peeta is already playing the Game and strategizing, and that his kindness is his attempt to position himself to kill her when the time comes.

Chapter Five Scenes

15. They are prepared for their introduction to the people. Her stylist, Cinna, is introduced and seems to be an ally. He talks about Katniss's costume and helps with her strategy: Katniss and Peeta will be presented as a united front. Peeta is all smiles and helpful.
16. The parade of Tributes for the citizens ... Peeta and Katniss are presented in flaming (literally) uniforms. This is a key moment in the story, in which the two are deliberately pitched to the crowd as a team (which everyone knows might result in one killing the other). Peeta takes her hand, as if he buys into this.
17. The immediate aftermath ... the flames are extinguished. We hear Katniss's interior monologue: So this is how it is. Peeta is luring her in, making her vulnerable. The closer he is, the more dangerous he will be.

    At the final moment in the scene, Katniss finally buys in to the strategy and returns the gesture of affection. She kisses Peeta on the cheek, "right on his bruise." It's on. Her journey just changed, shifting into a higher gear. She's now strategizing. She's in survival mode. For her, the Games have finally begun. (This occurs on page 72, at the 19.4 percent mark, almost exactly at the optimal twenty percent target milestone.)

This is the First Plot Point. The Part One setup is over ... we now move into Part Two, in which the overall context driving the mission of these scenes is how Katniss *responds* and reacts to her new quest. Notice how all the scenes in Part Two align with this context.

Chapter Six Scenes

18. A lot of orientation for us and for Katniss ... with further insight into the politics of the Game (sponsors, favorites, etc.). Here the author introduces the other Tributes. Katniss isn't encouraged by what she sees. A theme of social/class prejudice, already on the table in this story, now comes into play.

19. At dinner with the District Twelve "team" Katniss sees a servant girl (a muted criminal) that she thinks she recognizes. This is a catalyst for Peeta to step forward and have her back, which confuses Katniss further. Is it strategy or true friendship? She's sure it's the former, yet she has her first hint of doubt.

20. Talking with Peeta and the mute servant girl after this dinner (which includes a scary explanation from her handlers that contributes to the stakes). Peeta lied for her and had her back, because it would be dangerous for Katniss to admit she knows the girl.

21. A flashback to when she really did run into the girl while hunting in the woods with Gale. The girl was victimized by the Peacekeeper forces.

22. After the flashback, Peeta talks about his recollection of Katniss back home, and how he gave her the bread that day.

23. A short scene in which Katniss goes back to her room. The mute girl is there, distant. Katniss is guilty—out of fear, she had watched the Peacekeepers kill the mute girl's friend and then mutilate the girl herself, just as if Katniss was watching the Games. Just like the people who will watch her suffer and die. She wonders if this girl will enjoy watching that happen.

Chapter Seven Scenes

24. The next morning, Katniss prepares for the day, her first in her training. She eats alone, remembers home.

25. Peeta and Haymitch arrive. Peeta is dressed identical to Katniss for the introduction of the Tributes. Haymitch offers to coach them separately. They discuss their respective skills. Peeta is supportive of Katniss. Haymitch agrees with him—people will be clamoring to help her. Haymitch instructs them to stay together always, in and away from training. This is strategy, the only thing that will keep them alive.

26. Training begins. She sizes up the other Tributes, now out of their intro uniforms, and finds some of them intimidating, especially the boy from District Two (a "Career," bred for the Games since early childhood) ... more foreshadowing. The Gamekeepers show up to observe. We learn about eating protocol, which is tied to politics (deliberately like a high school clique). She and Peeta are grateful to not be alone. (This is a time-spanning scene that delivers several periods of the day, an example of time compression within a single scene.)

27. Second day of training. We meet Rue (who will be a player in this story later).

28. Later they review the day's events with Haymitch and Effie.

29. Katniss and Peeta are alone, and Katniss finds herself laughing with him. She catches herself and tells him they should stop pretending when they are alone, rejecting him and the strategy... she knows it's all just part of the Game.

30. Third day of training. Katniss tries to impress the Gamekeepers with her bow-shooting skills. They seem not to notice, which angers her. She shoots an arrow into their midst, momentarily terrifying them. She has their attention now. (A genius scene idea, by the way.)

Chapter Eight Scenes

31. Alone afterward, Katniss reflects. She's sure she's made a fatal error.

32. At dinner her act is discussed. Haymitch is supportive.

33. After dinner they gather to view the scoring (results from the training). She gets an 11, the highest score of all. She's now the favorite to win, which she knows will put her in the bull's-eye of the other Tributes.

34. A flashback of the day she met Gale connects to her proficiency with the bow and hunting (giving her and us a sense of hope).

35. Moving forward in time, Katniss realizes that she feels for Gale.

36. The next morning, Katniss is greeted with the news that Peeta has requested to be trained separately from now on.

Chapter Nine Scenes

37. Katniss feels betrayed but glad the "strategy" and the charade are over. She meets with Effie to talk about wardrobe.

38. She meets with Haymitch to talk strategy, now that she's the favorite. Haymitch believes gaining favor with the people is an advantage, as they (through sponsors) can send help to her in the Games. Peeta's strategy is to be "likeable," and Haymitch reminds her that she's not. She needs a story.

39. The next day, with Cinna, her stylist. Her training with Effie and Haymitch is over. Haymitch dresses her, tries to cheer her up, and coaches her toward being more likeable. He wants to be considered a friend.

40. A press conference, televised. Haymitch tells Peeta and Katniss they must continue to present themselves as a couple, which Katniss doesn't like. Caesar, the host, interviews the other Tributes, while Katniss sizes them up. She nails her own interview and establishes herself as a crowd favorite. When Peeta is interviewed, he makes it clear that they're a couple, and that he'll die before she does.

PART 2: THE GAMES

Chapter Ten Scenes

41. Peeta is still being interviewed. He's affirming this as a love story between them, one that she (Katniss) wasn't aware of … until now. Hearts flutter.

42. As the Tributes are transported back to their quarters, Katniss confronts Peeta, outraged by what he said during the interview. They debate this with Haymitch, who says she's just been helped. Peeta has given her a much stronger chance at survival, because now people love her. They will root for her, and sponsors will step up.

43. The Games begin the next morning. Effie and Haymitch say their farewells, though they'll continue working on their behalf to line up sponsors (this is important foreshadowing). Haymitch gives last-minute critical advice: Run *away* from the opening confrontation at the Cornucopia, which is a blood bath.

44. Katniss can't sleep. She goes to the roof, reflecting on it all. Peeta is there, too, doing the same thing. He's resigned to dying; he wants to die as "himself." They discuss how the Gamekeepers can manipulate the Games from behind the scenes to achieve the most popular outcome (foreshadowing).

    Note that the *First Pinch Point* occurs in this scene, on page 141, almost exactly at its target point at the thirty-seventh to thirty-eighth percentile mark. This story is densely populated with many pinch-point moments (when the antagonistic force comes front and center for the reader, reminding us of what's at stake), but notice how this moment is different: It relates to the depth of the characters' most inner selves, the desire to not give in and to die as themselves, which will be their only victory. You'll notice later how the other Tributes turn into blood-lusting sadists in the arena … while our heroes will die before they allow themselves to sink that far. It all comes front and center in this scene.

45. Cinna prepares Katniss to enter the arena. In a warm exchange, he gives her Prim's mockingjay pin (foreshadowing, both for this and subsequent books) as she enters the chute and hears the announcement: The Games have begun.

Chapter Eleven Scenes

46. Katniss is elevated into the arena. The Tributes await the opening horn. She considers going in, trying to score a weap-

on. When it sounds … she runs as fast as she can away from the Cornucopia, where weapons await, and where half the Tributes will die within the first few minutes. She does exactly as Haymitch advised. (Interesting note here: This is perhaps the biggest expositional transition in the story, and yet it is not one of the major story milestones. Why? Because we're still in Part Two, which began right after the First Plot Point. The mission-driven context of the story hasn't changed, and she's still in response mode to the subtextual contrived relationship with Peeta and the Games themselves. Only when she turns into a proactive attacker will Part Three of this story be underway.)

47. She does decide, however, to snatch up some supplies and reverses ground to get a backpack. She has to fight for it, but her adversary is killed from behind. She's next. A knife is thrown, but it lodges in the backpack, now hers to use. She runs.

48. Katniss flees through the woods. Later, she hears the cannons sounding, indicating the number of dead Tributes: Eleven, nearly half. She wonders if Peeta is among them and is not sure how she feels about it. At least she won't have to kill him if he has already died. She stops and inspects the pack, hoping for water. No luck. Twilight is coming. She sets some traps to get food.

49. It's night now, and Katniss is perched in a tree, strapped in. The death recap is broadcasted into the sky holographically, showing her who has died and who hasn't. Peeta is alive, and so are five Careers. And Rue. She isn't aware that she's dozed off.

50. She's awakened by snapping sounds nearby and sees a pack of aligned Tributes. She hears them kill another Tribute and hears their conversation—they're after *her*. To her surprise and horror, Peeta is among them.

Chapter Twelve Scenes

51. The pack of Tributes is right below her. They send Peeta back to the Tribute they killed to look for supplies, and they con-

sider killing him now. They decide not to, as he's their best chance of finding *her*.

52. Dawn. The pack moves on. Before Katniss can get out of the tree, a hovercraft appears to fetch the body of the girl the pack killed the night before.

53. Katniss runs, hunts, and tries to find water. She knows she's being televised, and that the viewers are rooting for her and/ or rooting for her death. She tries to impress them. She feels weak and sick. She almost eats deadly toxic berries. She climbs a tree for the night.

54. Morning. She feels worse and needs water. She considers the lake near the Cornucopia and sets off.

55. She finds mud, which means water, and then finds a pond. She slowly drinks, eats a rabbit, and rests. Night comes and she climbs a tree and sleeps. She is awakened suddenly ... by a wall of fire.

Chapter Thirteen Scenes

56. She flees the fire and considers it all as she runs, realizing the Game has changed and the odds are being manipulated off-stage. Her leg is burned badly. The fire ceases, and quiet returns. She rests, feeling helpless, until dawn.

57. She bathes in the small pond, washing away blood and assessing the damage. Fatigue overcomes her and she dozes off.

58. She's awakened when the pack that includes Peeta finds her, but she has time to hide. She climbs a high tree, but they stop directly beneath her. Resigned to her death, she calls down to them with a mocking tone, playing to the television audience. They try to climb after her, but can't make it. One girl shoots an arrow and misses; the arrow is now hers. They decide to leave her until morning, striking a camp at the base of her tree.

59. Then she hears something, not from the ground, but to the side, up in the next tree. It's Rue, who has seen the whole thing. Rue points to something, signaling her help. Katniss is no longer alone.

Chapter Fourteen Scenes

The next scene is the Midpoint. This new context has changed the story. It transforms Katniss from the *responder* that she has been into a proactive *attacker* of her problem.

This happens on Page 185 ... at 49.5 percent of the story's total length, almost *precisely* on target. (I can't be sure if it was Collins's awareness of this principle or her killer story instincts that caused her to be this closely on target. What matters most is that it happens as it does, almost precisely according to the structural principles being defined here, and the effectiveness of the story attests to the power of the story physics being employed. Less effective stories are usually those that play loose with both structure and story physics.)

60. Rue has shown Katniss a hive of deadly genetically engineered wasps hanging directly over the sleeping pack below. If Katniss can cut it, allowing it to fall on them, she'll have a chance. But doing so without getting stung herself will be nearly impossible. She waits until the nightly anthem plays over the arena loudspeakers to mask the sounds of her cutting, using the knife from the Cornucopia attack.

61. The anthem finally sounds, and she begins to cut. But with her injuries it is too painful and slow—it's not going to work. (Notice how, very literally, she's not running here, but *attacking*. This is the contextual difference between Parts Two and Three: the shift from responder to attacker.)

62. Then she notices that something has been delivered to her, resting on her bag in the tree. It's a salve from Haymitch, which will heal her wound very quickly. Her pain vanishes immediately.

63. She returns to cutting loose the hive of wasps but is stung in the process. She knows this will result in great pain and possible hallucinations, but she keeps at it ... and the hive finally falls. The pack panics and runs, but two of the girls are stung to death. Katniss is alone and safe ... for now. But she's already feeling the effects of being stung herself.

64. She descends and finds a bow next to the body of the newly dead pack girl. The warrior now has a weapon, the weapon of her choice.

65. But the poison stings overcome her. She falls, just as one of the hunters arrives … but it's Peeta. He tells her to run, saving her after all.

66. She flees in a poisoned haze, just as one of the Careers almost reaches her. She falls into a nest of stinging ants and passes out.

Chapter Fifteen Scenes

67. Katniss awakens in agony. As she comes to her senses, she flashes back to a discussion with Gale, debating on leaving the District. They should have left. Then she remembers she has the bow, her strong suit. She has a chance.

   Note how she thinks to herself that having the bow gives her "an entirely new perspective on the Games," which is precisely the purpose of the post-Midpoint scenes. Not a coincidence.

68. Rue comes to her as she tends to her wounds and refreshes with water from the pond where she's woken. Rue wants an alliance and tends to Katniss's stings with some medicinal leaves she has. Katniss shoots game, and they eat.

69. Rue tells Katniss that the "sunglasses" in her pack are actually for night vision. They decide they need an offensive (attacking) plan.

Chapter Sixteen Scenes

70. The death cannon wakes them. There are eight Tributes left, including Peeta, wherever he is. They decide to raid the Careers' food stash so they hatch a plan. They'll use the mockingjays to communicate from a distance.

71. They separate to implement their plan, an attack on the Cornucopia fortress where the pack is stockpiling their booty from the kills they've made.

72. Katniss reaches the Cornucopia and assesses the situation. She sees the booby traps and overhears the Careers talking about

her, their rage and intent to kill her—slowly. (That is a deliberate touch by the author to ratchet up the dramatic tension and stakes.)

73. She finally sees her opportunity and takes it, shooting an arrow into the stockpile and releasing apples, which tumble onto the surrounding land mine. The whole thing blows up.

Chapter Seventeen Scenes

74. Aftermath of explosion ... Katniss wants to flee, but she's dazed. Another blast knocks her down again. She hides as the Career pack returns to the devastated pile. She remains overnight to wait this out and seek her next opening.

75. She wakes in the morning and sees one of the girls going through the pile, laughing. The others are gone for now.

76. Katniss returns to where she and Rue separated, climbs a tree to wait for Rue to return, eats, and waits.

77. After a while, she goes to the next agreed-upon meeting place. Soon she hears a scream and runs toward it. Rue is in a net. Just as Katniss gets there, a spear pierces Rue's body. (Note: This is the Second Pinch Point, on page 232, which marks the sixty-second percentile mark, the optimal target for this moment. This is the first time Katniss must directly kill another combatant, and both she and the reader directly experience the darkness of the circumstances—which is the mission of a pinch point—as Rue's fate is sealed.

Chapter Eighteen Scenes

78. Katniss quickly shoots the boy who threw the spear. She sings a comforting song to Rue as she dies (hero empathy). Katniss reflects on Rue and her own progress within the Games so far. She decorates Rue's body so the Gamekeepers will show it and leaves the spear embedded in it so that the Careers can't use it later. The hovercraft comes for Rue's body. (This is a single scene consisting of a sequence of connected events, all aligned under a single scene mission.)

79. Katniss regroups, staying in hiding. A tiny parachute arrives with a loaf of bread. It's from Rue's district, in gratitude. She climbs a tree and settles in for the night. The evening anthem shows the dead for that day: Rue and her killer. Six Tributes are left.

80. She returns to the site of Rue's third fire, consolidates supplies, and waits. She kills some birds and eats, then goes to the water source and camps. It's an uneventful day. She reflects on the boy she killed.

81. And then the unexpected happens: She hears an announcement from the Gamekeeper over the public address, stating that a rule change has been made: If two Tributes from the same district survive as the last two standing, they will be declared co-winners. She calls out Peeta's name.

Again, don't be fooled—this *isn't* a Plot Point along the dramatic and character arcs. It's new information, certainly, and a new subtext for Katniss. This is an example of an author inserting as many twists, subtext shifts, and plot turns as she wants, which doesn't negate the overall four-part, context-driven model or the major milestones that separate them. One of those milestones—the Second Plot Point—is still to come.

PART THREE: THE VICTOR

Chapter Nineteen Scenes

82. Katniss is happy at this news, which fills her with hope. Peeta's love story strategy has worked after all. She reflects on it all, then goes to sleep.

83. She begins looking for Peeta, sees blood, and follows the trail. She finds him hiding in camouflage (which was foreshadowed back at the Training Center). He's injured. He cracks a joke about her kissing him. She rolls him into the stream to clean him up and feeds him. He makes another kiss comment.

84. Katniss moves Peeta into a cave to hide. She kisses him to get him to stop talking about dying. It's her first kiss ... ever.

Haymitch sends food, as if to encourage them to keep this up, because the audience will love it.

Chapter Twenty Scenes

This entire chapter plays like one long scene, with no discernible breaks. You could argue there are several scenes here, but that's not a critical call, provided one sees what's going on strategically. It's written as a time compression, a narrative device Collins uses frequently to rapidly move the story forward. She's trying to achieve pace and exposition.

I've broken this chapter into four scenes here to show how the mission of the story beats changes and evolves.

85. Katniss cares for and feeds Peeta, then sleeps. When she wakes, she checks his leg, which is worse. She feeds him again and tells a story from the past.
86. An announcement is made: A backpack with essential supplies awaits each Tribute at the Cornucopia. It's a ploy to force the combatants together. Peeta and Katniss argue: He wants her to stay with him, fearing she'll be killed. She wants to go, because they need those supplies.
87. Haymitch sends medicine to speed Peeta's recovery.
88. Katniss drugs him with some berries she knows will knock him out. She's free to go.

Chapter Twenty-One Scenes

89. Katniss prepares for her trip to the Cornucopia. She visualizes people at home in District Twelve rooting for her and heads out into the woods.
90. She arrives at the staged scene and sees the waiting backpack. As she watches, one of the other Tributes dashes out, grabs a pack, and runs off. This inspires Katniss to go for it.
91. But she's sideswiped by yet another Tribute (Clove, a knife specialist), who pins her down, taunts her about Peeta, and prepares to kill her.

Just in time, Thresh, Rue's district mate, pulls Clove off her. He's furious at Clove, believing it was she who killed Rue. He kills her. He then turns to Katniss and says he'll let her live—a one-time pass—for her kindness to his friend Rue. (Notice that for this to work, the author would need to make sure the reader saw Thresh and Rue as friends earlier in the story.)

92. She returns to the cave. She has a syringe full of the city's best medicine to cure and save Peeta. She administers it, then falls asleep. They have new hope. She and Peeta will now be a team, after all.

Chapter Twenty-Two Scenes

This change in the story—the *Second Plot Point*—sets the stage for a final countdown, then a showdown. Something had to happen to change the course of Katniss's quest and her relationship with Peeta (which has from the beginning been the spine of this structure), and this is it. This is on page 297 … the seventy-ninth percentile, very close to being right on cue.

93. Katniss wakes in the cave, delirious from her injuries sustained at the Cornucopia. Peeta, now healed, nurses her. They have a rambling discussion about the situation, Thrash and Cato, and one of them needing to die to save the other. In her inner dialogue, Katniss doesn't want to lose Peeta now (this is the mission of this scene, but it needed to occur organically in context to their discussion). They kiss, but this time it's different.

94. Later that evening, they return to the topic of their suddenly real romance. Then a parachute delivery comes … a feast. They assume it's from Haymitch as a reward and sign of approval of their new level of love for each other. This was his strategy and hope all along.

Chapter Twenty-Three Scenes

95. More banter about their relationship, playing to the audience. They ponder how Haymitch won when he was a Tribute and

consider life back at home if they survive as a winning couple. They eat more and gather their strength.

96. They finally leave the cave to hunt for food. They talk about cheese missing from Peeta's stash outside the cave. The cannon sounds, the hovercraft comes to pick up the body of the other lone girl survivor (Foxface); she's eaten the poisoned berries (from earlier foreshadowing) Peeta had stashed.

    Katniss tells Peeta the berries are poisonous; he would have eaten them himself at some point. They plant the berries in a pouch and leave it behind in the hope that Cato will find them and eat them, too. They light a fire to try to draw him close, knowing he's looking for them. Soon they decide to return to the cave.

97. Katniss contemplates where she and Peeta are at this point. (Notice how much of the narrative, especially here in Part Four, is inner dialogue, which allows us to experience both her fear and her courage as she considers options ... as well as her deepening feelings for Peeta. This is the mission of this and several other scenes in this section.)

98. They return to the lake for water, but the Gamekeepers have dried up other water sources; they are forcing a final showdown with Cato, who appears to them now (the mission of this scene). But he's running *from* something: A pack of wild wolflike creatures (genetically engineered "muttations") has been chasing him ... and now they're chasing down Katniss and Peeta as well.

99. Katniss, Peeta, and Cato run to the safety of the Cornucopia, climbing to the top of the structure where the muttations can't reach them. Peeta has lagged behind, and Katniss must help him up before the muttations tear off his legs. Upon closer examination, Katniss realizes these muttations are, in fact, the actual life forces of the dead Tributes. (This little twist isn't in the movie, which treats the muttations with more focus and a different approach; in the book the dogs are a metaphor for the Gamekeepers turning these children against each other.) They reach Peeta as he's climbing, and he kills one with his knife.

100. Cato, who has been reeling from his own injuries, gets Peeta in a death headlock. They square off. Katniss draws an arrow and aims at his head. A stalemate: If she shoots him, both he and Peeta will fall into the open jaws of the muttations who await at the base of the Cornucopia.

    Katniss shoots an arrow into his hand, and Peeta gets free just as Cato falls into the pack of vicious mutts. She grabs Peeta and saves him from falling.

101. Cato is fighting off the mutts in a bloody confrontation.

102. Cato's fight and death take a disturbingly long time, much to the delight, Katniss assumes, of the television audience. As this happens, Katniss cares for Peeta's wounds while still atop the Cornucopia.

103. At dawn, there's enough light for Katniss to see Cato, still barely alive. She uses her last arrow to end his suffering. The mutts disappear into a hole in the ground. Katniss and Peeta have won the Hunger Games.

104. Or so they think. The Gamekeepers announce that they've changed their minds, and that the earlier rule revision has been revoked: Only one Tribute can win after all. (How much do we *hate* the people behind all of this? That hatred is part of the appeal of the story, and the author prompts us to feel that hatred frequently, along with our empathy for Katniss.)

105. Katniss and Peeta discuss this new twist and come up with an idea. They won't let the Gamekeepers win. Using the berries, they'll commit simultaneous suicide (setting up a possible Romeo and Juliet outcome). They have every intention of following through … Katniss actually puts the berries in her mouth. This is no bluff.

    The Gamekeeper suddenly, urgently, orders them to stop … and announces that the *two of them* have just won the Hunger Games.

    Katniss and Peeta, however, have won more than that, and they have defeated more than the other Tributes in doing so.

Chapter Twenty-Six Scenes

106. The hovercraft comes for them, and they are taken back to the Training Center for medical treatment and rest. Katniss narrates her inner feelings the entire time, contemplating what this means.

107. She gets closure with the mute servant girl she had recognized earlier. It turns out the girl didn't wish her dead after all. Humanity resides with the meek and oppressed, not the oppressors. (Note: This isn't in the film version.)

108. Time passes and Katniss heals. (This isn't really its own scene, but simply a part of the time compression narrative strategy applied here, which can play as if it's a scene in a narrative sense, since it bears a single mission.)

109. She finally reunites with her team. Cinna prepares her to be presented to the people through another televised event. She is still a product to be used by the Gamekeepers, who want to alter her physically through surgery, giving us our first sense that Katniss is not out of the woods.

110. Haymitch warns she is still in danger. She's beaten the Game and in the process humiliated the Gamekeepers and the President. They will try to get even with her and punish her in some way. His counsel is to make sure she explains that her actions were motivated by her love for Peeta, and to go nowhere near the politics and her need to defy and beat the Gamekeepers.

111. Katniss decides that this is actually worse than being hunted in the arena.

Chapter Twenty-Seven Scenes

112. We are shown the televised documentary hosted by Caesar (who couldn't be any creepier). The program includes video footage of Katniss's journey, hitting the highlights. Katniss notices they omit anything that could be perceived as rebellion (such as her covering Rue's body with flowers; this is a statement on Big Brother politics and media spin).

Katniss and Peeta are taken to the President's celebratory dinner gala. Haymitch is there, and he has Katniss's back. (This is a one-paragraph aside—not a separate scene—before Katniss moves us forward to her next experience.)

113. It's time for her interview with Caesar. After a brief greeting from Peeta (who is concerned because it seems the Gamekeepers are keeping them apart), they are on the air, sitting together. The context of their answers to all of Caesar's questions and prompts is that of their great love for each other and how this love allowed them to survive and ultimately triumph.

114. Peeta reveals he's been fitted with a prosthetic leg (which explains why they had been kept apart; Katniss had no idea). In the end, the final moment is all about love, a perfect P.R. ploy for the Games. Katniss and Peeta hang between the truth and the illusion and pander to this expectation in order to save themselves long enough to get back to District Twelve.

115. During the journey home, Haymitch assures them that they barely dodged a bullet with the Capitol, who thought the stunt with the berries was rebellious.

116. Peeta realizes Katniss's affection toward him in the arena was, after all, just a survival strategy. Now that it's over he senses her distance, something Katniss can't completely refute. She's confused about her own feelings now that she's going home.

117. There remains one more parting shot for the television audience. They manage one final, somewhat forced, gesture of unity for the crowd.

The remainder of this story analysis refers to various milestones in the story. I recommend you use this beat sheet to fit each milestone in its proper narrative place.

For now, though, take an inventory of how the story physics worked for you, and how the structure and narrative strategies played to the power of those forces. Notice how the story was told in major blocks: Katniss at home (the Tribute selection and flashbacks) ... transport to the Capitol city ... training and preparation ... opening of the

Games and Katniss's initial period of running ... her alliance with Rue and attacking ... Rue's death and Katniss's reunion with Peeta ... their attack on the Cornucopia, leading to the showdown with Cato ... and the aftermath of the Games.

As a writer looking to plan a story, this is precisely what you can do to make it happen. Create the narrative blocks, then juxtapose them to (and integrate them with) the contextual four-part sequence: setup ... response ... attack ... resolution. When you apply the Six Core Competencies as tools to define the elements of the story (you need to cover these four bases: concept, character, theme, and structure), and then keep the ever-present potential of story physics in mind as you finalize your scenes and your beat sheet and when you actually draft the scenes. That's a process that will lead you toward a draft that actually works. It will be something you can revise and/or polish into a submitted piece of work.

THE FIRST PLOT POINT

Why is the First Plot Point the most important moment in a story?

Because it fully launches the hero's *story-specific journey*. Everything prior to the First Plot Point has been part of a *setup* for this moment.

I say "story-specific" because your hero may indeed be on a compelling path prior to the First Plot Point (which is a good thing), and the actual "plot" of the story may already be in play as well. The First Plot Point suddenly and more fully (or initially) *defines* the forthcoming hero's quest, need, problem, or journey in context to two things: *stakes* and antagonistic *opposition*.

The job of your Part One setup scenes is to put all of this in play while investing the reader in your hero on an emotional level.

No small feat, that.

If your First Plot Point is soft, in the wrong place, or nonexistent, it plays havoc with the story's underlying story physics. You won't hear an editor tell you your novel or screenplay is being rejected because of First Plot Point issues ... but if they bother to tell you the reason at all (rare), it *will* connect to those very same compromised story physics that your mishandled First Plot Point caused, guaranteed.

"Takes too long to get going." "Didn't care about the hero." "Stakes are weak." "Story treading water." "Just not compelling enough."

In *The Hunger Games*, the First Plot Point is masked behind a series of prior *Inciting Incidents* (yes, they can and often do pop up in Part One prior to the First Plot Point). It doesn't matter if Collins uses or doesn't use this terminology, but her story sensibilities absolutely do put a textbook First Plot Point right where it should be (page 72 of the trade paperback, as reflected on the beat sheet).

Some have challenged this. It doesn't look like a First Plot Point … *if* you're looking for the wrong thing, which is easy to do in this story. The key to finding a First Plot Point in a story—and more importantly, to *writing* one properly—is to understand what the *core story* is.

And in *The Hunger Games* it may not be what you think it is.

Both *Titanic* and *The Hunger Games* have highly dramatic plot turns that deal with that dramatic landscape. But in both stories—even though there are twists specific to the more obvious danger threatening the characters—the core structure revolves around the hero and the love story. Those sinking ship-related—*and* Games-related—twists and transitions are *catalysts* for the core story: In the case of *The Hunger Games*, it's the relationship between Katniss and Peeta.

Whoa. That changes everything, at least if you were looking for obvious story transitions as plot points, which isn't the case here. Those transitions are terrific and forward the plot. But they aren't evolutions of the love story, which is the core story that drives its four-part contextual structure.

The point is that you have to know which thread is the *core story* of your novel or screenplay and then build your plot points and milestones around it.

When something massively transitional happens in the story prior to the First Plot Point, it's an *Inciting Incident*. In *The Hunger Games*, we see a bunch of them: Prim gets picked as a Tribute … Katniss volunteers in her place … Peeta gets picked … they leave their home for the Capitol facing nearly certain death … and (this is a big one), they are set up to be a couple as a strategy to win favor with sponsors and the audience.

None of those are the First Plot Point. All of them are Inciting Incidents.

They all contribute to the effectiveness of this story: They hook us ... they make us feel it ... they allow us to see deep into Katniss and really root for her ... and (here's an example of story physics in play) we begin to take this journey with her in a *vicarious* way.

So why aren't any of these the First Plot Point (FPP)? Two reasons.

One: Placement. All of these scenes occur too early to be the milestone FPP. They do change the story and help define the forthcoming hero's quest ... but only as building blocks within a setup context. None of them define the *core* journey ... they all merely help set it up. The real launch of the core story journey (and it's *not* the beginning of the Games themselves) is about to come. Because the real structural *core* of this story, and thus the hero's core journey, is the *love story*.

On page 72, Katniss finally gives in to the "couple" strategy she's been fighting. She's suspicious of it and of Peeta, who may be playing her, making her vulnerable to an opening where he can put a knife in her heart. She doesn't know what to do with this, and it conflicts her.

Until page 72, when she buys in, accepts it, and begins to engage with it, at least from outward appearances. She declares to us (through her actions) that she'll play Peeta's dark game and beat him at it. Notice the story physics in play here: We empathize with her, we root for her (dramatic tension), we wonder what will happen next (dramatic tension), we feel that anxiety that comes with the prospect of love (vicarious experience), we sense that this could be as strategic as it is real (compelling premise), and because we're not exactly sure about it all, we want more (execution X-factor).

When she kisses his cheek as his partner, she does so on an existing bruise. It's nice visual poetry and irony at work. From that action, from the way it's set up and written, the story *changes* right there. This is the First Plot Point. It begins her journey and defines her core quest: to survive not only the Games, but the deception of her closest ally and supposed partner. It does so in context to those two things: stakes and the opposition. The dramatic tension just got higher, the empathy just got complicated, and the vicarious experience just shot to the moon.

The brilliance of Collins here is that the exterior plot, the Games themselves, is so strong and compelling on a story physics level that this core love story disappears into it, yet remains the spine of it. A reader has two emotional tracks available, and their melding exceeds the sum of their parts.

CONCEPT TO COMPELLING PREMISE

In interviews Collins admits her original idea for this story came from watching reality television. But that idea wasn't a story yet. It had to become a concept before a *story* was available.

The concept was this: "What if, in a futuristic dystopian society, young people are pitted against each other by a cruel ruling elite class in a televised death match to avenge and control formerly revolutionary districts?"

There's more, of course, but that's the point: The first idea, and the first concepts that result from it, always grow into what will become the nuances and layers of the story.

It became a premise when she added this: "When a young woman volunteers to take her sister's place in this almost-certain death match, her district partner is a boy she's noticed before, and who claims to be falling for her as the Games grow nearer, presenting a possibly lifesaving strategy if she perpetrates this illusion and leverages it to glean the favor of the viewing audience and sponsors."

Idea ... to concept ... to layers of concept ... to a compelling premise housed within the contextual framework of the collective hierarchy of concepts.

At any given point, writers should check in with this sequence to see where they are.

We can look at Suzanne Collins's structure—or the structure of any bestseller—and *learn* from it. See the moving parts at work. Juxtapose it against the principles of mission-driven, four-part, milestone-reliant exposition and sequencing.

But when we look at concept, what is there to *learn*?

In the case of *The Hunger Games*, the concept in play is huge and compelling. This is the case with most bestsellers (exceptions include more literary works, like those of John Irving and Jonathan Franzen). But why? What makes this concept the platform for a *great* story? *That's* what we can learn from analyzing it.

Concept is like an engine. But without wheels, a transmission, an undercarriage, a seat to sit in, a steering wheel, and some pedals, the vehicle doesn't function. It just sits there making a lot of noise while emitting toxic fumes. An engine, just sitting on blocks bellowing smoke, is easily misunderstood and perceived as useless.

And, of course, a *vehicle* goes nowhere without one.

DID SUZANNE COLLINS *BEGIN* WITH *CONCEPT*?

We can't be sure. But we can say why we enjoyed the ride.

You came for the Games. You stayed—you gasped, you kept turning pages—because you *cared*. That was because of the love story and the horrific thematic resonance. Because of the story physics.

It doesn't matter where Suzanne Collins *started*. Stories almost always begin with one of three story elements: a concept ... a character ... or a theme. Sometimes, especially in the case of "based on a true story" projects, it begins with structure or a sequence of events.

But in each case this is also true: It doesn't *become* a great story, or even an effective one, until *all* of those elements are in place. It doesn't matter where you *begin* your story development, as long as you eventually nail all Six Core Competencies.

Even then, though, you'll need more than that to elevate the story to greatness. More on this topic—and how Collins did it—in a moment.

Rumor holds that Collins was watching television one night, switching back and forth between a war documentary and a reality show, both of which, it seems, pushed her buttons.

And thus the concept for *The Hunger Games* was hatched. That wasn't Collins's first idea. No, the first idea, whatever it was, *led* her to this concept.

While perhaps implied, that "what if?" statement does not introduce a character, or even a theme. Those had to be added, wrapped around, and melted into the concept (this stirring process is the *art* of storytelling), which is certainly what Collins did. Neither that concept nor these elements arrived fully realized—they were both products of an evolving *process of development*: the incubation of elements and the melding of the elements into one another.

You can engage in the process through story planning or through story drafting. Both can get you there, because both depend on the power of story physics to make the story work.

Resist the temptation to jump the gun, or the shark, which is easy to do, especially if you are a drafter, because: a) it's harder to see the elements working within a draft, as opposed to an outline, and b) it's daunting to revise a draft that shows itself to be deficient in midstream, making it oh-so-tempting to *settle*, or worse, to start over after 400 pages of carpel-tunnel-inducing typing.

Whatever element you begin with (and it is often *concept*), play with it, poke it, fertilize it, until is grows into something more, something where character and theme emerge in a completely logical and compelling way. Allow story physics to drive that process, always shooting for more and better levels.

The mistake—the common shortcoming of unpublished manuscripts—is to write almost exclusively *about* your concept or your theme without the visible, visceral presence of the other elements. Without a plot. Notice how *The Hunger Games*, while a very character-driven story, leverages dramatic tension (plot) to give the characters something to do and challenge them to change (arc). Briskly paced dramatic tension is the fuel for high levels of empathy and vicarious experience.

In *The Hunger Games*, while Collins almost certainly began with this concept, the story ended up being *about* a love story at its core, with dramatic tension escalating throughout because of the huge *stakes* attached. The exterior drama unfolding within the arena of the Games is, in essence, the tapestry upon which the stitches of this love story emerge.

The First Plot Point, in fact, is driven by the love story. Call it an "A Plot" and a "B Plot" if you wish (how you label these things is less important than how you understand and implement them), but their sum is vastly in excess of their individual parts.

Without the love story, the Games become nothing more than a weekly episode of *Survivor* with knives. Without the Games, the love story is just another afternoon soap opera.

Without the heinous Gamekeepers and the dystopian society they serve, none of this has much weight, and their presence gives the reader something to root for, and—importantly—something to root *against*. This is what lends the story its powerful themes and thus how it emotionally engages (and *enrages*, in this case) the reader ... perhaps the strongest aspect of this story.

RELATING THIS TO STORY PHYSICS

Story physics are the *powers of narrative* that move the reader toward engagement and response. And that's part of the lesson we take from this story: Like the Six Core Competencies that allow you to work with them, you need to nail the six essences of story physics as well. No matter how strong your concept, it doesn't rise to this level without *all* of those story physics in play. And *that* can't happen unless you bring strong characters, powerful themes, and solid structure to the execution of your concept.

Powerful story physics are what you're going for. The Six Core Competencies are how you get there. It's a circular, paradoxical dance, one that you need to engage in.

Without the Games, this love story has little dramatic tension and absolutely no stakes (the key to reader empathy). In fact, it doesn't exist.

Without the love story, we have less reader empathy and a more shallow vicarious experience. In fact, without the love story, this book plays more like a video game.

Without the dystopian society, less reader empathy is achieved.

The outcome of your understanding of all of this—as demonstrated so ably in *The Hunger Games*—leads to a checklist you can use to vet and improve your story. How are you dealing with each of the Six Core Competencies? How do your story elements optimize the major modalities of story physics?

You can plan for and command them, or you can wrestle your story toward them as you write. But in the end, what will make your story more effective is never a mystery.

How you get there is your call. If you're willing to look closely and recognize the inner machinations in play, stories like *The Hunger Games* become a clinic on how to do so.

PHYSICS IN THE PART ONE SETUP SCENES

You've heard me say that the First Plot Point is the most important moment in your story. Now that we know what the First Plot Point is in this story, we can examine how the scenes prior to it—which comprise the entirety of the Part One setup—fulfill this mission.

The contextual mission of all Part One scenes is to *set up* two things: the forthcoming First Plot Point ... and the story to follow. The First Plot Point is the trigger, the catalyst, for the rest of your story. Which is why, in turn, it is the most important moment in your story.

Here's a provocative truth: The degree to which you succeed with your Part One setup scenes defines how successful your story will be overall. Of all the places you shouldn't settle, or worse, write without an awareness of the importance of context, this is it.

These setup scenes (usually about ten to eighteen or so) need to accomplish a number of critical missions:

- Hook the reader (compelling premise)
- Introduce the concept of the story (compelling premise and dramatic tension)
- Show us setting, time, place, and (as necessary) some backstory (vicarious experience)
- Introduce the main character (your story's *hero*) (hero empathy)
- Show us the hero's situation, goals, worldview, and emotional state prior to the launch of the path that lies ahead (hero empathy)

- Make us care about the hero through the establishing of stakes (hero empathy)
- Foreshadow as necessary, including the presence (perhaps implied, maybe in the reader's face, your call) of the antagonist (dramatic tension)

All of which leads to the First Plot Point (pacing, dramatic tension, hero empathy, vicarious experience).

With all of this in place, you are ready to lower the boom, ignite the fuse, and launch the journey with your First Plot Point, which comes in context (and an emotional investment) to these same objectives. This is all the foundation of your novel or screenplay's story physics. It all starts here, in Part One.

If you deliver your First Plot Point too soon, without adequate setup, you risk compromising reader empathy for the hero (which is essential to success), as well as putting all of those bulleted missions at risk.

If you engage in too much setup, then you risk compromising pace, which (especially at this point in the story) is also essential.

Let's see how Collins does this in *The Hunger Games*.

The narrative style and flow Collins uses in this series makes it challenging and imprecise to identify and segregate scenes. She uses what I call a "deep first-person" voice, meaning it is presented like a stream of consciousness flow of thoughts from Katniss, during which she might reflect on something that happened in the past. When that occurs, you could consider it a flashback, as its own scene … or not. Normally a "scene" announces itself with a shift of time, place, or both … but in *The Hunger Games* this becomes a fuzzy line.

That said, I've identified seventeen scenes in Part One. All of them are clearly, in terms of context, used to *set up* the forthcoming First Plot Point, as well as the rest of the story. Go back to the beat sheet and look for this context in play in all the Part One scenes. They're all leading to the First Plot Point, which is how Katniss plans on surviving the Games.

The kiss-on-the-bruised-cheek moment is the First Plot Point because it defines their journey going forward, and it does so in context to known stakes and opposition. Katniss has made a shift that launches the core spine of this story, which, along with its location in the story, defines it as the First Plot Point.

THE POWER OF SEQUENCING SCENES

To prepare for this section, I watched the DVD of *The Hunger Games* again. I first heard about this story through the media ... then watched the movie... then watched the movie again and read the novel casually ... then read and broke down the novel slowly and analytically ... and then watched the film again. Every phase of this immersion illuminated something new and taught me something more.

It occurs to me that the way I experienced this story, in which I became familiar enough to write about it, is almost the same evolving manner in which we experience our own stories as we write them. We don't know enough about a story until we've immersed ourselves in it several times, to a point where we can validly estimate our understanding to be complete enough to conclude we are done. Pantsers risk this because changes are made on the fly, and you really can't nail them until you reenter the story in another draft. This exposes a potential pitfall on that path: It's easy to settle, to quit learning about our stories before we've discovered all of their inherent potential.

One of the most powerful narrative tools at our disposal is scene *sequencing*, which in essence breaks down a block of action into distinct scenes, each with its own story beat contributing toward the block in question, and each leading seamlessly and urgently into the next. Once again, *The Hunger Games* is a transparent laboratory to study this narrative device at work.

A chase scene in a movie is a great example: Is this a collection of scenes or a single scene broken down into a sequence of moments and revelations that comprise a whole narrative mission? I think it's the latter. These scenes don't involve a time, location, or point of view shift, all of which are benchmarks for a new scene.

Often those sequence blocks use time and place shifts to segregate scenes, but a *sequence* links these scenes together into a microstory.

For example, consider the sequence in *The Hunger Games* when Katniss is sleeping in the tree with the hunter pack camped below and Rue awakens her, silently pointing out the hornets' nest a few feet away, signaling that she could cut it loose and drop in on the others below … and then Katniss climbs up and begins sawing at the branch, and is stung in the process (which sets up the subsequent sequence) … and then the nest falls and all hell breaks loose … and then Katniss climbs down and claims the bow from one of the dead girls.

End of sequence.

Was this all one *scene*? You could argue that it was. But when you look closely, you see it can also be accurately described as a series of linked scenes creating a sort of *microstory* with beginning, middle, and ending beats that propel the *macro*story forward.

This sequence, which is the Midpoint of the story (both in the book and the film), has the structural and expositional mission to evolve Katniss from her Part Two reaction/wandering self into a Part Two attacker/warrior self. In a narrative sense, the mission of the scene is to have Katniss gain possession of the bow and arrows, which allows this transition from wanderer to warrior to happen.

When you know what your scene or mission must accomplish, and when that mission fits structurally, contextually, and narratively (as it does here), *something wonderful happens for the writer*: You are then free to blow it out of the water, to *optimize* the story physics of dramatic tension, pace, and empathy through a more vivid vicarious experience.

Did those wasps scare the bejesus out of you? They did me. Collins could have created anything she wanted as a means for Katniss to get the bow and arrow from the girl (who, not coincidentally, had been presented as sadistic and arrogant, making her demise gratifying in its violence), but she optimized the moment with this particular choice.

When we are mission driven in our scene and sequence choices, that optimization and gratification is what can lift our stories to a higher level. When we are *searching* for purpose within a scene, optimization is harder to achieve.

Other sequences in this story.

One of the cool things about the use of sequences is that they really fill up your pages. In a sixty-scene novel, for example, if you have six sequences of five scenes each, they become *half* of the story itself. You don't have to come up with sixty units of dramatic setup and action; instead, you can cover half of those with six microstories that move the overall narrative forward in an optimized way.

Here are some other sequences in *The Hunger Games*. Notice how much of the story they occupy: The reaping ... the train ride ... the training ... the opening of the Games ... Katniss fleeing... the hornets' nest sequence described above ... Katniss's reaction to the stings (where Peeta appears as her savior) ... the strategy with Rue and the attack on the food ... healing Peeta in the cave ... the unleashing of the vicious digital dogs ... the end battle at the Cornucopia ... the aftermath.

They're all sequences. These thirteen sequences alone take up about half of the total scenes in the story. They are blocks of narrative. If you can envision and sequence the blocks first, injecting the right missions and then breaking them down into component beats, you can tell your story at the beat sheet and outline phase, even before writing a draft. And if you're an organic drafter, if you have these sequences in mind as you write, you will be much closer to a structurally optimized and physics-intensified story when you're finished, with fewer drafts required to reach the point where you can call the draft "final."

Once your sequences are defined in terms of their mission or what they need to achieve and deliver to the reader, you can break them down into scenes.

It's all mission driven, contextually empowered, and narratively seamless.

FROM BOOK TO FILM

Sometimes the coach calls a time-out to lecture a player about footwork. About mechanics. Sometimes the coach calls a time-out to say a few words about how the game is approached, or about mind-set, or about how to avoid getting in your own way, or about how to get the most of the talent you are bringing to your game.

This is one of those times.

I've called out several ways and specific instances in which *The Hunger Games* movie is different than the book upon which it is based. Suzanne Collins received a screen-writing credit (which may or may not mean anything in terms of who actually wrote the final shooting script, and it only very rarely signifies a collaboration), so let's assume she was in on this very deliberate departure. Or at least signed off on it while sitting on a yacht in Cannes.

But why change anything, one might ask? A good question, that.

There's always a pat answer for that: What plays in a novel may not play as well on the screen. And that's almost certainly, to some extent, part of it. But there's more to it. In fact, there's a lesson for storytellers—novelists *and* screenwriters—that's just itching to make us better at what we do.

Here's a truth nobody involved will admit to out of respect to Suzanne Collins: The movie was changed not just to optimize it for the screen, but to make the story *better*.

But wait, I hear you crying out. How can you make a thirty-million-copy-selling novel *better*? Why change what has proven to be magic, what is universally loved?

Because—get ready for it—it *can* be better.

As novelists, we are a creative committee of one.

We alone get to say what stays, what goes, what changes, at least in *our* "final" draft. Editors hop on the team at that point, but they're not likely to make the types of changes that filmmakers make to a novel they're adapting. Which means the author lives and dies by her creative decisions, which are always made in light of, and in context to, what she knows and believes about storytelling craft.

Suzanne Collins was no rookie when she penned this story. No matter how the filmmakers switched some things around, her decisions were stellar. But her experience, her craft—the very qualities that empowered her to write this great story—are precisely what played into her *acceptance* of the changes themselves. That, and perhaps an eight-figure direct deposit to her savings account.

The point: One mind alone, especially the mind of a newer writer or an unpublished writer, rarely *optimizes* each and every creative decision that must be made in the course of writing a story. We nail some, we get by on others, and a few we tank. The real problem—and the opportunity I'm putting in italics here —is that *when we unknowingly, or because of ignorance, haste, or blinders that fit tighter than a muzzle, settle for the first organic idea we have, our stories suffer for it.*

Happens all the time. To all of us. Even Suzanne Collins, to some extent.

Why else would the filmmakers tell her story differently than the book did, even slightly so?

To make it better. To raise the level of story physics. To jack dramatic tension. Heighten stakes. Intensify reader empathy. To elevate thematic resonance.

As a footnote, it should be noted that Collins was actively involved in the writing of the film script based on her novel, receiving a credit (and a paycheck) for doing so. She was aware of, participated in, and signed off on every story change noted here.

Every change in the book-to-story evolution points directly to one or more of these underlying motivations. It's all about story physics, the forces that make a story work ... and those are always up for grabs.

We, as writers, need to do the same with our stories.

Hopefully you do it before you stuff it into an envelope or hit the SEND button once you get a nibble from an agent or editor.

The Hunger Games was told in rigid first person. This was Collins's choice. We aren't privy to anything that transpires beyond the curtain of her hero's awareness, which limits the ability to fully understand the motives and Machiavellian cruelty of the folks who are pulling the strings of the Games.

The more we understand *that*, the more emotion we're likely to invest. This is what the filmmakers knew, and why they changed the story.

In the book we only get a historical overview from Katniss's POV. We never meet President Snow or the head Gamekeeper. We never see the machinations of folks with crazy facial hair pulling levers that result in fires and parachute deliveries and digital hounds from hell. (While in the book these dogs were representative of dead Tributes, in the film they were simply generically terrifying. The film took great liberties with this concept by creating new laws of physics—not *story* physics, but actual classroom laws-of-nature physics—that pushed the story into the realm of fantasy).

Limited first-person POV limits the story on almost all the elements of story physics cited above. And so, the filmmakers added scenes from behind that curtain, including a subplot with its own dramatic tension that pits the President against the head Gamekeeper.

If you saw the film, you know how that turned out. But if you only read the first book in the series, you didn't. That dynamic and its outcome aren't revealed until the second book, and even then, without the up-close-and-personal cache of the film.

There were other changes.

Many of Katniss's backstory flashbacks were combined and compressed.

Gale, who occupies Katniss's thoughts, is given almost no airtime in the film after she departs for the Games. And in a major addition, the film shows us a moment in which Katniss gives a sign of respect to the people of District Eleven, whose Tribute Rue has just been killed and mourned by Katniss, resulting in a rebellious riot (connecting to stakes and theme).

Imagine a room full of people wearing cool clothes, sitting in front of iPads, sipping designer water and lattes. That's the team of screenwriters, producers, and even actors as they discuss the script they are about to write and shoot, based on your book. When it happens to you, a film based on *your* book, you may or may not be there … probably not.

They must love your story, right? Why else would someone driving an Aston Martin have optioned and then given it a green light? Why else would Michael Douglas and Meryl Streep be sitting in that room?

Answer: They're trying to make your story *better*.

They are playing with options on all fronts, asking "what if?" questions, firing off ideas. They aren't settling for your last and best creative decisions, even if they are in love with the general concept and arc of your story. Even if your name is Suzanne Collins.

There shouldn't be a difference.

Write your story. Let it rip.

But then—either in the moment, or via another pass—ask yourself if your decisions, your story moments, are the absolute very best they can be. If the story physics pack a significant punch. If what you've written, moment by moment, optimizes dramatic tension while forwarding exposition, both at the macrostory level and the sequence and scene level.

Do your scenes and sequences have their own tension and stakes? Are they compelling? Will your reader be right there in those moments?

Are you maximizing point of view? Does what happens behind the curtain enhance the story? How are you handling that ... and backstory ... and foreshadowing ... all within the infinitesimal subtleties of your characterizations?

Have you asked yourself why anyone will *care*? What level of emotion are you plucking at in any given moment? Can you make what you've written even better? You need to make that your highest priority at some point in the process, over and above moving forward.

THE "RISK" OF *THE HUNGER GAMES*

As someone who advocates writing fiction from a context of structural story architecture, mission-driven elements, and aesthetic discipline driven by market standards, I am sometimes pitted against others who advocate "taking risks" with our stories, as if, somehow, these philosophies are not aligned.

I suppose it depends on how you frame the issue.

Is breaking certain principles and laws in this life a risk ... or is it suicide? The question applies to our stories as much as it does anything else.

Is jumping off a bridge onto a freeway a risk, or is it certain death that will appear, to anyone looking in, to be suicide? The act violates all the known laws of physics and survival, which is always suicidal.

That analogy, without compromise, accurately frames the question of risk-taking in our stories.

Don't be fooled or seduced.

Risk is good. Suicide is tragic and stupid. Death by naiveté is even worse.

Those who encourage us to *take risks*—a group to which I belong—are not suggesting we write stories that violate the basic tenets of dramatic physics, structural integrity, or creative license. Go ahead, write a story with no conflict, lackluster pacing, zero inherent compelling interest, and nobody to root for ... then see what happens.

That manuscript lying on the freeway, right next to the guy who just jumped off a bridge? That's his novel.

Risk taking, in this context, has everything to do with *courage* and *bold vision*.

It has to do with the bucking of belief systems, social boundaries, and the occasional use of creative narration techniques. It relates to the boldness with which an author takes a theme and explodes it into a dramatic framework that challenges, frightens, disturbs, grips, and entertains.

The Hunger Games is a prime example of this.

I've heard some writers wax outrage about *The Hunger Games*, saying that the book is obscene in the violence and darkness perpetrated on the children who inhabit it, and that as authors we have a responsibility to hold our fiction to higher standards. People seem to take pride in hating it, as much because they don't believe Suzanne Collins is all that good (they're wrong, based on results, which stem directly from her bold vision and keen sense of craft; every iconic bestseller brings the green out in a certain percentage of lesser writers and critics) as because their worldview has been challenged.

The risk, then, is this: Whose standards *are* they?

Yours? Society's? Risk comes when we challenge norms, speculate on alternative realities, and show consequences, and do so with the full knowledge that it very likely will piss off a certain percentage of the market.

Suzanne Collins, who wrote a story about children killing children, took significant risks. Dan Brown took similar risks in *The Da Vinci Code*, challenging the spiritual views of a few generations of practicing Catholics in the process. If that's all you see in these stories, then frankly, you didn't get it. You didn't get what millions of other readers *did* get.

For Collins, let's just agree that the risks she took paid off, at least in terms of commercial success. There are still plenty of haters, the fact of which, I'm assuming, makes Collins smile widely from the comfort of her 40,000 square foot home with a killer view and a helipad.

The Hunger Games, by the way, took no risks when it came to story physics. It is, in fact, a *model* for it.

It's gut check time: Are you being seduced in the wrong way by the *"take-risks-in-your-writing"* mantra? Are you tempting fate by jumping off a literary bridge? Or are you framing this properly as a challenge to take your book to new places, with bold ideas that explore relevant themes and then empower the story through a fierce adherence to the very principles that will make it work?

Here's hoping it's the latter.

May all your risks turn out to be survivable, and just possibly, a catalyst for your success. May you be accused of writing with vision and courage. Never forget that your parachute, the thing that will save your story's life, has strings called the Six Core Competencies, which connect you to the very things that will allow you to land safely, and on target ... a literary parachute boldly emblazoned with these words: *Story Physics*.

May your landings be soft and your stories be ... amazing.

INDEX

and context, 52–58
and core competencies, 153–155,
  157–159
defined, 29–51
exercise in, 142
and *The Help*, 168–200
and *The Hunger Games*, 201–242
importance to story, 16–18
key elements of, 31
as narrative benchmarks, 78–88
optimization of, 7, 8, 20, 59, 88,
  147–150, 235–236
shift toward, 13–20
six basic realms of, 22, 79
as storytelling truths, 18–20
and structure, 105–113
turning idea into concept, 15
storytelling
  art of, 230
  character-driven, 172–173
  context of, 57–58
  core competencies of, 79–88, 152–167
  forces of, 78–79
  mission-driven, 127–133
  objective of, 63
strategy
  narrative (*See* narrative strategy)
  and structure, 108–109
structure, 10, 61, 76, 79, 84–85, 90, 153,
  157–158
  closer look at, 162–167
  defined, 84, 161
  and *The Help*, 170, 173, 187
  and *The Hunger Games*, 228
  principles of, 109–111
  and story physics, 105–113
  and strategy, 108–109
  weak, 105–109
style, 153, 158
subplot, 11, 56, 92, 130, 180
  and *The Help*, 183, 190–191, 193
  and subtexts, 196–198
subtext, 19, 87, 92, 96–99, 103, 114, 120,
  180
  examples of, 98–99

and *The Help*, 172, 183, 185–186,
  197–198
and *The Hunger Games*, 202,
  203–204
optimizing, 97–98, 99
and subplots, 196–198
and theme, 97
surprise, 60
talent, 8, 27, 34, 112
Tarantino, Quentin, 61, 110
tense, 74, 75
tension. *See* dramatic tension
theme, 10, 11, 39, 74, 79, 83–84, 90, 92,
  102–103, 107–108, 153, 157
  defined, 83, 161
  and *The Help*, 173, 181, 186
  and *The Hunger Games*, 202–204
  and subtext, 97
third person narrative, 86, 116
time sequencing, 130
Time to Kill, A (Grisham), 98
timing, 178
Titanic (film), 122
Top Gun (film), 46–47, 121
transitions, 226
Twilight saga, The, 121
twist, plot, 60, 84, 184, 194, 226
Updike, John, 86
vicarious experience, 46–48, 74, 79,
  119–123, 157, 158, 178, 187, 230, 231
  and *The Help*, 48, 185, 194–195
  and *The Hunger Games*, 227, 228
vision, 77
voice. *See* writing voice
"what if?" statements, 70, 71, 74, 81, 160,
  230
Wolf Gift, The (Rice), 121
writing
  highest goal of, 125–126
  with power, 147–148
writing voice, 10, 48, 59, 79, 86, 130, 153,
  158, 161, 168